# STATES OF DISORDER

*For Morag*

# States of Disorder

## Understanding State Failure and Intervention in the Periphery

DAN HALVORSON
*Griffith University, Australia*

Routledge
Taylor & Francis Group
LONDON AND NEW YORK

First published 2013 by Ashgate Publishing

Published 2016 by Routledge
2 Park Square, Milton Park, Abingdon, Oxfordshire OX14 4RN
711 Third Avenue, New York, NY 10017, USA

First issued in paperback 2016

*Routledge is an imprint of the Taylor & Francis Group, an informa business*



**British Library Cataloguing in Publication Data**
Halvorson, Daniel.
States of disorder : understanding state failure and intervention in the periphery.
1. Failed states – History. 2. Intervention (International law – History.
I. Title
327.1'01–dc23

**Library of Congress Cataloging-in-Publication Data**
Halvorson, Daniel.
States of disorder : understanding state failure and intervention in the periphery / by Dan Halvorson.
p. cm.
Includes bibliographical references and index.
ISBN 978-1-4094-5188-4
1. Failed states. 2. Humanitarian intervention. 3. Intervention (International law) I. Title.

JC328.7.H35 2013
327.1'17—dc23

2012031360

ISBN 13: 978-1-138-26927-9 (pbk)
ISBN 13: 978-1-4094-5188-4 (hbk)

# Contents

# Acknowledgements

I would like to acknowledge a number of people for their help and encouragement in the development of this book. Special thanks are due to Jason Sharman and Michael Wesley for their generous mentorship. I would also like to thank a number of my colleagues at Griffith University: Martin Griffiths, Michael Heazle, Haig Patapan and Stephen McCarthy for commenting on various aspects of the study. The project would not have been possible without the support on my family. I thank my parents, Bob and Rhonda Halvorson for providing me with the educational opportunities and confidence to pursue such an undertaking. Most importantly, I thank my partner, Morag, for her love, steadfastness and belief in me. Finally, I would like to express my thanks to the anonymous reviewer and publishing team at Ashgate for their useful suggestions in improving the manuscript.

Dan Halvorson

# List of Abbreviations

| | |
|---|---|
| *AFNWS* | *All Africa News* |
| *AFP* | *Agence France-Presse* |
| AIPO | American Institute of Public Opinion |
| *AP* | *Associated Press* |
| ARVN | Army of the Republic of Vietnam |
| AU | African Union |
| BBC | British Broadcasting Corporation |
| BWIs | Bretton Woods Institutions |
| CAB | Cabinet Office Records (UK) |
| CIA | Central Intelligence Agency |
| DFID | Department for International Development (UK) |
| DRC | Democratic Republic of Congo |
| DRV | Democratic Republic of Vietnam |
| EC | European Commission |
| ECOMICI | Economic Community of West African States Mission Ivory Coast |
| ECOWAS | Economic Community of West African States |
| ESDP | European Security and Defence Policy |
| EU | European Union |
| *FN* | *Forces Nouvelles* |
| FO | Foreign Office (UK) |
| *FPI* | *Front Populaire Ivoirien* |
| *FRUS* | *Foreign Relations of the United States* |
| GATT | General Agreement on Tariffs and Trade |
| GDP | gross domestic product |
| GVN | Government of Vietnam |
| ICBM | intercontinental ballistic missile |
| ICC | International Criminal Court |
| ICG | International Crisis Group |
| IMF | International Monetary Fund |
| IR | International Relations |
| JCS | Joint Chiefs of Staff |
| LMP | Presidential Majority |
| MAAG | Military Assistance Advisory Group |
| MACV | Military Assistance Command Vietnam |
| MIT | Massachusetts Institute of Technology |
| *MJP* | *Mouvement pour la Justice et la Paix* |

| | |
|---|---|
| *MPCI* | *Mouvement Patriotique de la Côte D'Ivoire* |
| *MPIGO* | *Mouvement Populaire du Grand Ouest* |
| NATO | North Atlantic Treaty Organization |
| NGO | non-government organization |
| NIE | new institutional economics |
| NLF | National Liberation Front |
| NSAM | national security action memorandum |
| NSC | National Security Council |
| OAU | Organization of African Unity |
| OECD | Organisation for Economic Co-operation and Development |
| OEEC | Organisation for European Economic Co-operation |
| PAVN | People's Army of Vietnam |
| *PDCI* | *Parti Démocratique de Côte d'Ivoire* |
| PLA | People's Liberation Army |
| PRC | People's Republic of China |
| PRO | Public Records Office (UK) (now The National Archives) |
| RAMSI | Regional Assistance Mission Solomon Islands |
| *RDR* | *Rassemblement des Républicains* |
| RFCI | Republican Forces of Côte d'Ivoire |
| RPF | Rwanda Patriotic Front |
| RVN | Republic of Vietnam |
| SNIE | Special National Intelligence Estimate |
| SVN | South Vietnam |
| *UMP* | *Union pour la Majorité Présidetielle* |
| UN | United Nations |
| UNOCI | United Nations Operation Côte D'Ivoire |
| USSR | Union of Soviet Socialist Republics |
| VC | 'Viet Cong' |
| VWP | Vietnamese Worker's Party |
| WMD | weapons of mass destruction |

# Chapter 1
# Introduction

State 'failure' is the label currently applied to the perennial problem in international politics of disorder on the periphery. This book is about why great powers intervene with armed force to reverse state failure in peripheral regions of the world. Such regions may be geographically near or far, but states of disorder on the periphery are not an existential threat to great powers (Taliaferro 2004b: 184). The survival or territorial integrity of great powers is not threatened by present disorder on the periphery be it post-Cold War ethnic conflict in the Balkans or in sub-Saharan Africa, or even by violent transnational activity that strikes at the core, such as the al-Qaeda terrorist attacks of 11 September 2001 directed from Afghanistan (Jervis 2002). During the Cold War, Washington's security posture toward the Third World was characterized by repeated commitments to strategically marginal areas out of a symbolic concern to maintain credibility. These were often in support of 'weak states of dubious legitimacy', riven by 'internal conflicts over religion, ethnicity, class, status, and ideology' (Linantud 2008: 638). Disorder on the periphery is a problem of weakness not strength. This distinguishes failed states from so-called 'rogue' states that seek to develop the material capacity to directly threaten great powers or their vital interests. This is not to say that great powers do not have important interests in peripheral areas. But peripheral disorder is not a direct material threat to great powers in a traditional security sense that necessarily calls for a military response. Interventions in the periphery are military actions of choice rather than of necessity.

But a policy choice to intervene in the periphery to restore order is not taken in the expectation of material gain or even to directly avert losses. To the contrary, these military operations are costly in economic and human terms. They hold unforeseeable and unintended consequences, and are often damaging to the material interests of the intervening power. In this they confound rational explanations for state behaviour. They are also different from conquest or colonization. Their objective is to restore or build a viable state in conformity with the norms of appropriate statehood in the international society. The choice to intervene with military force in the periphery – assuming responsibility for an uncertain outcome – is mostly taken reluctantly by policy-makers, but often taken nonetheless. In each of the case studies of intervention examined in this book, rational alternatives to the military actions undertaken were available to policy-makers, but were ruled out for intangible prestige-based motives.

The meaning of state failure in any historical period, and why major powers might intervene to restore order, cannot be understood in a narrow materialist sense. Neither can assessments of state fragility based on the empirical conditions within peripheral states comprehend the meaning of state 'failure'. What failed states do threaten is intangible, but far more important to the most powerful states than the material interests they may hold in the periphery. Failed states threaten the ideas, values and principles on which the international society is ordered. Material conditions are not irrelevant to questions of state failure, but are indirect. Andrew Phillips (2011: 23–4) argues that the normative complexes of international order must rest 'on a permissive *order-enabling* material foundation'. Or as Torbjørn Knutsen (1999: 2) puts it, power is the 'decisive background determinant of order'. The distribution of capabilities provides the material structural conditions for international order. Power and norms are intimately connected. All sovereign states have an in-principle concern for the maintenance of an international society. But it is the great powers of the era that establish the normative criteria on which that society should operate. Great powers define the standards of legitimacy for state identities and behaviour within the international society. Their domestic institutions serve as models for appropriate statehood that others must approximate. The ordering principles of international society reflect the values and serve the interests of those powerful states that gave rise to them. Because of this, international orders are marked by varying degrees of interpretation, contestation and legitimacy.

Intervention in international relations is typically defined as the 'dictatorial or coercive interference, by an outside party or parties, in the sphere of jurisdiction of a sovereign state, or more broadly of an independent political community' (Bull 1984: 1). Interventions in the periphery, as considered here, are certainly coercive, but less overtly dictatorial than this definition allows. The three interventions examined in this book were all consensual, in that they took place at the invitation or acquiescence of the legitimate government of the targeted state as recognized by international law. Intervention in the periphery is also a broader concept in its objectives than the above definition stipulates. Its protagonists usually seek a measure of control over present and future governance outcomes from targeted states through the restoration or promotion of enduring institutional arrangements, rather than the temporary manipulation of internal events or processes for short-term objectives.

In this context, Elizabeth N. Saunders (2009: 123–5) makes the distinction between 'transformative' and 'non-transformative' strategies of intervention. Both share the definition of military intervention 'as an overt, short-term deployment of at least 1,000 combat-ready ground troops across international boundaries to influence an outcome in another state or an interstate dispute; it may or may not interfere in another state's domestic institutions' (Saunders 2009: 122–3). The objective of transformative interventions is to interfere with or determine the domestic institutions of the targeted state. Non-transformative interventions, as the label suggests, seek to deal with a particular crisis or alter a foreign policy action without the intention of altering institutional structures (Saunders 2009: 123–5). Definitions like this are shown in this book to be problematic because embarking on an intervention in the periphery is rarely a clean-cut policy decision, the attributes of which become operative at a particular point in time. In the cases examined here, each intervention evolved haphazardly in response to events on the ground, the political climate at home, and the mounting concerns of decision-makers. On the other hand, interventions in the periphery by great powers to restore order do seem to be genuinely transformative, regardless of their intent, in that shoring up weak state structures prevents institutional changes that might otherwise occur (Saunders 2009: 124).

The term 'international order' is used here in a specifically English School sense as the 'pattern' or set of normative principles on which the international society is ordered. Following Hedley Bull (1966), this pattern may be pluralist or solidarist. Pluralist orders embody thin normative claims. They accept a variety of regime types and hold minimal standards for state behaviour. In solidarist international orders, states operate within a thick legal and normative environment densely packed with rules and expectations reflecting the values of leading actors. This creates a high normative standard for states' identities and behaviours (Buzan 2004: 46–51, Hurrell 2007). This approach to international order differs somewhat from more expansive understandings that equate it with the constitutive structures of the international society and their transformations over time on a world historical scale (e.g., Reus-Smit 1999, Phillips 2011). My purpose in this book is narrower. Patterns of international order are used as an interpretive framework to enable a more historically-informed understanding of the nature of state failure in international society and why great powers persistently intervene with military force to restore order in the absence of existential threats to their security. When the term international order is used throughout the book, it refers to the pattern of order in the international society, whether pluralist or solidarist. Chapter 3 elaborates a more substantive account of this concept of international order, and its dynamics in historical context.

Chapter 4 presents the book's first case study focusing on the 1882 British intervention in Egypt, which took place on the periphery of the multipolar European international system of the late-nineteenth century. The identities of the great powers ranged from absolute monarchy in Tsarist Russia to democratic republicanism in France. This plurality of state forms in the multipolar European system was reflected in an international order codified in the classic 'standard of civilization'. The standard provided explicit normative criteria that held minimal requirements for state identity but stringent criteria for international conduct. The standard enjoyed wide legitimacy within the international society and formed the criteria against which non-European states such as Japan could be admitted. Its provisions were, however, subject to a degree of interpretation by the great powers. The British variant considered here, for instance, placed particular emphasis on sound finance and the sanctity of international treaties as providing the discipline and character for good government (Cain and Hopkins 2002: 45–8).

By contrast to the legitimacy of the 'standard', Washington's vision during the Cold War of a non-communist, 'free world' order in the modernizing Third World periphery was heavily contested. The second case considered in Chapter 5, the 1965 US combat intervention in South Vietnam, was undertaken in the postcolonial international order that emerged in the early decades after World War II. The foundational United Nations (UN) Charter principles of sovereign equality, non-intervention and national self-determination provided for a pluralist international order. Again, this featured minimal requirements for state identity but stringent standards for behaviour. While both protagonists in the Cold War struggle shared anti-colonial convictions, international order was heavily contested in the bipolar international system. Each side had a clear ideological vision and sought to exclude that of the other within their strategic spheres of influence. Power and order were tightly interlocked within the zero-sum bipolar structure.

The liberal international order that emerged at the end of the Cold War with the collapse of the Soviet Union is solidarist and universalizing, underwritten by US unipolarity. In the post-Cold War period, normative principles of appropriate statehood such as democratization and liberal governance have come to enjoy high levels of international consensus and legitimacy, but with less room for contestation and interpretation. The book's third case study in Chapter 6, the 2002 French intervention in Ivory Coast, was undertaken in the solidarist liberal international order of the first decade of the twenty-first century. The French view of state failure, which is mainly concerned with violent ethnic conflict, differs somewhat from the Anglo-American emphasis on ungoverned political spaces and transnational security threats, but liberal-democracy as the standard for appropriate statehood remains uncontested.

Once established, international orders become path dependent and status quo-oriented. The great powers that established them and benefit most from them will be most concerned for their preservation. More important than this, being a source and exemplar of international order is integral to the identity and ontological security needs of status quo great powers. It imbues their national identity with a meaning that gives a sense of purpose and agency in the world. Rather than their physical security, disorder on the periphery threatens the ontological security of status quo great powers by challenging their role identity as the source and guarantor of international order. Taken at face value, 'disorder' could mean many things depending on the standpoint and assumptions of the observer. What resonates for great powers as 'disorder' is a breach of the ordering principles by which they seek to manage the international society. While there may be some similarities in the empirical characteristics of disorder over time, such as military coups and violent civil unrest, the meaning and significance of this to great powers is relative to the prevailing international order.

Identities are shaped, routinized and sustained through social relationships. This process is reflected in the biographical narratives states develop to maintain a coherent sense of national identity through the flux of time and historical events (Steele 2008: 2–3). Both individuals and collectivities understand themselves and find meaning through the stories they tell about themselves. Stories provide the necessary shape through which collective energies and anxieties can be channelled. In framing or constructing narratives, motifs and archetypes are deployed as recurring anchors that bind stories together, giving them meaning and coherence across time. Meaning is important because it 'determines how people will react to, interpret, or deal with any event and force' (Reeves 2004: 78). States' identity narratives provide the evaluative frameworks through which events are interpreted and motives formulated by political decision-makers. Political leaders will typically have a strong identification with their state's identity narrative (Sasley 2011).

Stable, ordered patterns of relationships are also crucial for ontological security because they allow for predictability about the future, which in turn is required for a meaningful sense of agency in the world. This is particularly important for status quo actors that are satisfied with the present state of affairs. The ontological security of status quo great powers is challenged by disruptions to routinized relationships, role identities and the narratives that ground and support them, through 'normative threats' to international order (Creppell 2011). Such disruptions to international order impinge directly on the prestige of status quo great powers – on their reputation, credibility and national honour. Under certain conditions, these become powerful motives for action because of the disjuncture created between a negative turn of events and the identity narratives within which political actors find meaning (Steele 2008: 2–3, 13).

Failed states are not a direct security threat to major powers. They are a normative threat to international order, which is why they are taken so seriously. The meaning of state failure in any historical period is judged against the principles of appropriate statehood promoted and legitimized by the great powers. In this sense, 'failed' states are a socially constructed category. The norms of international order are constitutive of state failure in a given period. They also provide the threshold conditions for permissible intervention in the international society. A more interesting observation explored in Chapter 2 is that not all states are able to be socialized to international order norms at any given time. Normative pressures within the international society to transform the internal character of peripheral states often results in the disorder currently characterized as state failure. For example, in Chapter 6, post-Cold War pressures for democratization in Ivory Coast directly prompted a political crisis that resulted in two military coups, foreign intervention, the partition of the country, and violent civil unrest in what had previously been West Africa's most stable and successful state. This observation is also borne out in the historical case studies where modernizing pressures coming from outside contributed to the breakdown of order in peripheral states.

## A Challenge to Orthodoxy

Placing state failure and intervention in a historical context of international orders is a challenge to the academic and policy orthodoxy that has developed since the end of the Cold War. The orthodox view of state failure began to emerge in the early 1990s. Robert Kaplan (1994: 45) depicted the dire consequences of state failure along a string of West African states in an influential 1994 article, 'The Coming Anarchy', and predicted that this was 'what the political character of our planet is likely to be in the twenty-first century'. Kaplan's article foreshadowed the intense academic and policy interest that built throughout the 1990s about a crisis of governance and order in large swathes of the postcolonial and post-communist world. By the turn of the century, the 'pathologies' of state failure, exemplified by the cases of Sierra Leone, Liberia, Afghanistan, Somalia and Haiti, had become a commonplace in the academic literature. Internally, failed states were characterized by corrupted and disintegrating institutions, endemic civil war often along ethnic lines, human rights abuses and intractable poverty. Externally, failed states generated massive cross-border refugee flows and disease epidemics, facilitated transnational crime, and exported a contagious instability and disorder to regional neighbours.

It was only following the 11 September 2001 terrorist attacks on the United States, planned and directed by al-Qaeda from Afghanistan, that the failed state transcended its previous humanitarian dimension to acquire its current status as a profound transnational security threat (Rotberg 2002: 127, Wolff 2011: 954–5). The failed state underwent a redefinition consistent with the 'securitization' of governance in the post-9/11 international climate (Newman 2009: 434). Rather than denoting a state with chronic internal conflicts giving rise to acute human security concerns, state failure since 2001 has increasingly been viewed as the failure to provide 'security from the types of societal disorder that provide ideal conditions in which malevolent transnational forces can operate' (Wesley 2005: 68). It is now a routine assertion that weak and failed states rather than strong revisionist states pose the gravest threat to international security. This has prompted a plethora of literature examining the perceived causes and indicators of state failure and policy prescriptions for state-building.

The interventionist norms that coalesced in the 1990s around democratization and humanitarianism were superseded at the height of the war on terror by those of preventing state failure, transnational terrorism, the proliferation of weapons of mass destruction (WMD), and in promoting 'good' governance as the cure for these problems. In failed state contexts, 'best practice' in state-building adopts a progressive approach that seeks to restore physical security before moving through institutional capacity building in budget and finance; administrative, legal and judicial; market economy, and democratic electoral functions (François and Sud 2006: 149–50, Rubin 2006: 175–85, Wesley 2008: 373). This greater attentiveness to shaping governance outcomes is also evident in arguments for international arrangements such as shared sovereignty (Krasner 2004), neo-trusteeship (Fearon and Laitin 2004), and in calls for a return to a benign imperial tutelage (Ferguson 2004). At the time of writing in early 2012, recent developments such as the North Atlantic Treaty Organization (NATO) intervention in Libya in 2011 have seen a shift in liberal interventionist norms back toward a firmer responsibility to protect civilians. These shifts are consistent with the historic pattern identified by Martha

Finnemore (2003) that the purpose of armed intervention changes over time in line with changes in international order norms.

## Interpretive Framework and Arguments

International order provides the normative criteria for state failure and permissible intervention. The distribution of capabilities provides the structural conditions for order and the geographical focus of great power attention. As the case studies in the book demonstrate, disorder in these areas may be a risk to the material interests of great powers, but this is not a sufficient condition for military intervention. In parts of the world where great powers see themselves as the indispensable source on international order, failed states are a normative threat to their identity and ontological security needs. International order, capabilities and ontological security are the conceptual foundations necessary for understanding state failure and intervention in the periphery. Prestige is the intangible link that connects these large, diffuse conditional factors to a concrete policy of intervention to restore order in failed states. Prestige is conceptualized in the book as encompassing normative (reputation), instrumental (credibility) and emotional (honour) dimensions, which align with the conceptual building blocks of the study. The rationale and justification for these claims is elaborated further in Chapter 3.

The book has two main arguments. The first is that state failure is not an empirical condition unique to the post-Cold War world, but a historical interpretation of disorder. The significance of disorder from the periphery, however defined in historical context, is contingent on the pattern of international order in a given period. The second argument is that prestige is the primary motive for interventions in the periphery to restore order. The book does not claim that prestige was the only motive for the cases of intervention examined, but that it was the dominant consideration within a mix of motives and taken to some degree as an end in itself. For status quo great powers, there is an intrinsic association between prestige and upholding international order norms in what they consider to be their spheres of responsibility (Löwenheim 2003: 27–8). In a relational sense, disorder in these areas challenges the reputation of great powers for maintaining order and therefore engages their more instrumental concerns for credibility in other parts of the world.

More importantly though, our imagining of the way that others see us can deeply affect the way we feel about ourselves. Richard Little (2009: 115) notes that 'there is a very marked tendency in international relations to ignore the fact that decision-makers are individuals who possess emotions, and that they are potentially also in a position where they can act out these emotions on the world stage'. Rationalist approaches to explaining human behaviour divide cognition from emotion and relegate 'the latter to the status of invisible, unapproachable, or unimportant'. This leads to an 'impoverished and inaccurate conception of human motives'. Emotions are central to the shaping of decisions and the triggering of actions (Keys 2011: 592). Normative threats from the periphery that disrupt stable expectations about the future are experienced emotionally by political decision-makers typically in the form of anger or frustration. These emotional reactions are sometimes available to the observer as direct statements or observations. But more commonly, they are expressed as social gestures of 'affront' or 'insult' to self-respect and national honour. This may extend to humiliation and the desire for retribution if normative threats result in tangible consequences.

## Case Selection and Method

The book takes a holistic approach suited to understanding the complex historical phenomenon of state failure and intervention. As the arguments suggest, the research design is theoretically pluralist, drawing on English School, neo-classical realist and constructivist perspectives. The study has involved deep and sustained historical inquiry across a number of settings in both diplomatic and intellectual history. The importance of both material and ideational factors, and the interplay between the domestic politics of leading states and their foreign policies, is also necessary to understanding state failure and intervention in the periphery. The book incorporates all these elements at various stages.

The historical case studies in the book are based on original archival and documentary research. Many theoretical works in International Relations (IR) identify and seek to explain historical patterns based solely on interpretations made by historians. While hard to avoid because of the breadth of material that must be covered, this is not always satisfactory because the generalizations or patterns drawn are abstractions of historians' interpretations, distant from original sources, and necessarily coloured by historiographical debates and preoccupations of the time of writing. It denies the chance to draw new perspectives from valuable primary source evidence by bringing to bear alternative 'problem frames' and theoretical assumptions. Historical interpretation 'means attributing significance to events, or, more broadly, attributing meaning to human experience' (Puchala 2003: 5). For IR scholars a close reading of the historical sources within a reconstruction, however imperfect, of the worldview and social imaginary of policy elites of the time, can be meaningful in both understanding the past for its own sake, and in providing historically-informed insight into present concerns and future trajectories. As E.H. Carr (1964: 68–9) noted, historical knowledge cannot predict specific events, but regularities in collective human behaviour over time can provide a valid and useful guide for future action.

Placing the concepts of state failure and intervention within a comparative historical context goes some way to countering the charge of 'presentism' that is often levelled by historians at political scientists (Elman and Elman 1997: 8–9). This is taken up further in Chapter 2. The academic and policy literature on failed states and state-building intervention focuses for the most part on present policy imperatives and lacks sensitivity to the historical continuities in assessing institutions of governance against external normative standards. On the other hand, using contemporary themes to inspire an investigation into the past to uncover or demonstrate patterns leaves the researcher open to the charge of ahistoricism (Buzan and Little 2000: 19–20). This seems unavoidable, however, in approaching historical material from a comparative perspective across time. To identify regularities and differences across cases, a framework for understanding must be imposed at a level of abstraction above the specific events in question in each individual case (Puchala 2003: 7). The problem of ahistoricism is partly overcome in this study by locating the meaning of disorder and the response of great powers within their respective historical milieus, which are reconstructed in Chapter 3.

The three case studies in the book are selected on the basis of differing patterns of international order underwritten in each period by the structural conditions of polarity. To advance the argument, this is intended to illustrate the contingent nature of state failure across time and divergent patterns of international order. On the other hand, the case selection also shows that, conditioned by prevailing international order norms, material capabilities and ontological security, the prestige motive remains a constant in understanding interventions in the periphery over more than a century's time-span of profound social and political change. One of the purposes of the book is to challenge conventional accounts of state failure and intervention by placing the phenomena in a historical context of international orders. On this basis it was decided to reinterpret two well-known historical cases of military intervention.

Marxist and liberal historians consider the 1882 British occupation of Egypt to be one of the archetypical examples of modern economic imperialism. Historians of European geopolitics attribute the intervention to the protection of the Suez Canal route to India and the British Empire in Asia. By applying an interpretive framework of international order, capabilities and ontological security, I demonstrate that neither of these dominant explanations is sustainable compared with a prestige-based interpretation. The British intervention in Egypt was undertaken to restore national honour at home, and to maintain imperial credibility abroad, on which the Empire in India, with its large Muslim population, was believed to rest. The US combat intervention in South Vietnam from 1965 is often interpreted as a tragic and misguided attempt by the Johnson administration to arrest Chinese communist expansionism in Southeast Asia in what was really a Vietnamese national struggle against foreign domination. By applying the book's interpretive framework, I offer an alternative prestige-based perspective. The decision to intervene in South Vietnam was ultimately taken by the Johnson administration to avoid personal and political humiliation by demonstrating US reputation for resolve in maintaining 'free world' order in the postcolonial periphery.

The book's third and contemporary case study remains in place at the time of writing in early 2012. The 2002 French intervention in Ivory Coast fits more readily into the orthodox account of post-Cold War state failure outlined above. French military actions to restore order in Ivory Coast were justified on the shifting bases of protecting French nationals, enforcing internationally-sanctioned peace agreements, promoting regional stability, and ultimately, the protection of civilians caught up in fighting. My analysis of the French case shows however, that prestige concerns remain paramount, even in the current liberal international order. The intervention in Ivory Coast was undertaken to reverse the shame and dishonour of French policies and actions that were implicated in the genocide in Rwanda. The intervention in Ivory Coast was a litmus test of a new French policy in sub-Saharan Africa; the pursuit of a meaningful sense of *grandeur* through the robust promotion of liberal order norms.

Within each case study, a 'process tracing' method is applied in identifying and analysing selected evidence from relevant archival materials, public documents and media reports. This is supplemented with secondary sources where appropriate. Process tracing allows the researcher to examine chains of events or decision-making processes by which 'case conditions are translated into case outcomes' (Van Evera 1997: 64). My interpretation of the evidence in the book's case study chapters reveals how the pressures of international order, strategic constraints, and ontological security needs, influenced policy processes and the decision-making of political leaders. Each case shows how events on the ground in the periphery were progressively interpreted by policy elites as a state 'failure' requiring military intervention to restore order. Each case study demonstrates how prestige across its normative, instrumental and emotional dimensions was engaged by events and expressed by political leaders as the primary motive for intervention.

## Contribution

The book seeks to make a number of academic and policy contributions. It first makes a substantial contribution to the contemporary literature on state failure by adding a layer of historical richness and theoretical nuance. The literature on failed states, governance and state-building interventions is for the most part based on flawed definitions and questionable assumptions about the concept of state failure. With notable exceptions (e.g., Holm 2001), it is driven mainly by practitioner concerns and is theoretically underdeveloped from an IR perspective. By subjecting the concept of state failure to a rigorous analytical and philosophical critique in Chapter 2, a theoretical reformulation in Chapter 3, and a historically-informed treatment in the case studies, the book reveals a number of timely policy implications that are canvassed briefly below and more substantially in the book's conclusion.

The book also makes a contribution to the theorization of prestige in international relations, particularly from a constructivist perspective that emphasizes the importance of norms and emotions. Prestige and related concepts such as honour and glory are generally seen as anachronisms in world politics, or as having been replaced by more contemporary concerns for international standing or esteem. When it is invoked, the prestige motive is assumed to apply specifically to great power rivalries, particularly in driving the behaviour of revisionist states (e.g., Wohlforth 2009). This book demonstrates, however, that prestige is also a crucial factor in the relationship between status quo major powers and disordered states in peripheral areas. An important implication of this is that the prestige motive is far from irrelevant to the current security focus on 'fragile' states, governance and transnational problems.

If current ideas about state failure are as deeply flawed as this study suggests, this holds serious implications for the security policies of Western states. These flawed understandings inform all current efforts at state-building at the cost of thousands of lives in places like Afghanistan, and to the tune of billions of dollars. And in some cases, it only seems to make the situation worse. How we understand state failure is of critical importance because it shapes practical approaches to the problem. Ideas about state failure only acquire their meaning in relation to international order norms, which change over time with shifts in the distribution of capabilities. If the international system moves toward multipolarity and greater acceptance of plurality in regime type with the continued resurgence of China and other non-Western great powers, the principles of international order will become increasingly contested. An evolution toward a pluralist order will see different understandings and new descriptors for state 'failure'. Permissible reasons for intervention will again become more stringent. The 'good' governance concerns elicited by contemporary failed states, and the liberal state-building agenda, will diminish in importance.

For Western policy elites, breaking the intellectual prism that assumes a global liberal-democratic order as normative will be an acute and visceral threat to ontological security needs. Because of this, as international order becomes more contested, we are likely to see greater pressures from within the West for intervention in the periphery to promote liberal norms. The book demonstrates that the objectives of interventions in the periphery are less likely to be achieved successfully where international order norms are contested. The historical patterns identified in the book suggest greater future pressures for armed interventions by Western states in circumstances where success is highly uncertain, along with greater multipolar competition and strategic risks. The insights generated from the study can help security practitioners in rethinking their approaches to state failure for the coming decades. A closed policy mindset assuming conflict over the nature of governance has ended will be ill-prepared to manage disordered states on the periphery in an emerging and complex multipolar system, the ordering principles of which will be increasingly contested.

## Plan of the Book

The following chapter reviews and challenges the orthodox view of state failure that has emerged as dominant in the academic and policy literature since the end of the Cold War. Chapter 2 argues that state failure cannot be defined by empirical indicators that seek to measure its causes or consequences. The case is made that failed states are not unique to the post-Cold War era, nor are they uniquely threatening compared with earlier historical periods. More controversially, I argue that state failure does not derive from a failure of formal institutions of governance. Neither is it a result of the failure of the state to provide public goods to its citizens. The main conclusion of Chapter 2 is that the current failed state phenomenon is a product of the post-Cold War change in international order that sees universal movement toward liberal-democracy as normative for all states. This suggests that the meaning of state failure in a given period must be relative to the principles of international order, which are historically contingent.

Chapter 3 develops an interpretive framework for understanding state failure and the imperatives informing decisions to intervene in disordered states on the periphery. I first define and elaborate the conceptual foundations of international order, the distribution of capabilities, and ontological security, the dynamics between them, and locate them in their respective historical and case-specific contexts. Chapter 3 then introduces the prestige motive as the linkage connecting these conditional factors into a concrete policy of military intervention. The concept of prestige is disaggregated into three dimensions: the normative (reputation), instrumental (credibility) and emotional (national honour). I make the argument that normative threats to great powers in areas where they see themselves as the purveyors of international order are experienced as a challenge to their reputation, and consequently, to their national honour and international credibility. Maintaining prestige across these dimensions is the primary motive for military interventions in the periphery to reverse state failure.

In Chapters 4, 5 and 6, three empirical case studies of intervention in the periphery are interpreted through this framework. Chapter 4 re-examines the 1882 British intervention in Egypt in the late-nineteenth century pluralist international order. Chapter 5 reconsiders the 1965 US intervention in South Vietnam in the postcolonial international order of the Cold War. Chapter 6 examines a contemporary case study of intervention in the solidarist international order of the early twenty-first century – the 2002 French intervention in Ivory Coast. The analysis in each case shows how state failure is best understood as a normative threat to status quo great powers in areas where they see themselves as the source of international order. Each chapter illustrates how the three dimensions of prestige are engaged in failed state contexts to advance the book's argument that interventions to restore order in the periphery are taken primarily for prestige-based motives. Chapter 7 summarizes the findings from the study, draws out the larger patterns and implications from the case study analysis, and offers concluding reflections for the future.

# Chapter 2
# Rethinking State Failure

The orthodox way of thinking about state failure introduced in Chapter 1 represents a chronic case of what in historiography is termed 'presentism'.[1] The fallacy of presentism is the notion that we in the present either stand at the apex of human achievement and virtue or that our problems are of greater importance than those faced in the past. The current failed state phenomenon is held to be either unique to the post-Cold War era, or after the shock of the terrorist attacks of 11 September 2001, especially pernicious in an increasingly interconnected world. However, even the most cursory historical survey shows that peripheral disorder and harmful transnational activity has been a ubiquitous feature of past international systems. Due to its policy resonance in the global 'war on terror', the proliferating literature on state fragility, governance and state-building interventions has in large part been practitioner driven. Focused on the problems at hand, it lacks historical sensitivity.

There have always been weak or fragile states in the modern period or poorly governed and disorderly political communities in earlier times. This raises the question of why state failure has acquired such importance in academic and policy circles after the end of the Cold War? Why, for example, would the Democratic Republic of Congo (DRC) be considered a 'failed' state in 1995 or 2005, but not in 1965 when there may be no meaningful difference in its observable empirical conditions? This chapter seeks to answer these questions. In doing so, it reconceptualizes state failure and lays the foundation for the interpretive framework developed in Chapter 3. The position argued here is that state failure is not new and cannot be located empirically at the unit level in weak or fragile states. The chapter first demonstrates that empirical indicators seeking to measure causes or consequences of state failure cannot adequately define the concept. I then argue that the 'failed state' cannot be considered unique to the post-Cold War era, nor is the current failed state phenomenon uniquely threatening when compared with disorder on the periphery in earlier historical periods. The critique then proceeds to the more deeply held assumptions about state failure. I make the argument that state failure is not primarily a failure of institutions of governance. Neither is it a result of the failure of the state to provide public goods to its citizens.

The chapter's main conclusion is that the current failed state phenomenon is a product of the post-Cold War change in international ordering principles that sees universal movement toward liberal-democracy as normative for all states. This normative shift is a consequence of the change in the structure of the international system from bipolar to unipolar with the collapse of the Soviet Union. The internal

1 An earlier version of this chapter was published in Halvorson (2010a).

conditions of many failed states were independent of these systemic changes. Many postcolonial states in Africa and elsewhere have demonstrated the material conditions of state failure since their inception (see Jackson 2000: 296, Anderson 2004: 10–14, Caplan 2007: 231, Englebert and Tull 2008: 111–13). For others, external pressures for democratization and liberal governance norms contributed to the breakdown of relatively stable neo-patrimonial political structures into violent and chronic disorder. Whether socially constructed or having an empirical basis, the contemporary failed state phenomenon is relative to the change in international order after the Cold War.

## Definitions of State Failure: Confusion and Conflation

One of the most striking features of the orthodox view of the failed state is the lack of consensus on its definition. The concept of state failure has proven difficult to delineate and define with clarity (Call 2008). Two main approaches have been used to define the failed state empirically or statistically (see Newman 2009: 425–9, Sanin 2011, Wolff 2011: 953–61 for recent and comprehensive reviews of these approaches). The first, such as that of Robert I. Rotberg (2003: 2–10), bases its assessment on the relative presence or absence of the perceived 'pathologies' of state failure. Categories of state are then arranged on a continuum from weak or fragile, through failing to failed, and finally, to collapsed. The continuum implies movement either way, and that the strong or capable state lies at the other extremity. Placing states or peoples along a continuum in this way is deeply resonant with earlier schemas of ranking societies against a normative standard set down by the most powerful states. For example, the European standard of civilization differentiated between savage, barbarous and civilized polities. This same continuum was carried into the inter-war period with the A, B and C Mandates of the League of Nations. With decolonization in the decades after World War II, theories of modernization and development gave rise to the continuum of less-developed through developing to advanced industrial states. The Cold War struggle gave us the First, Second and Third Worlds. Placing states along a continuum is imbued with Western-centric liberal assumptions about progress and improvement, which colours the selection and inferences drawn from empirical data, and determines the policy prescriptions for state-building.

Another approach conflates definition with identification. The annual 'Failed States Index' (2010), commissioned by the Fund for Peace and *Foreign Policy*, assesses states at risk of 'collapse' against 12 empirical indicators such as demographic pressures, uneven development, numbers of displaced people, economic decline, human rights abuses, deterioration of public services, factionalized elites and external intervention, among others. States of concern are then arranged in a league table with the top ten deemed as failed or collapsed. These approaches to defining state failure are problematic. The continuum is positional rather than definitional. It places categories in relation to one another, rather than specifying the attributes of each category. Both the league table and continuum method also derive their categories or identifications of state failure from empirical indicators that are analytically imprecise. Indicators such as refugee flows, economic decline and human rights abuses measure both possible causes and consequences of state failure (Newman 2009: 425–6). Another problem is that certain indicators are present in some cases and not others. A number of the indicators used to identify state failure are also present in strong or capable states. Methods that rely on a context-specific set of shifting, amorphous indicators cannot adequately define the concept of the failed state in a positivist sense.

## Failed States: Unique or Uniquely Threatening?

The current idea of state failure began to acquire prominence in academic and policy circles from the early 1990s. In 1992, Gerald B. Helman and Stephen R. Ratner (1992: 3) described a 'disturbing new phenomenon': 'the failed nation state, utterly incapable of sustaining itself as a member of the international community'. Stephen D. Krasner and Carlos Pascual (2005: 153) claimed that state failure presents 'one of the most important foreign policy challenges of the contemporary era'. Mark T. Berger (2007: 1203–4) asserted that 'the growing number of collapsing/collapsed or failing/failed nation-states in the world today' means 'that we are in the midst of a crisis of the nation-state system as a whole'. While recognizing that 'weak, failed, and defeated states have long been a part of the international landscape', Robert C. Orr (2004: 7) argued that 'the threat they pose today to the United States and the civilised world is greater than ever'. The assertion that the most serious security threats in a globalized and interconnected world are now transnational, and emanate from the small, weak and failed, has become something of a mantra in the wake of the 9/11 terrorist attacks.

The empirical indicators that are used to define contemporary state failure and its transnational security consequences cannot however be considered substantially new or unique. Nor is the human security cost of state failure in the present greater than comparable disorder in the past. The disintegration of the Austro-Hungarian and Ottoman Empires, and the First Chinese Republic, for example, exhibited many of the same characteristics over much longer periods of time and at a human cost far exceeding that of contemporary state failure. More recently, the 'failure' of South Vietnam between 1959 and 1975 cost the lives of up to three million people across Indochina and 50,000 US servicemen. It is unclear why the transnational issues preoccupying us in the present should be the only ones of importance in thinking about state failure.

Similarly, the 'new' (Kaldor 1999) or 'network' (Duffield 2002b) wars of the post-Cold War era of globalization are often described as identity or ethnic-based internal conflicts weaving 'back and forth across borders to form regionalized systems of insecurity'. Parties to these conflicts deliberately exploit and target civilians as part of their war strategy dedicated to the pursuit of narrow sectarian interests (Duffield 2002a: 1051). But again, it is difficult to discern how these material conditions differ in any meaningful way from the ethnic cleansing, irredentist claims, persecution of minorities, warlord violence and refugee flows characteristic of these past examples (e.g., Marten 2006/07).

Profoundly misleading also is Mark Duffield's (2001: 15–16) thesis that 'the modalities of underdevelopment have become dangerous and destabilising' in the post-Cold War era, leading to the 'radical' merger of development and security. Duffield (2005: 20) argues that 'with the crisis of state-based security' after the Cold War, 'development has discovered a new strategic role'. Yet modernization theory was deployed by the United States during the Cold War for precisely this reason. Communist insurgencies in the Third World were believed to be directly linked to underdevelopment; they were 'scavengers' on the dislocation and instability generated by the inexorable forces of global modernization (see Packenham 1973: 52, Gaddis 1982: 208, and more generally Latham 2000). Samuel P. Huntington (1968: 41) pointed out that in the decades 'after World War II American foreign policy toward the modernizing countries was in large part devoted to promoting economic and social development because these would lead to political stability'. Berger and Heloise Weber (2006: 202) have also noted in the current failed state context that there 'has been a rediscovery of the earlier cold war preoccupation with viewing poverty and underdevelopment as a threat to global order'. These Cold War 'modernizing' approaches are directly analogous to current claims that the only answer to the security challenges of fragile and failing states in a 'globalizing' world must lay in development, hence the dominant focus on institutions of governance.

A sharp distinction is also erroneously made between the inter-state security risks of weak governments during the Cold War and the transnational security risks transmitted by contemporary state failure. Both derive from the same empirical source: the presence of transnational risks due to the inability of weak governments to effectively control the territories and populations for which they are responsible to the international society. Joseph S. Nye and Robert O. Keohane (1972: xii) define transnational activity as 'the movement of tangible or intangible items across state boundaries when at least one actor is not an agent of a government'. Arnold Wolfers (1962: 23) observed as early as 1962 that a host of transnational actors augmented nation-states in the international arena and on occasion acted in competition with them. Nye and Keohane (1972: xvi) cite the examples of multinational enterprises, revolutionary movements, and trade unions as purveyors of such transnational activity. They further make the important point that transnational activity 'increases the sensitivity of societies to one another and thereby alters relationships between governments'.

In the multipolar and bipolar international systems of the past with pluralistic order norms; transnational security issues generated by revolutionary or terrorist activity; political instability and civil unrest; or ethnic conflicts and people movements; have been viewed by states as potential risks in strategic calculations, whether as an opportunity for a competitor or a liability to their own interests. In the absence of intense strategic competition in the present unipolar system these same empirical conditions are interpreted against liberal norms primarily as a human security concern, whether to the people living in failed states and neighbouring regions, or to foreigners that may be affected by harmful transnational activity. Again, it is not the empirical character of these activities that has profoundly changed, but the frameworks through which they are evaluated, and that they can now impact on powerful and wealthy states rather than only the poor and vulnerable. States have also routinely sponsored or co-opted transnational actors and movements as elements of their foreign policies (Atzili 2006/07: 140, Salehyan 2007: 225, San Akca 2009). The presence of 'transnational' activity cannot differentiate the present failed state phenomenon from earlier examples of disorder on the periphery.

There is little evidence, however, that the actual terms state 'failure' or 'failed state' were used in the past although analogous discourses and descriptors can be found in the documentary records and in historical accounts. This suggests that the label is likely to change in the future along with the evolution of international order norms. As mentioned above, European international law differentiated between civilized, barbarous and savage polities based on their relative capacities to demonstrate appropriate properties of statehood to the international society (Gong 1984). Discourses of 'anarchy' and state 'collapse' were common in nineteenth century British foreign policy dealing with the Ottoman periphery and in US Cold War diplomacy relating to the Third World. Delegitimizing labels were also attached in particular cases. The Ottoman Empire was the 'sick man of Europe'. Republican China was a 'foreign office attached to chaos'. President John F. Kennedy was warned by J.K. Galbraith not to become involved with 'jungle regimes' whose writ runs as far as the international airport (Ninkovich 1994: 267).

The dire situation in West Africa reported by Robert Kaplan in 1994 was presciently forecast by George F. Kennan and described by the historian, Hugh Tinker, during the process of African decolonization some thirty years earlier. For example, in a 1962 letter to Walt W. Rostow, Kennan (in *Foreign Relations of the United States* [*FRUS*] 1961–63, vol. 8, doc. 85) then US Ambassador to Yugoslavia, observed,

> You have a vision … of a humane Africa, divided into God knows how many independent states, all with neat borders, U.N. membership, and all the other trappings of sovereignty on the western pattern … I see ahead in this area, no matter what we do: primarily … bewilderment, inexperience, violence, racial hatred, and internecine strife of every sort … we should have a policy towards these people … devoid of illusions about their probable future, devoid in particular of any fond belief that they are going to grow in our image …

In 1964, Tinker (1967: 44) accurately foreshadowed the contemporary 'failed' state with his depiction of the 'broken-backed' postcolonial states of East Africa:

> The State will enjoy full international recognition and membership of the United Nations … both the 'free world' and the Communist bloc will provide aid and advice … with total absence of effect. The government may be elected or self-appointed. The ministers will promote enlightened legislation which will never be implemented … Representatives of the central government will be stationed in the districts … but their writ will not run as far as the compound wall. The real power in the districts will be exercised by the men of force … [who] run their own small private armies … Then there will be the underground of resistance leaders, who are quite frankly bandits, and who levy their tribute from the peasants as well as the townspeople. Finally, there will be army or military police … exercising their protection with a heavy hand.

The internal conditions of state failure typified in the contemporary literature cannot be considered unique to the post-Cold War or post-9/11 periods. Nor is it plausible to assume that the transnational security risks generated by state failure in the present are uniquely threatening or dangerous compared with those of the past.

## The Poverty of Institutional Approaches to State Failure

The greatest flaw in the current idea of the failed state is the taken-for-granted assumption that it is caused by a breakdown in institutions of governance. In this section I challenge the assumption, largely unquestioned in much of the policy and academic literature, that formal institutions of governance are the primary causal factors for state effectiveness or fragility. The institutional approach to state failure represents a direct importation into political science of the 'new institutional' economics (NIE) prominent since the early 1990s. Although related, the NIE is to be distinguished from the various 'new institutionalisms' in political science (see Hall and Taylor 1996, Peters 1998). The institutional approach to state failure sees economic development as the ultimate remedy for state fragility. The formal institutions to be promoted or reconstituted are directed towards economic development and reflect the assumptions of the NIE. It has become an article of faith that state failure represents a failure of governance, and that appropriate institutional promotion can therefore 'fix' failed states (see Ghani and Lockhart 2008).

A 2005 paper from Britain's Department for International Development (DFID), for example, asserts unequivocally 'that the central driver of fragility is weak institutions. All other factors associated with fragility are in themselves linked to weak state institutions as a driving force' (Vallings and Moreno-Torres 2005: 7). The European Union's (EU) (2003: 4) inaugural Security Strategy attributes 'state failure' to 'bad governance – corruption, abuse of power, weak institutions and lack of accountability'. The intense renewal of emphasis on formal institutions rests on the presumed direct correlation between development and security discussed above (see Rotberg 2004: 71). This has resulted in the flawed assumption that institutions of governance are the primary causal variables for state effectiveness and sustainable development – that underdevelopment and fragility are causes rather than consequences of state failure.

The basic assumptions of the NIE are that institutions are not neutral and exert a significant effect on economic behaviour. Individuals will be utility-maximizing 'subject to the limits imposed by the existing institutional structure' (Furubotn and Richter 2005: 36). In short, institutions matter: 'they influence norms, beliefs, and actions; therefore, they shape outcomes' (Przeworski 2004a: 527). Institutions, according to Adam Przeworski (2004a: 527), are also 'endogenous: their form and their functioning depend on the conditions in which they emerge and endure'. Douglass C. North (1997: 224), perhaps the most influential scholar in the field of NIE, asserts that the institutional and organizational structures of a political economy are its primary source of economic productivity and growth. States are underdeveloped because their institutional structures lack the appropriate incentives to encourage entrepreneurial activity (North 1990: 110).

Institutions are defined as the 'rules of the game' that reduce the uncertainty inherent in human interaction by establishing stable and orderly behavioural patterns. The institutional framework of a society is conceived as having 'three components: formal rules, informal rules, and enforcement mechanisms' (Yeager 1998: 9). Formal institutions consist of the rules codified in constitutions, legislation and administrative regulation, and the organizations necessary for their enactment and performance. Informal institutions are the society's unwritten rules of conduct. They are defined by culture, norms, and shared attitudes and assumptions, some of which will be more conducive to development than others. The third component of the institutional framework is enforcement. Some institutions will be ineffective if not enforced. In cohesive societies, informal rules based on moral or cultural norms will be self-enforced by the majority of people (Yeager 1998: 9–10).

The NIE recognizes that informal cultural institutions may impede the effectiveness of formal institutions in facilitating development. Indeed, prominent scholars such as Lawrence E. Harrison (1985, 2000, 2006), focus specifically on the relationship between culture and development. However, the predominant approach of the NIE relegates culture to the margins and assumes that formal institutional frameworks, based on the model of advanced industrialized democracies, can profoundly shape behaviour and thereby alter development outcomes (Helmke and Levisky 2004: 725–6). For example, Mancur Olson (2000: 59) stresses that an appropriate structure of incentives is crucial for economic development. Institutions must provide an impartial rule of law, foster creativity and entrepreneurship, reduce transaction costs in capital markets to encourage domestic and foreign investment, and allow for a competitive economic environment that forces continual improvement by firms.

Institutional economics tends to downplay the reverse causation that formal institutional frameworks are expressions of power relations and cultural forms, or, as in the United States, the constitutional expression of a political philosophy (Fukuyama 2004: 113). In arguing that all development is 'inescapably political',

Adrian Leftwich (2000) makes a compelling recent case for the primacy of politics in development. He argues that development cannot be 'managerial or administrative' in a neutral sense. Altering the distribution of resources in a society through changes to formal institutions or regulations cannot help but change power relations (Leftwich 2000: 5–6). Leftwich (2000: 106) concludes that 'the promotion of good governance and "institution-building", explicitly detached … from a politics that can sustain it, is bound to produce feeble and flimsy developmental results'.

In critiquing the current international passion for technocratic 'institutional engineering', Przeworski (2004a: 527) makes 'the embarrassingly obvious observation that if endogeneity is strong, then institutions cannot have a causal efficacy of their own'. Conditions shape institutions. Formal institutions, whether indigenous or externally imposed, can only transmit the effects of 'the conditions that gave rise to them'. Institutions are epiphenomenal. They transmit social power relations and cultural norms that lie elsewhere (Przeworski 2004a: 527–8). At best, formal governance institutions can only be an intervening rather than a primary causal variable in any explanatory schema.

Dominant approaches to the issue assume that states fail because of corrupted and ineffective institutions of governance. Yet if institutions are endogenous, with form and function contingent on the historical conditions in which they emerge and endure; state failure must then derive from these underlying conditions. The power relations and cultural norms that shape states' institutional structures have an international and domestic dynamic. What constitutes appropriate state institutions in any historical period is defined by the most powerful actors in conformity with the ordering principles of the international society. To enjoy genuine international legitimacy, a state's domestic political institutions must approximate prevailing norms of appropriate statehood, whether the stable rational-bureaucratic framework of the nineteenth century or the liberal-democratic capitalist institutional architecture of the present.

State failure and its 'pathologies', such as underdevelopment, derive from the incongruence of informal institutions, that is, local power relations and cultural norms with externally-generated formal institutional structures. The patterns of the past suggest that not all political communities can be socialized to international norms of statehood as defined by the most powerful actors at any given time. For example, in the nineteenth century the Ottoman and Habsburg imperial states were unable to adapt to the emerging international norm of nation-statehood. Conversely, if formal institutional structures, such as those inherited by African and Melanesian states on decolonization do not reflect indigenous power relations and cultural values, they will not function as intended or deliver the governance outcomes anticipated (Przeworski 2004b: 167). This is not to suggest that cultural forms are immutable, but that their evolution occurs only at a glacial pace. The efficacy that indigenous power relations and cultural values will transmit through institutional structures is immediate, whereas reciprocal influence is weaker and may take generations.

A necessary congruence between power relations, cultural forms and formal institutions has long been recognized. The Roman philosopher-statesman Cicero (1976: 131) held that the 'deliberating authority' of a commonwealth 'must always be relative to the peculiar grounds which have brought the particular state into being'. St Thomas Aquinas (1970: 133), the scholastic theologian and medieval philosopher made the similar point that 'laws when they are passed should take account of the condition of the men who will be subject to them ... the law should be "possible both with regard to nature and with regard to the custom of the country"'.[2] On a similar note, Edmund Burke (1910: 38) argued in 1790 that 'no artificial institution whatsoever, can make the men of whom any system of authority is composed any other than God, and nature, and education, and their habits of life have made them'.

NIE perspectives, however, put their faith in the assumption that 'change in formal institutions can lead to ... change in long-held cultural values and beliefs' (Yeager 1998: 44–5). This is clearly a reversal of the direction of causation in the development of institutional structures in advanced industrial states. Historically, the establishment and evolution of successful formal institutional structures has been the product of culture-bound informal institutions and deeper belief systems. While there are some successful cases in East Asia of formal institutional promotion and adaptation, the chronic underdevelopment and insecurity of large parts of the 'developing' world should sound a cautionary note. It should be remembered that states such as Japan and South Korea that have successfully assimilated Western institutional structures are culturally homogenous, and have long 'national' histories and rational-bureaucratic traditions (Fukuyama 2004: 30, Duara 2008). These attributes fortuitously coincided with the conceptual boundaries of the postcolonial sovereign state. These conditions are not present in many parts of the developing world where social allegiances may be sub-state to tribe, clan or ethnicity, supra-state in Islamic societies, or a combination of these. And as I argue in the following section, these social allegiances are prior to any imagined or contrived 'social contract'.

## The 'Perverse Rationality' of the Social Contract Approach

Former US Ambassador to the United Nations, Jeanne Kirkpatrick (1982: 11) made the observation that 'rationalism encourages us to believe that anything that can be conceived can be brought into being. The rationalist perversion in modern politics consists in the determined effort to understand and shape people and societies on the basis of inadequate, oversimplified theories of human behaviour'. The 'rationalist perversion' is stark in social contract approaches to state failure and state-building. In this conception, state failure is the failure of the state to

2 In the second part of this quotation, Aquinas is citing St Isidore (d. 636), Archbishop of Seville.

provide public goods to its citizens (e.g., François and Sud 2006: 143, Dorff 2005: 22–3).

One of the early academic writers on the contemporary failed state phenomenon, Jean-Germain Gros (1996: 456), argues that failed states are 'those in which public authorities are either unable or unwilling to carry out their end of what Hobbes long ago called the social contract'. Rotberg (2004: 75) considers 'the social contract between ruler and ruled' to be at 'the core of interactions between states and their citizenries'. Rotberg (2004: 75) assumes that states and their governments 'exist primarily to provide for their taxpayers or inhabitants'. Britain's DFID (2005: 7) defines fragile states as 'those where the government cannot or will not deliver core functions to the majority of its people, including the poor'. State legitimacy is performance-based, a product of how effectively utilitarian functions are carried out. Stein Eriksen (2011: 230–31) describes this approach as the 'service provider' view of the state.

The Commission on Weak States and US National Security (2004: 13) focuses its attention on the 'three functions that effective governments must be able to perform: ensuring security, meeting the basic needs of citizens, and maintaining legitimacy'. Stewart Patrick (2011: 9) posits four 'core functions'. These are the provision of physical security, effective and accountable institutions in which civil rights can be realized, an economic regulatory environment conducive to private sector growth, and a basic social welfare system. For its part, the Organisation for Economic Co-operation and Development (OECD) (2008: 14) defines state-building as '*purposeful action to develop the capacity, institutions and legitimacy of the state in relation to an effective political process for negotiating the mutual demands between state and societal groups*'. The OECD (2008: 14–15) recognizes that a state's domestic legitimacy may to some degree rest in less tangible historical or identity-based resources, but nonetheless claims it is principally an outcome of a state's effectiveness in public goods provision.

Ashraf Ghani and Clare Lockhart (2008) have elaborated one of the more prominent recent examples of the social contract approach to state failure. Their 2008 book, *Fixing Failed States*, posits an abstract and exogenous ideal state. The state is composed by ten utilitarian functions drawn from the recent experience of successful states in the present era of 'intensifying global flows and value chains'. The authors argue that weak and failing states can then be empirically measured against this standard. The 'sovereignty gap' between the ideal type and the actual situation represents the extent to which the state has failed. The functional deficiencies comprising the sovereignty gap are then the focus for state-building. Ghani and Lockhart (2008) make the claim that unlike blanket approaches to capacity building theirs is particularly sensitive to local conditions. The sensitivity to context they are concerned with, however, relates not to the form of state that may emerge from the end of the process, but to the targeting of expertise and resources to the specific functional areas in which individual states deviate from the ideal type.

The state in this rationalist conception has been stripped of all politics. This is consistent, according to David Chandler (2006: 53), with the current policy consensus on governance and state-building, which sees 'unguided domestic political processes' as a 'problem for strengthening state capacity rather than central to it'. Paradoxically, liberal state-building has become anti-democratic because it 'inevitably means restricting the importance of the political sphere of political party competition and policy-making by elected representatives' (Chandler 2006: 53). Similarly, Shahar Hameiri (2007: 114) notes that in the rationalist view of state effectiveness, 'social and political relationships are not seen as intrinsic to institutions, but only as constraints or obstacles to performance'. State and society are seen to exist in a competitive rather than mutually-supportive relationship. This competitive relationship runs counter to political sociology approaches that see effective states as those embedded within their societies. Socially 'embedded' states have a greater capacity to maintain themselves domestically and conduct themselves internationally than state forms that are separate from their underlying social dynamics (Hobson 1998: 293).

It is also interesting to note how current technocratic approaches to state-building are diametrically opposed to the political development theories prominent during the 1960s despite their underlying affinities about modernization and progress. Huntington (1968: 24–5) argued that successful state institutions must have both moral and structural dimensions, and it is explicitly the political rather than legal-regulatory institutions of a society that give it a cohesive moral direction. Societies cannot define meaningful common interests in the absence of strong political institutions. The 'public interest' is not something that can exist without an institutionalized *political* process. An effective government that gives substance to the public interest must derive from political rather than technocratic processes.

Contrary to this, however, Ghani and Lockhart (2008: 68) suggest that social conflicts are best brought to compromise solutions through the 'reframing' of 'politics to create a technical space'. They argue that 'politics can be either constructive or destructive'. Yet politics is always both. To those without it, political power is never in the right hands. The content and direction of state functions and their distributional outcomes are under continuous social and political contestation, even in the most successful states. Effective states are not legitimate because of the utilitarian functions they perform (Gray 2003: 95–6). The foundation of an effective state's domestic legitimacy precedes any imagined or contrived social contract. It is not a product of it.

Writers that invoke social contract theory in the failed state context display a meagre understanding of its antecedents in political philosophy. The social contract is not simply that between state and citizen. At first principles, the contract refers to the covenant made between prospective citizens to constitute the state. The Hobbesian contract rests on the proposition that '*a man be willing, when others are so to ... as for Peace, and defense of himselfe he shall think it necessary, to lay down this right to all things; and be contented with so much liberty against other men, as he would allow other men against himselfe*' (Hobbes 1996: 92). In the Lockean version, the individual 'puts on the bonds of civil society' by way of 'agreeing with other men to join and unite into a community for their comfortable, safe, and peaceable living one amongst another' (Locke 1980: 54). Jean-Jacques Rousseau (1968: 59–60) posits that the only way in which individuals 'can preserve themselves is by uniting their separate powers in a combination strong enough to overcome any resistance'. It is this first principle of social contract theory that is of most salience in thinking about state failure. The subsequent relationship between state and citizen is secondary and derivative.

Ghani and Lockhart (2008) make the point that they are not looking for the 'Platonic essence' of the state, but fail to recognize that their neo-utilitarian approach can then only ever be partial, necessarily confounded by the non-rational attributes of political community. Historically, the political community has been viewed predominantly as a natural or organic, rather than contractual entity, and dedicated to a particular moral or metaphysical conception of the good (see Aristotle 1962: 25–9, Cicero 1976: 128–31, 169, 173, Augustine 1972: 890–91, Aquinas 1970: 191, Bodin 1955, 1–8). States have always had a moral purpose (Reus-Smit 1999). They are expressions of collective identity. They are the means to achieve collective justice. The Palestinians and the Kurds do not seek statehood for purely functional reasons. States are also the vehicles for myths (Gilby 1958: 319). These myths form part of the identity narratives integral to states' ontological security. The United States embodies a deontological claim: it is the exemplar liberal state, the 'shining city upon a hill' to lead and inspire others (e.g., Reagan 1989). It is not the particular content of the 'good' that is important in this sense, but that all cohesive political communities are defined by a broad moral consensus about what is right and just. This shapes and defines their institutional structures.

Social contract theorists write as though the contract presupposes only the freely chosen rational choice of atomized individuals. However, the founders of an explicit or implied social contract must have already established themselves as a form of political community enabling them to determine who should participate in their future and who should not. Analytically prior to any imagined social contract there must be a modicum of value consensus and shared identity, a bond that makes the state coherent as a political community and considered legitimate by its members (Scruton 2002: 12–13). This element seems essential to the long-term successful orderly functioning of a state but has always been in short supply in weak states. If a state's territorial boundaries, institutional arrangements or system of positive law is incongruent with the values of its antecedent political community, or if it lacks the basis for any centred political community at all, it will be weak and ineffective. This problem is further compounded for weak states in the present liberal international order. The violent and protracted state-making processes that allowed for today's powerful and cohesive modern states to form are no longer acceptable within the international society (Ayoob 1995: chapter 2).

The rationalist perversion critiqued in this section of the chapter is to think that state legitimacy can derive solely from function or 'service provision'.

In successful states, political legitimacy is the prior basis for their effective functioning in defining and giving substance to the public interest. States with strong antecedent bases of political and social legitimacy will not lose control over their territories and populations even if there is a near complete breakdown in the provision of public goods, such as, for example, in Vietnam from the late 1970s to the mid-1980s.

## State Failure and International Orders

State failure has been shown to be a condition with long historical antecedents. It is not caused by a failure of governance institutions or by a breakdown in the social contract. Much more useful as a point of departure in thinking about state failure is Robert Jackson's concept of the postcolonial 'quasi-state', which was created by changes to international order after World War II. According to Jackson (1987: 528), quasi-states are essentially nominal political entities with largely abstract constitutions and institutions. Their existence is maintained and protected by courtesy of a permissive international society. This was made possible by normative changes to the meaning of sovereignty that evolved during the post-1945 period of rapid decolonization. Jackson (1987: 531) characterizes this normative shift as 'the ascendancy of a highly accommodating international morality which, at its centre, contains the principle of self-determination as an unqualified, universal human right of all ex-colonial peoples'.

The earlier requirement under international law that positive criteria of empirical statehood be demonstrated was largely abandoned under the powerful moral pressures generated by anti-colonial principles of self-determination and racial equality. Nearly all colonies gained independence within existing and often arbitrary state boundaries regardless of their lack of effective domestic institutions, and any substantive capability to control their territory, provide public goods, or foster socio-economic development beyond a narrow group of elites. Quasi-states acquired an unprecedented exemption from the power competition hitherto characteristic of international politics (Jackson 1990: 15–23). Most postcolonial states were weak, and according to the above empirical definitions of state fragility, many would have been considered 'failed' from their inception.

That the 'failed' state has only emerged as a serious concern to Western policy-makers in the post-Cold War period is again due to changes in international order norms underwritten by a shift in the distribution of capabilities. Core Western states led by Washington assumed that with the end of strategic bipolarity, the pattern of international order would move from pluralism toward liberal-democratic solidarism. For instance, the preamble to the 2002 US National Security Strategy explicitly states that the political system of 'freedom, democracy, and free enterprise' is the 'single sustainable model for national success' (The White House 2002).

From a more explicitly constructivist perspective, with the easing of both the deeply entrenched ideational frameworks and material constraints of the Cold War, cultural change in the post-1945 international system accelerated from the early 1990s. The international culture of permissiveness toward Jackson's postcolonial 'negative sovereignty' regime shifted to one of surveillance and intervention in the internal processes of weak states to discipline them to the norms of identity and behaviour of the emerging liberal international order. The relational ontology of a constructivist approach allows the 'role' of failed state to be constituted only in relation to a social structure of shared knowledge. Structures place social facts 'in relationships of conceptual necessity' to others, in that they are mutually constitutive. In this sense, the 'failed' state could not 'exist' until externally constituted as such in relation to the 'appropriate' or 'successful' state, as defined within a structure of shared knowledge (Wendt 1999: 84–5, 227–8). The failed state has been ideationally constituted in relation to the redefinition of the appropriate properties of statehood in the post-Cold War era. The condition of state failure must then be relative to the normative principles of international order, which are historically contingent.

## Conclusion

This chapter has demonstrated that current empirical definitions of state failure are inadequate and that the focus on state institutions and functions is flawed, able to provide at best only a partial understanding of the failed state phenomenon. I have shown that state failure is not unique to the post-Cold War era, nor is it uniquely threatening in comparison with earlier historical periods. More controversially, the chapter challenged some of the more deeply entrenched assumptions about the purpose and function of the state, which are used to frame current approaches to state 'failure' and reconstitution. I demonstrated that the concept of state failure cannot plausibly be explained as a failure of formal institutions of governance. Neither is it a result of the failure of the state to provide public goods to its citizens. These are symptoms or consequences of state failure, not causes.

Finally, the chapter concluded from an analysis of Jackson's idea of the quasi-state, and constructivist theoretical perspectives, that changes in the nature of legitimate statehood in a given period are driven by material and ideational changes independent of the empirical conditions within weak states. The current failed state phenomenon is a result of the post-Cold War change to solidarist international ordering principles that assumes universal movement toward liberal-democracy as normative for all states. This normative shift is a consequence of the change in structural conditions from a bipolar to unipolar international system. With the shift from a pluralist to solidarist order, weak states are caught in a double bind. The pressures of liberal international order norms both contribute to state weakness on the periphery and frame the evaluations of state failure made by the core actors of international society. But, at the same time, status quo great powers require conformity to this pattern of order, however deleterious it may be for weak states, for their own ontological security needs. The themes of international order, distribution of capabilities and ontological security are elaborated further in Chapter 3 as the conceptual foundations in developing the book's interpretive framework to take into the case studies presented in Chapters 4, 5 and 6.

# Chapter 3
# International Order, Capabilities and Ontological Security: An Interpretive Framework

In the previous chapter I concluded that state failure is not new to the post-Cold War period, nor is it uniquely threatening in historical terms. It is not caused by a failure of institutions of governance or by the failure of the state to provide public goods to its citizens. What counts as state failure in a given period is relative to the norms of international order, which are historically contingent. The nature of international order, whether it embodies thick or thin normative claims, is conditioned by the structure of the international system. This chapter develops these claims further into an interpretive framework for understanding state failure and intervention in the periphery. I first define and elaborate the conceptual foundations of international order, the distribution of capabilities, and ontological security, the dynamics between them, and locate them in their respective historical and case-specific contexts.

The prestige motive is then introduced as the link connecting these diffuse conditional factors into a concrete policy of armed intervention to restore order in failed states on the periphery. I first disaggregate the concept of motive into three dimensions: the normative, instrumental and emotional. Emotions are taken here to have an object and involve both feeling and reflection. They are to be differentiated from objectless moods or affective states. I argue that norm violations will produce negative emotions among members of established social orders while positive emotions will be expressed when norms are revalidated. The strength of these emotions will demonstrate the value of the normative complex in question. For status quo actors, normative 'threats' to established orders will evoke the emotional expressions of affront or insult at a perceived challenge to their social status.

These three dimensions are then applied to the concept of prestige. First, I note that prestige has traditionally been viewed in its instrumental dimension as credibility. From a review of recent literature on ontological security, respect and honour, I establish the normative dimension of prestige as reputation for upholding international order norms. Reputation is external and relational in that it is a perception held by others. But more importantly, our imagining of the opinions others hold of us can deeply affect the way we feel about ourselves. An important insight from the ontological security perspective is that states are moved to social action to fulfil non-instrumental identity needs that are internally-focused. I call this internal sense of self-worth, national honour. This is the emotional dimension of the prestige motive.

I argue that normative threats to great powers in areas where they see themselves as the source of international order, are experienced as a challenge to their reputation, and consequently, to their self-respect and national honour. National honour can be considered in two ways. Disruptions to reputational norms are an affront to a status quo actor and will produce the 'negative' emotional expressions of insult or humiliation. Status quo great powers feel frustration and anger more acutely than other states because their perceived reputation as an indispensable source of international order is an integral and meaningful part of their identity narrative. Disproportionate behaviour in response to this will highlight how intensely a humiliation is felt. On the other hand, the 'positive' emotion of glory may be expressed when norms are re-validated and national honour restored. The final section of the chapter briefly reviews a number of recent studies that seek to explain interventions in the periphery. I first demonstrate that these are inadequate either because the complexity of the prestige motive is neglected or ignored altogether; or, where it is invoked, it can only explain a very narrow set of cases because it overlooks the element of normative threat.

## Pattern of Order in International Society

Sovereign statehood is the constitutive institution of international society. It divided Europe and later the world into a plurality of independent political entities each with absolute jurisdiction over mutually recognized territories. Overlaying the institution of sovereignty are the power relations between states. Henry Kissinger (1964: 1) defines international order as the balance of power along with a doctrine of legitimacy. Legitimacy, in the sense, does not imply justice. Rather, it denotes 'international agreement about the nature of workable arrangements and about the permissible aims and methods of foreign policy'. Such agreement will reflect the preferences of those states positioned favourably in the balance of power. The elements of this agreement provide the normative framework for international order. Once established, an international order is path-dependent and status quo in character. It will be threatened by weak states that are unable to meet its normative requirements or by revisionist or recalcitrant states unwilling to conform to it, or that seek to overturn it.

For Hedley Bull and other writers of the English School, legitimacy and order are found in an international society of states, which presupposes the existence of a states-system in strictly realist terms. Similar to Kissinger's doctrine of legitimacy, states that are members of the society 'conceive themselves to be bound by a common set of rules in their relations with one another, and share in the working of common institutions' (Bull 2002: 13). These rules are intended to promote the fundamental goals of the international society: the maintenance of a society of sovereign states, the preservation of each state's independence, the promotion of peace as the normal condition of international affairs and the promotion of the necessary conditions for order in all social life (Bull 2002: 16–19). These basic social conditions are protection from arbitrary violence, reliable expectations that agreements will be carried out and security from challenges to possessions that are constant and without limit (Bull 2002: 5). The preservation of the international society overrides all other goals, even at the expense of peace or the sovereign integrity of individual states. According to Bull, the institutions used by international society to achieve these goals are the balance of power system, international law, diplomacy, the special managerial responsibility of the great powers and war (Bull 2002: 71). The understanding by major powers that they carry a special burden of responsibility for the international society is particularly important for the arguments developed here. The responsibility to maintain international order is deeply implicated in the prestige and identity narrative of status quo great powers.

The idea that international order is based on a certain 'pattern', or set of principles, gives normative direction to Kissinger's 'legitimate aims and methods of foreign policy' and to Bull's 'goals' of the international society. Bull (1966: 52) suggested that patterns of order in the international society may be pluralist or solidarist. Also writing in 1966, Raymond Aron (2003: 99–104) advanced the similar notion that international systems may be ordered on heterogeneous or homogeneous patterns. A pluralist or heterogeneous international order is best explained by Michael Oakeshott's concept of a 'civil association', where a relationship among members exists in their acceptance of institutionalized rules governing mutual interactions. These rules are conditions of conduct only, and 'indifferent to the pursuit or achievement' of any particular purpose or common interest (Oakeshott 1975: 201–3). Pluralist international orders recognize, at least in principle, the ontological equality of all states and incorporate norms of self-determination and non-intervention (Wheeler 1992: 467). The provisions of the 1945 UN Charter are the definitive statement of a pluralist international order. Patterns of order that are pluralistic, with acceptance of differing regime forms and minimal standards for state behaviour, will produce a high normative threshold for state failure and permissible intervention. Pluralistic patterns of order are possible in all international system structures whether multipolar, bipolar or unipolar. Solidarist orders, however, are the sole preserve of unipolar international systems and will reflect the deontological claims of the hegemon.

A solidarist or homogeneous pattern of order may be equated with Oakeshott's (1975: 115) concept of an 'enterprise association', defined as a social relationship among members dedicated to not only a 'common purpose' but also to 'the "management" of its pursuit'. In solidarist international orders, states operate within a legal and normative environment densely packed with rules and norms reflecting the values of leading actors. This creates a high normative standard for state behaviour (Buzan 2004: 46–51). In the immediate post-Cold War era, core liberal actors led by the United States hold that an idealized version of their own form of governance is universal. State identities and behaviours that deviate from this normative standard attract moral and sometimes material sanction. Non-intervention has increasingly become conditional on the responsibility to conform to these standards. In patterns of order based on assumptions of convergence in regime forms and state behaviours, the threshold for state failure and intervention will be much lower than in pluralistic orders.

States with the greatest interest in maintaining the prevailing pattern of international order, and with the greatest capacity to intervene, will carry the burden of responsibility to do so. Status quo great powers will therefore be the actors most concerned with disorder from the periphery. This is in the form of state 'failure' in the present, with similar labels applying in the past, as shown in Chapter 2. The pattern of order in the international society is the criteria against which political leaders evaluate state failure and it also sets the normative conditions for permissible intervention to restore order.

It is important to reiterate that failed states do not present any direct material security threat to great powers in a traditional sense. This raises the question of why do states mount military interventions to restore order at substantial cost and risk, rather than quarantining the transnational problems emanating from failed states. I argue that the actual or anticipated breach of international order norms by a 'deviant' social actor gives rise to a 'normative threat'. Creppell (2011: 455) advances this idea to explain the perception by a group of harm or destruction to something valuable or essential to them but not concrete or physically tangible: a '[n]ormative threat portends a change in one's way of life or in the patterns or rules one expects to govern relationships'. As we have observed, order is both functional, in that it provides for stable and predictable behaviour, and normative, in that beliefs about the right principles of order are extremely important. The international reputation of status quo great powers, and also their sense of national honour, is heavily invested in their role as purveyors of order. For such powers, failed states, however defined in historical context, are a normative threat to their expectations for international order in areas they consider within their sphere of responsibility. Crucially, this also impinges on great powers' identity and ontological security needs, a theme developed further below.

### *The Standard of Civilization in the Late-Nineteenth Century*

The book's first case study, the 1882 British occupation of Egypt, took place on the semi-colonial Ottoman periphery of the European international society of the late-nineteenth century. The ordering principles for the international society were based on the emerging 'standard of civilization' in international law. The 'classical' standard consisted of five criteria: the first was that Europeans anywhere should be afforded protection of life, liberty and property consistent with the rule of law in Europe. The second was that a civilized state must retain a rational-bureaucratic structure, uphold its international commitments and exercise control over a defined territory. The third was that a state must accept the prevailing system of European international law. The fourth was the maintenance of adequate and permanent channels for diplomacy. A fifth, more subjective criterion ruled out social practices deemed unacceptable by Europeans such as suttee, slavery and polygamy. The necessity for international administration and extraterritoriality became symbolic of a polity's less than civilized status relative to international society members (Gong 1984).

The pattern of order institutionalized in the 'standard' was pluralistic, underwritten by strategic multipolarity. Among international society members it provided for mutually-agreed, rules-based conduct without the pursuit of a common purpose or conformity in regime type. This did not preclude a European Concert on periodic questions of mutual concern, which was the strong preference of British liberals (Medlicott 1969: 33–4). The disposition of the international society toward those outside, was, however, solidarist to the extent that other polities were also judged against the European standard. This provided for a continuum from the 'savage' polities of sub-Saharan Africa and the Pacific Islands through the 'barbarous' decaying empires of the Orient to the 'civilized' states of Europe. The British variant of the standard considered in Chapter 4 placed particular emphasis on sound finance, public frugality and the sanctity of contract and international treaties as providing the discipline and character for good government (Cain and Hopkins 2002: 45–8). Prime Minister Gladstone's (1971: 115–17) principles of foreign policy outlined in his 1879 Midlothian election campaign firmly subordinated 'freedom' and the 'equality of nations' to economy, the preservation of peace, the will of 'civilized' Europe and international law.

Egypt was considered 'semi-barbarous', not yet ready for full self-government or membership of international society, but *was* expected to abide by its rules under European supervision. Left to its own devices, it would rapidly return to a state of 'anarchy' (Gong 1984: 62, *The Times* 1881: 4). By defaulting on its debts in 1876, the Egyptian Khedivate had failed to uphold its international financial commitments, a serious breach of the standard.[1] The establishment of an Anglo-French dual 'Control' over Egyptian finances in 1879 had restored the fiscal viability of Egyptian administration. Its continuation ensured the maintenance of a functioning, de facto independent Egyptian state under the nominal suzerainty of the Ottoman Empire.

### *The Cold War Postcolonial International Order*

The second case study in the book, the 1965 US combat intervention in South Vietnam, was a product of the Cold War bipolar international system (1947–89). The post-1945 pattern of international order that underlay the Cold War was pluralistic, based on the foundational UN Charter principles of self-determination, sovereign equality and non-interference in states' internal affairs. The 'self' in self-determination was no longer national, however, but referred specifically

1 The 'Khedive' was the title of the Ottoman viceroy of Egypt. The Khedivate was made hereditary in Egypt within the Muhammad Ali dynasty in 1866.

to colonies, many of which were multiethnic artefacts created by the European empires. The impetus for gradual and orderly decolonization through the UN trusteeship process was overtaken by the mid-1950s. Demands for rapid, universal decolonization were brought to bear through the UN General Assembly which was steadily accruing a postcolonial majority. This shift to a postcolonial normative framework produced a rights-based rather than performance-based model of Third World statehood (Jackson 1993: 121–6). Decolonization ignited a sea of turbulence and destabilization in large swathes of the periphery, which, by the early 1960s, had become the main theatres of the Cold War.

Overlaying this final phase of the modern transformation to a universal system of formally independent states was the ideological bipolarity that also defined the post-World War II international order. The ideological disposition of both superpowers was anti-colonial and both engaged in anti-colonial rhetoric in seeking support from emerging states (Jackson 1993: 128). During the formative period of the Cold War, however, the opportunities and problems of decolonization were a second order consideration for US policy-makers, who acquiesced to the restoration of British, French and Dutch rule in Southeast Asia (Leffler 1992: 92–4). In 1945, the United States had emerged as the world's most powerful state. Washington's expectations for a broadly liberal, global multilateral order, constituted and regulated through the new United Nations, Bretton Woods Institutions (BWIs) and the General Agreement on Tariffs and Trade (GATT), were by 1950, thwarted by the consolidation of the antithetical Marxist-Leninist bloc (Knutsen 1999).

Outside the communist sphere, the United States fashioned an 'open and loosely rule-based international order' focused primarily on Western Europe and Pacific Asia, with emphasis also on the Eastern Mediterranean and Middle East. This pluralistic 'free world' order was grounded on the consent of North Atlantic and Asian partners and 'organized around open markets, security alliances, multilateral cooperation', and at least in the case of Western Europe, 'democratic community' (Ikenberry 2005: 133). In Europe, the emphasis was on multilateral economic cooperation through the Organisation for European Economic Co-Operation (OEEC) (later OECD) and a security community through NATO. In East Asia and the Middle East, the emphasis was on bilateral economic linkages and a hub-and-spoke array of security alliances (Knutsen 1999: 213). Washington's Cold War national security doctrine encompassed a large range of intangible security referents that cannot be understood according to calculations of material interest. Normative threats to national security were subjective and limitless and closely tied to perceptions of US reputation for resolve. Adverse events or disorder anywhere on the globe were a potential risk to core American 'interests' defined in a normative language of values (Yergin 1990: 196, Layne 2006: 119).

Modernization theorists in the Democratic administrations of the 1960s, such as Walt W. Rostow and Roger Hilsman, saw communist insurgencies as insidious attempts to capitalize on the dislocations of the transition to modernity, of which decolonization was a necessary aspect. This view was also strongly shared by

President John F. Kennedy (e.g., 1961c: 444–5, 1961d: 461, 1961g: 397). Hilsman in particular believed that modernization conceived as socio-economic development was not in itself sufficient to bolster weak postcolonial governments and suppress insurgencies. The building of physical security and administrative efficacy were also essential to a state's legitimacy and its resistance to communist subversion. Most postcolonial governments lacked capacity in these areas (Blaufarb 1977: 58–62).

By August 1962 a counterinsurgency and nation-building doctrine had been developed based on four elements: a comprehensive appraisal of the political and economic circumstances of the at-risk country; the development and implementation of measures to ameliorate the major causes of social discontent; effective military and police forces for internal security; and the building of administrative capacity to support these measures (Blaufarb 1977: 63–4). Under the intellectual auspices of modernization theory, counterinsurgency doctrine formed the basis for rural 'pacification' and nation-building in South Vietnam. The inculcation of South Vietnamese 'nationalism' and state legitimacy was seen to be instrumental and performance-based, rather than primordial or constitutional (Latham 2000: 204). There are clear parallels between US approaches to nation-building during the Cold War and the current technocratic approaches to state-building critiqued in Chapter 2 (Latham 2006: 39–40).

### *The Post-Cold War Liberal International Order*

The book's third case study, the 2002 French intervention in Ivory Coast, took place in the liberal international order of the early twenty-first century. In contrast to these earlier historical periods, the international order in the immediate post-Cold War period was solidarist and homogenizing. The claim by Washington that liberal-democratic capitalism is the sole legitimate form of governance forms the normative basis of a liberal international order. Strategic unipolarity underwrites the current international order. Preponderant US strategic power provides the necessary coercive authority for the functioning of a global market economy. The neo-liberal ideology underpinning this is consistent with the interests and worldview of mobile financial capital, the transnational managerial classes of affluent OECD states, and also privileged elites in the less developed world (Gill 2003: 123). At the time of writing in early 2012, the US is slowly emerging from the recession following the financial crisis of 2007–08 while the European Union (EU) remains mired in the Greek sovereign debt crisis. Despite the return of Keynesian stimulus packages and multiple proposals for financial sector reform, an alternative worldview to post-Washington consensus neo-liberalism has yet to emerge.

Another defining element of liberal international order is the complex network of global governance which now ranges across many spheres of planetary life. As an adjunct to the globalization process, the agents of global governance are represented as supraterritorial or nonterritorial and to some extent autonomous from state power. Yet most aspects of global governance are undertaken by intergovernmental or Western state agencies in partnership with private transnational or local non-government organizations (NGOs). Governance implies universal, technocratic and value-neutral criteria for efficient state administration. Contemporary notions of good governance, however, are synonymous with the ideological preferences of the wealthy states of the West. Good governance is equated with multiparty democracy, the rule of law, an open market economy, private property and human rights norms (Ignatieff 2005: 68–9). But as William Brown (2006: 360) points out, in the most underdeveloped parts of the world such as sub-Saharan Africa, the governance prescriptions of a solidarist liberal international order are not neutral reforms but amount to a program of radical, revolutionary social change.

In the realm of ideas, the liberal international order represents the endpoint of Enlightenment teleology, most famously articulated by Francis Fukuyama in the 1989 essay, 'The End of History?' In the post-Cold War era, various strands of liberal thought in the spheres of human rights, human security, cosmopolitanism, democratic peace theory and neo-liberal economics have converged to form a renewed standard of civilization, sometimes termed a 'global civilization'. But different from the classical standard, which was mainly concerned with states' behaviour, global civilization is fundamentally concerned with states' 'identity'. This has implicitly reinstated a hierarchy that overlays states' formal UN Charter equality (see Reus-Smit 2005: 72, Simpson 2004: 81, Mozzafarai 2001). The shift from a pluralist to a solidarist international order allows states to be differentiated and ranked according to how closely they conform to the model of liberal-democratic statehood. The internal characteristics of states determine their standing and treatment against the liberal standard set down by core Western states and increasingly reflected in international law. This treatment, particularly with respect to the legitimate use of force, sees 'rights to self-determination and non-intervention' qualified for certain categories of state, such as 'rogue' or 'failed' (Reus-Smit 2005: 72).

France sits uneasily within the liberal international order of the post-Cold War era under US dominance. Historically, France maintains a competing claim as the exemplar liberal republican state (Gordon 1993: 14–17, Krotz and Sperling 2011). Both the United States and France consider their respective liberal projects to be universal and that they occupy a position of exceptionalism in world affairs. These differences became starkly apparent during the period of the Bush administration (2001–09) where Washington claimed that the values of freedom, democracy and human rights were of essentially American origin. By contrast, and reflecting its diminished power in the world, France now sees its universal liberal values reflected in international law and institutions, especially the UN and EU (Bowen 2005: 112). The conflict between US unilateralism and French multilateralism was most clearly displayed in the lead up to the 2003 invasion of Iraq. The French position on the legitimacy of multilateralism was somewhat disingenuous, however, given that France at that time retained and exercised a claim to unilateral action, especially in Africa.

The French experience of decolonization in sub-Saharan Africa was relatively tranquil compared with the trauma of Indochina and Algeria. In the postcolonial international order, the imperial *mission civilisatrice* in Africa continued to be understood as a French duty and also a 'noble end' of policy because it 'was appreciated and accepted as necessary' by indigenous elites (Chipman 1989: 85). Decolonization in francophone Africa was undertaken by the metropole and local elites 'in a spirit of collaboration with the former colonizer' that rejected the non-aligned, anti-colonial message of the 1955 Bandung Conference (Chipman 1989: 103). France's continuing 'management' of a sphere of responsibility in Africa was central to its residual claims to great power status. Perhaps because it was ultimately self-serving, at the end of the Cold War, France's civilizing mission in Africa appeared to have failed. Neither peace nor development had been brought to many of its former colonies (Charbonneau 2008: 1).

In the immediate post-Cold War period, France at first retained a traditional realist and Gaullist foreign policy outlook. In Africa, the end of the Cold War had little immediate impact on French policy. Existing patterns of relations and troop levels were maintained until 1994 when things began to change due to the national shame and denigration of France's reputation because of complicity in the genocide in Rwanda (Gregory 2000b: 438–9). By the end of the 1990s, however, a transformation in the worldview of French political elites had taken place. France was a committed supporter of the EU position on democratization, respect for ethnic and religious diversity, and progress in human rights. French policy had changed quite radically during the brutal wars of ethnic cleansing in Bosnia and Kosovo to one that supported 'the liberation of oppressed nationalities and the right of intervention against governments guilty of violating human rights' (Soutou 2002: 83). The current French Defence and National Security White Paper explicitly predicates military operations on the 'responsibility to protect' civilian populations (*Présidence de la République* 2008). The French intervention in Ivory Coast examined in Chapter 6 was in part justified by a robust mandate to protect civilians.

## Distribution of Capabilities

The distribution of capabilities, or structure of the international system, is also essential to understanding state failure and intervention in three important ways. The first is that power is the background condition for international order. Great powers define the standards of international legitimacy and serve as a model for others to follow. Benjamin O. Fordham and Victor Assal (2007: 31–2) argue that the '"prestige" of powerful states' is manifested in 'the demonstration effect of their institutions and practices in the international system'. The prestige of major powers is heavily invested in the prevailing international order, whether pluralist or solidarist, which reflects their values and serves their interests. Second, armed interventions in states deemed to be failed will only occur in geographical locations where the interests of status quo major powers are engaged, or that they consider a strategic sphere of influence. In each of the cases examined in the book, the intervening power held important material interests in the area, but this was not a sufficient condition for military intervention. Alternative interest-based courses of action were available to policymakers in each case. Third, interventions in the periphery are constrained by the distribution of capabilities. Prudential calculations operate in both the decision to intervene and in the scope of military action that can be undertaken. This is a compelling consideration in multipolar and bipolar systems.

### *Multipolarity in the Late-Nineteenth Century*

The 1882 British intervention in Egypt took place in the multipolar international system of the late-nineteenth century. Multipolarity in the European context meant that three or more states were considered pre-eminent and no single state could survive an alliance of the others against it. In multipolar systems, a state's primary strategic concern is a division of potential gains or losses that may favour others more than itself (Waltz 1979: 106). Britain's position in the 1880s was of a status quo power in relative decline. The margin of capabilities between Britain and its industrial rivals had narrowed since the height of its ascendance in the 1850s. Britain lacked a mass conscript army comparable to the Continental Powers and had stood aside from 'the series of wars which culminated in the crushing defeat of France by Germany in 1870–71' (Evans 1968: 190). London was disconcerted by the recasting of the systemic structure brought by Italian and German unification but remained slow to appreciate the intensity of the renewed strategic competition precipitated by these profound changes in Central Europe.

Events of the 1870s also challenged the longstanding British interests in the Near East of safeguarding the routes and communications to the Indian subcontinent by keeping Russia out of the area and preventing any other Power from encroaching militarily on Egypt (Lowe 1969: 38–9). After the defeat of France in 1870, Russia renounced the Black Sea clauses of the Treaty of Paris, enabling the Straits to be closed to British shipping. On Bismarck's initiative in 1872, Russia also entered the *Dreikaiserbund* ('Three Emperors' League'), with Germany and Austria-Hungary, further heightening traditional British Russophobia. The closure of the Straits meant that the British navy had no alternate means to check a Russian advance to the Persian Gulf or an attack on India through Afghanistan (Clayton 1971). Matters briefly came to a head with the Anglo-Russian war scare of 1878, in which the British Mediterranean fleet was despatched to the Dardanelles to challenge a threatened Russian attack on Constantinople.

The French Third Republic had moved closer to Britain in the wake of the country's humiliating defeat at the hands of Prussia, but the relationship was deeply problematic. The informal 'liberal alliance' was needed to prevent German hegemony of the Continent, though this imperative also drew France closer to Russia. British and French interests also diverged sharply in North Africa, a sphere in which Italy was also interested in competition with France (Lowe 1969: 40). Britain sought a Mediterranean ringed by independent states. The French, already ensconced in Algeria, saw in North Africa an Empire encompassing Morocco, Tunis, Tripoli and Egypt (Taylor 1954: 285). The result, by the early 1880s, was a sporadically expanding French sphere across the Maghreb and a tense Anglo-French rivalry of influence at Cairo.

Meanwhile, Bismarck, in isolating France and tranquilizing Austro-Russian rivalries in the Balkans, had concluded the Dual Alliance with Austria in 1879, renewed the *Dreikaiserbund* in 1881 and added Italy to the Triple Alliance of 1882. Bismarck's other key objective was to keep Britain isolated by preventing 'any English dominated system of alliances or Concert of Europe' (Lowe 1969: 49). It was into this strategic context that the second Liberal government of William Ewart Gladstone (1880–85) took office in April 1880. Radical liberal opinion, including that professed by Gladstone himself, deprecated the value of India, and therefore of Egypt (the 'road to India'), as worth the risk of either a European war or a break with France (e.g., Gladstone 1877: 10, Osborn 1882: 30–31, Westlake 1882: 824).

### *The Bipolar Cold War System*

The United States' intervention with combat forces in Vietnam from 1965 to 1973 is considered to be one of the defining conflicts, or 'proxy wars', of the Cold War bipolar international system. The United States and the Soviet Union, as the leading actors of the opposing blocs, were pre-eminent, if far from equal, in aggregate capabilities. Bipolarity also meant that the Cold War balance could not be tilted by the defection of any third party to either side. Washington maintained a clear superiority during the 1960s in its capacity to deliver nuclear warheads to Soviet Bloc territory. However, the destructiveness of thermonuclear weapons and the deployment by Moscow of a second-strike capability by the early 1960s meant that only a small but credible deterrent force was required for effective parity (Johnson 1994: 91–3, 109). President Eisenhower's Basic National Security Policy of 5 August 1959 assessed that a condition of 'relative nuclear parity' was in existence (*FRUS* 1958–60, vol. 3, doc. 70).

In practice, bipolarity functioned more in the realm of perception. Decision-makers in Washington tended to view Cold War competition as a zero-sum game. More so than in the other case studies where the pattern of international order is clearly separable from the distribution of capabilities, zero-sum ideological and strategic bipolarity meant that order and power were tightly interlocked. Gains to communism anywhere through subversion or insurgency would lead to a symbolic erosion of US credibility everywhere, thereby contributing to even further losses (Johnson 1994: 25–6). Even though the United States remained overwhelmingly superior in strategic reach and material capability to both the USSR and China, any communist territorial or reputational gain, or technological advance, was interpreted by Washington as deeply threatening. Initiatives by Moscow to redress the strategic imbalance, such as the introduction of intermediate-range ballistic missiles to Cuba in 1962, were invariably perceived by Washington as highly provocative and aggressive.

To counter professed Soviet support for wars of 'national liberation', the Kennedy administration developed a counterinsurgency strategy to meet communist subversion directly and symmetrically. President Johnson followed this approach faithfully in Vietnam with graduated escalations in response to communist 'provocations'. The US response to the National Liberation Front (NLF) insurgency in South Vietnam was considered a critical test case of countering Maoist 'people's war' doctrine. Even if the international communist movement was no longer unified after the Sino-Soviet split of the early 1960s, the risk to global order remained acute. The 'loss' of South Vietnam would erode US national security by emboldening indigenous communist movements elsewhere in Asia, Africa and the Western Hemisphere (Horowitz 1971: 422, Lin 2009: 43–9).

### *Unipolarity in the Early Twenty-First Century*

The 2002 French intervention in Ivory Coast was mounted in the unipolar international system of the early twenty-first century. Following the end of strategic bipolarity in 1991, the defining characteristic of the current international system has been the global hegemony of the United States. Its core ideological preference for liberal-democratic capitalism forms the normative basis of a post-Cold War liberal international order. The unipolar system is also marked by the containment of overt security competition among second-tier major powers (Wohlforth 1999: 7–8). China's rapid economic growth and military modernization raises strategic uncertainty in the East Asian region and points to a future multipolar world, but in 2012 the United States remains by far the most powerful global player.

The events of 1989–91 that brought an end to the Cold War came as a shock to France. Its traditional realist foreign policy outlook was slow to adjust to the new strategic situation which was unfavourable to Paris in a number of ways. The end of the bipolar world and reunification of Germany destroyed the unique position France had carved out for itself during the period of the Fifth Republic. This was based on leadership in Western Europe due to the partition of Germany, an independent French nuclear deterrent, an autonomous relationship with NATO allowing Paris to escape elements of the Atlantic alliance it did not like, and a less antagonistic relationship with Moscow. This allowed France to continue to play a prominent world role and maintain a great power sphere of influence in Africa (Soutou 2002: 76–7, Bozo 1995).

These conditions, and France's strategic claims to great power status, largely evaporated with the end of the Cold War and the advent of US hegemony. The salience and prestige of France's nuclear arsenal was immediately diminished. The removal of one pole of the Cold War system meant that the role of France as an intermediate third player now lacked plausibility. France was now one of a number of second tier major powers (Maclean and Szarka 2008: 6–7, Howorth 1996: 384). The initial French response to this was to shift focus to multilateral forums, especially to the UN Security Council where France's permanent five membership allows for residual great power status. Reflecting this, French policy on the Security Council in the early 1990s was activist, with French troops comprising a majority of the world's peacekeeping contributions (Utley 2006: 63–4, Treacher 2000: 25–7).

In order to arrest its strategic decline in the post-Cold War era, France has also focused on its role in the EU, which is believed to multiply its power and strategic influence while also sharing the burden of security risks and costs. The French ambition for the EU is that of 'a *powerful* world actor, that is constructed by a *political* process, and which has a distinct *identity* in the global capitalist system' (Drake 2010: 187). The notion of *Europe puissance* sees the continent as an independent 'great power' in a multipolar world that can defend European interests worldwide across the full spectrum of capabilities and stand up to the United States when interests diverge (Irondelle 2008: 155–6). Thus, while France's post-Cold War emphasis on multilateralism contains a normative element, as discussed above, it is also tied to the idea of multipolarity suggesting a realist policy of power maximization to counter US unipolarity (Holm 2004: 486).

Along with Britain, France is the only EU member-state with the capacity to mount independent military operations and Paris therefore takes a natural leadership role in EU security policy. Doubts remain, however, as to the political will of member-states and the capacity of the EU to be a coordinated, independent strategic actor. French power in the EU has been diffused by the expansion in membership to 27 states. Most western member-states see the EU's normative and 'soft power' role as primary, while eastern European states give priority to their NATO membership (Irondelle 2008: 156). Another problem for France is that Britain's special relationship with Washington thwarts French ambitions for the EU to be a strategic counterweight to the United States in a multipolar world (Drake 2010: 193–5).

The strategic situation in West Africa became more complicated from the late 1990s. During the Cold War, France maintained a *pré carré*, or exclusive sphere of influence, in francophone West Africa with the acquiescence of the superpowers. There was little change to this until the period from 1994 to 1997. France's main competitor up until this time was Nigeria, the largest Anglophone country, with aspirations to African leadership and regional dominance (Obi 2008: 188–9, Howe 2005: 179–82). France's historic European rival in Africa, Britain, also maintained close ties with many former colonies although to a lesser extent than France in the defence and security spheres (Cumming 2004: 111). After the Cold War, Britain has also viewed sub-Saharan Africa as a venue to display an out-of-area strategic presence. This became more important with the Blair government's ethical foreign policy (Griffin 2007: 22–6).

Since the late-1990s, however, the enduring state fragility of Nigeria, and shared Anglo-French interests in reducing security costs, has tended to result in more cooperative relationships. Nigeria's role as a leading contributor to regional peacekeeping operations has been welcomed by Paris. Nigeria did not, however, deploy combat forces to the Economic Community of West African States' (ECOWAS) operation in Ivory Coast from early 2003 perhaps reflecting these earlier rivalries (see Obi 2009: 130–31, Adebajo 2008: 23–5). Along with the St-Malo Agreement of 1998 on the European Security and Defence Policy (ESDP), France and Britain also pledged to coordinate their Africa policies to reduce costs and duplication of effort, but perhaps more importantly to pool resources to maintain Anglo-French influence on the continent against newer entrants (Chafer and Cumming 2010: 1144–5, Chafer 2002: 350–51).

In the 2000s, the United States and China have become the main strategic competition for France in West Africa. This is largely due to both countries search for energy security and diversification of oil suppliers. Instability in the Middle East has prompted renewed interest by all major industrialized powers in fostering sources of oil in other parts of the world. There are extensive supplies adjacent to the West African coast and in the Niger Delta (Klare and Volman 2006). Promoting stability in West Africa has become increasingly important. After the 9/11 attacks, the assumed linkages between fragile states and transnational threats also mean that sub-Saharan Africa is of greater concern to Washington (Pham 2007, Mills 2004). France has tended to see US involvement in West Africa as encroachment on its traditional sphere of influence (Bowen 2005: 114).

China is also making inroads on the African continent. At the end of the 2000s, China was the continent's third largest trading partner after the EU and United States (Porteous 2008: 92). Similar to other parts of the world, a major problem for the West is that China's methods of buying influence with weak, vulnerable states ignores the normative concerns for democratization, human rights and good governance that are now dogma in Western capitals and international organizations. China's aid comes without strings attached and pointedly does not interfere in the internal affairs of African states (Lirong 2011, Bach 2008). Chinese penetration is therefore a direct erosion of the managerial role of France in African security policy by reducing compliance with the governance agenda the EU funds and seeks to promote.

The tensions and constraints of France's post-Cold War strategic position and its resistance to US hegemony are played out in its Africa policy in two ways. In the first decade of the twenty-first century, France's traditional great power role on the UN Security Council allows it to adopt a sovereign independent approach where necessary. But the trend in external military operations in Africa suggests a preference for action within multilateral frameworks (Bowen 2005: 94–7). Multilateralism bolsters French legitimacy and reputation by deflecting accusations of neo-colonialism while also reducing costs. In the early 2000s there was a resurgence of 'traditional' French interventions in Africa where bilateral defence agreements are still in place (Ivory Coast, 2002–present; Central African

Republic, 2003; Chad, 2004). But from the mid-2000s, the pattern of military activity suggests that France now seeks to play a lead or 'framework nation' role within EU military missions (e.g., Democratic Republic of Congo, 2003, 2006; Central African Republic and Chad, 2008–09) (Irondelle 2008: 463–4).

## Ontological Security

The pattern of international order provides the normative criteria for state failure and thresholds for permissible intervention. The distribution of capabilities provides the material structural conditions for the pattern of international order and the geographical focus of great power attention. Crucially, disorder in these areas also challenges the identity and ontological security needs of status quo great powers. Jennifer Mitzen (2006: 342) proposes that states 'engage in ontological security-seeking' in addition to the physical security imperative privileged by realism. This refers to the need for an actor to experience itself as a defined, whole and continuous entity through time, rather than something lacking definition and subject to constant change. Ontological security is required 'to realize a sense of agency' in the world. Identity insecurity is prompted by disorder and uncertainty because this sense of agency 'requires a stable cognitive environment' (Mitzen 2006: 342).

Identities are shaped, routinized and sustained through relationships with others. This is reflected in the accretion or construction of biographical narratives that are essential to maintaining a stable identity through the flux of time and contingent events (Steele 2008: 2–3). These 'self-identity' narratives also provide the subjective frameworks through which events are perceived and interpreted, and motives formulated by political decision-makers. According to Steele (2008: 19), '*ontological security obtains for states because state agents seek to satisfy the self-identity needs of the states which they lead*'. State identity narratives operate on two levels. Indirectly, they unconsciously underwrite longer-term cultural and historical 'sources of collective self-reference and self-preference that define the contours of the state and ultimately fashion its relations with others'. More directly, as 'a political template, national identity is consciously drawn upon as an extractive resource by the policy-making elite to justify, lend historical substance, motivate, and orient given foreign policies' (Hadfield-Amkhan 2010: 44–5). These two levels are evident in the case study chapters of the book, particularly in the historical examples where archival sources are available. State agents perceived and interpreted events through their respective identity narratives while also deploying the motifs emblematic of them in justifying their actions to domestic constituencies.

Stable patterns of relationships and habitual routines provide the 'cognitive certainty' required for a sense of agency in the world and therefore ontological security (Mitzen 2006: 342). Normative threats are a direct challenge to identity needs because 'a group's understanding of its identity is tied to basic orders or states of the world that are being disrupted' (Creppell 2011: 457). This is particularly the case for satisfied, status quo actors. The ontological security of status quo great powers is challenged by disruptions to routinized relationships and role identities through normative threats to international order. Such disruptions evoke emotions that become powerful motives for action because of the gap created between perceptions of events and how an actor needs to see itself consistent with its identity narrative (Löwenheim 2003: 28, Steele 2008: 2–3, 13).

Insights from the ontological security literature are important to this discussion of state failure and intervention because if states avoid certain 'moral, humanitarian, and honor-driven' actions, the feeling of disruption to their sense of self is just as important 'as threats to their physical integrity' (Steele 2008: 2). And as discussed, failed states present no traditional security threat to major powers. Steele diverges somewhat from Mitzen's account that self-identity is wholly dependent on social relationships. He emphasizes that while '[s]tates pursue their needs through social action', it is less to 'impress an external society' and more about satisfying 'their internal self-identity needs' (Steele 2008: 2). The insight that states are motivated to action in order to fulfil non-instrumental identity needs that are internally-focused is critical to understanding how prestige links normative ideas about international order to armed interventions. The role of prestige in understanding intervention in the periphery is elaborated further below.

Steele's thesis is, however, somewhat overstated in my view. For example, he argues without qualification that 'states pursue social actions to serve self-identity needs, even when these actions compromise their physical existence' (Steele 2008: 1). But in the cases examined here, especially in multipolar and bipolar international systems, the ontological security-seeking motives of prestige and related concepts of honour and retribution were pursued in tandem with prudential calculations. This observation is supported by Alexander Welsh (2008: 4), who, in 'considering honor as a moral imperative', argues that 'judgments about what actions to take have at some point to weigh likely results as well as felt obligations'. Assessments about state failure, and the timing and conduct of armed interventions, will be constrained by the distribution of capabilities.

For powerful status quo members of a society, normative threats to established orders will produce feelings of anger and corresponding social expressions of affront or insult at being treated with 'disrespect'. This may tend towards humiliation when such threats result in tangible consequences. Reinhard Wolff (2011: 115–16) argues that the experience of disrespect is intrinsically subjective. Of necessity, it relates to others' attitudes or behaviour towards us, but a feeling of disrespect is a result of how that behaviour fails to meet our 'subjective expectations' about our own 'social worth and importance'. It is disrespectful acts, especially if perceived as intentional, that provoke the sharpest feelings of humiliation and the desire for retribution (Wolf 2011: 128–9, Miller 2001: 536). A strong reaction to perceived insult can reconfirm the victim's sense of self-respect, '*regardless of any observers' perceptions, judgements, or reactions*' (Wolf 2011: 128). This internal emotional dimension of ontological security helps to explain why states may be moved to armed action that seems disproportionate or counter-productive in an instrumental sense.

### *Peace, Economy and Prestige: The British Self-Identity Narrative*

The archetypes and motifs of state identity that bind narratives together thematically remain stable over time while more transient elements are continually renegotiated in relation to the core themes (Hadfield-Amkhan 2010: 58). In the late-Victorian period, aspects of the British self-identity narrative were in flux. By the 1870s, the mid-century Pax Britannica had been eroded by European competition over the 'Eastern Question' of Ottoman decline. The character of the British Empire had also indelibly changed. It was no longer an 'empire of liberty' settled by peoples of British origin that shared similar values and institutions, but a territorial empire of conquest ruling over a myriad of cultures whose diverse peoples were largely without political representation (Marshall 1987: 115, Fieldhouse 1976: 4–5). This evolution in the character and expansion of the British Empire was coincident with the development of the European standard of civilization, which it also served to reinforce (Knorr 1963: 246–7).

In the 1870s, an acrimonious public debate had taken place between Tory 'imperialists' and 'non-interventionist' Liberals over foreign and imperial policy. The positions in the debate reflected the contradiction in British identity between liberty and imperial dominion. The Disraeli conservative government (1874–80) emphasized the prestige of Britain's 'Asiatic' Empire, the superiority of British civilization and focused jingoistic public attention on Anglo-Russian rivalries in Central Asia (Thompson 2000: 16, Eldridge 1973: 209, 232). This was much to the chagrin of the liberal non-conformist conscience to which 'the object of political life was to further good moral causes' (Lowe 1969: 2–3), not revel 'in military dominion over alien peoples' (Eldridge 1973: 229). In his victorious election campaign of 1879–80, Gladstone (1971: 115–17) had laid out six principles of a Liberal foreign policy: the creation of wealth through 'just legislation and economy at home'; the preservation of the European peace; the maintenance of a concert of Europe; the avoidance of 'needless and entangling engagements'; respect for 'the equal rights of all nations'; and a 'sympathy with freedom' founded 'upon the deepest and most profound love of order'.

The positions of both parties converged in the core themes of the British identity narrative based on preponderant naval power, geographical insularity and classical liberalism. These attributes enabled Britain's traditional role in European affairs as external balancer and its self-confident imperial assurance that free trade, law and civilization were a beneficent and necessary Anglo-Saxon gift to the world (Hadfield-Amkhan 2010: 81–3, 103). The posture of British liberal thought towards the outside world was inherently judgemental, the corollary to which was an evangelical impulse to reform humanity in an eschatological spirit of progress (Mehta 1999: 79). And despite their antagonistic rhetorical stances, the political elites of both parties in the 1880s sought to maintain traditional British interests abroad through informal influence (Durrans 1982: 267). Both continued to avoid entangling engagements on the Continent, and neither wished to bring 'more Oriental peoples into the Empire' (Robinson and Gallagher 1961: 85). Even if the mid-Victorian spirit of progress had weakened in the face of intransigent 'Oriental despotisms', both parties still regarded a liberal outlook in foreign policy as normative, differing only in degree (Robinson and Gallagher 1961: 1–10, Marsh 1989: 8).

As a status quo power, it was incumbent on British governments to 'respect the public's thirst for peace, economy and prestige' in their conduct of foreign and imperial policy (Robinson and Gallagher 1961: 23). The rapid advent of industrial modernity had revealed how acutely Britain needed 'the outside world – for resources, markets, as well as for physical and psychological space'. So while it was psychologically necessary for uncertainty and risk to be displaced and managed in potentially hazardous locations such as Ireland, the Orient or Africa, large parts of the world also needed to be represented as orderly and safe (Freedgood 2003: 9, 169). This was especially so for locations like Egypt, which were deemed essential to the prosperity and prestige of the British Empire.

### *To Preserve Freedom: The US Self-Identity Narrative*

By contrast to Britain, the US self-identity narrative up until the Vietnam intervention in 1965 was clear. The assumption of all post-1945 US administrations was that preponderant American power bestowed on it a unique responsibility to foster and maintain a world order in which liberal institutions could flourish (Gaddis 1982: 205). American exceptionalism and preponderant material capacity meant that failures to control international events produced 'greater anxiety and a greater sense of threat in the United States than in other countries' (Johnson 1994: 46). The perceived lesson of 1930s appeasement was the fundamental point of reference for US policy-makers in developing their national security doctrine, the policy of containment and the domino analogy (Yergin 1990: 197–8). Totalitarian states, aggressive and expansionist by definition were by their very existence a threat to national security, which at base referred to the preservation of the American way of life (Anderson 1993: 6, Layne 2006: 57, 61). An enlargement of the area of socialist autarchy, accelerated by the 'loss' of China in 1949, was also a direct threat to the historic US preference for an 'open door' system of world commerce and diffusion of liberal-capitalist norms, both of which had been unquestioned assumptions about the post-1945 international order (Williams 1972).

By 1950, the cumulative effects of the Czech coup and Berlin Blockade of 1948, the Soviet atomic detonation in September 1949, and the communist victory in China shortly thereafter, prompted a negative reassessment of US relative strength and served to heighten threat perceptions (Leffler 1992: 331, MacDonald 1991: 113–14). The Chinese communists were considered to be the Soviet Union's junior partner and were now poised to dominate Indochina and threaten insular Southeast Asia where communist insurgencies were already underway. This course of events accelerated the move away from George F. Kennan's 'strongpoint' containment to the strategic posture of 'perimeter' containment that prevailed until the intervention in South Vietnam. This was encapsulated in April 1950 in a National Security Council document known as 'NSC 68', arguably the most important US policy document of the Cold War.

NSC 68 is written in emotive, value-laden language indicative of the identity narrative held by American foreign policy elites in the 1950s. The document commenced with the apocalyptic assertion that in the Cold War struggle, not only the American Republic, but civilization itself was at stake (*FRUS* 1950, vol. 1: 238). The bipolar conflict was irreconcilable because the 'slave state' operated under the 'grim oligarchy of the Kremlin' could never be secure while the subversive idea of freedom existed in the world. The Kremlin's 'implacable purpose' must be 'to eliminate the challenge of freedom' and therefore the United States (*FRUS* 1950, vol. 1: 239). Zero-sum bipolarity, the indivisibility of interests, and the imperative to maintain credibility, were invoked in the assertion that 'the assault on free institutions is world-wide now', and that 'a defeat of free institutions anywhere is a defeat everywhere' (*FRUS* 1950, vol. 1: 240). In such a world, 'the absence of order among nations' was 'becoming less and less tolerable' (*FRUS* 1950, vol. 1: 263). Disorder on the periphery was antithetical to the US identity narrative of preserving freedom in the world.

By 1964, China had overtaken Russia in American public opinion as the greater threat to world peace (Levering 1978: 114–15, 126). While opinion polling indicated a clear desire to contain communism, after Korea there was little support for direct US military intervention in the Third World. On the other hand, initiatives toward belligerence such as in the Taiwan Straits and Lebanon crises, the abortive Bay of Pigs invasion, and the resumption of atmospheric nuclear testing in 1962, all significantly bolstered presidential approval ratings (Nathan and Oliver 1994: 159–60, Hughes 1978: 38). Arms control and peace initiatives were always supported in public opinion, but so were increases in military programmes and expenditures (Dumbrell 1990: 165). Similar to Britain, the American public required both peace and strength.

### Le Grandeur*: The French Self-Identity Narrative*

The fundamental purpose of French security policy in the Fifth Republic has been 'the pursuit and evocation of national *grandeur* and of an elevated global standing, or *rang*' ('rank') (Treacher 2001: 23). In De Gaulle's (1955: 3) famous words, 'France is not really herself unless in the front rank … France cannot be France without greatness'. Prestige, as an end in itself, is considered the strategic goal of French action in the world. For France, the tactics adopted in the service of this goal may change, but the pursuit of *grandeur* and assumptions about what it is, remain remarkably constant across time (see Treacher 2000: 23–4, Flynn 1995: 240–41). *Grandeur* is understood as *rayonnement*: the projection ('radiance') of French material power and cultural influence abroad. *Rang* implies a perception of hierarchy, superiority and distinction flowing from France's rich and glorious history (Sonntag 2008: 77). Assumptions about rank and *grandeur* are embedded in the French identity narrative and worldview of policy elites (Drake 2011: 197–8).

The intangible, aestheticized nature of French prestige means that actual declines in material power and wealth, or even defeats and setbacks, do not necessarily diminish the view that France continues to play, and indeed must play, a leading role in 'the drama of universal history' (Mahoney 1998: 60). The ontological security of France relies on its capacity and willingness to take independent action and on its ability to wield influence in the world. The causes to which such action is directed are influenced by the strategic constraints and opportunities considered above and normatively justified by France's universalizing civilizational narrative.

The notion of the French 'exception', that France is a country apart with an inherent 'greatness' or *singularité* dates from the 1789 Revolution, if not before (Treacher 2001: 28). The political basis of the French self-identity narrative is rooted in its vanguard Enlightenment role as progenitor of the modern nation-state. As is sometimes observed, the French state does not exist to serve its citizens; the citizens serve France (Chipman 1989: 26), which has a transcendent national identity based on its long historical and cultural legacy (Védrine 2001: 25). Because citizens were constituted politically by the state, the French liberal republican model could be universalized. From the outset, French nation-statehood was imbued with an external mission to spread its values. This was first reflected in the Revolutionary and Napoleonic Wars and later in the colonial *mission civilisatrice* (Keiger 2001: 17–20). De Gaulle (in Holm 2004: 472) believed that French goals, because they were French, reflected also the '"ambitions of mankind"'.

In the post-World War II period, the development by France of an independent nuclear arsenal was driven by the imperative to recover a sense of *grandeur* after the catastrophe of 1940. The capacity to ensure one's own survival through nuclear deterrence was the mark of great power status (Samaan and Gompert 2009: 487–8). Great powers also need to be able to project power internationally with an out-of-area strategic presence. To this end, France continued to self-develop and maintain high-prestige weapons systems, such as ballistic missiles, nuclear powered aircraft carriers, submarines and sophisticated strike aircraft. The retention by France in the postcolonial period of its overseas *Départements* and *Territoires*, and its African sphere of influence, was also integral to the maintenance of *grandeur* and therefore to its ontological security needs (Lansford 1996: 46–7, Utley 2002: 130). It also helped to reinforce French cultural power in maintaining a large French-speaking sphere on the African continent against 'Anglo-Saxon' influence (Chafer 2008: 38).

As mentioned above, France was slow to adjust to the new post-Cold War realities. Nuclear weapons no longer conferred international respect, attested to by the furore over Chirac's resumption of nuclear testing in 1995. Most damaging to France's international reputation, however, was its alleged complicity in the Rwandan genocide of 1994 in a misguided attempt to prop up the francophone Rwandan government against the English-speaking Rwanda Patriotic Front (RPF).

The subsequent French 'humanitarian intervention' to establish a secure zone for refugees allowed many of the Rwandan *génocidaires* to escape to neighbouring Zaire, where France continued to support the discredited dictator Mobutu Sese Seko until 1997. The genocide and regional wars that ensued claimed an estimated four million lives (Chafer 2008: 43–4, Utley 2002: 131–4).

With the catastrophic failure of French policy in the Great Lakes region, the Gaullist model of Africa policy was finished. It was the shame of Rwanda and Zaire that forced France to change tactics to a new policy of pursuing *grandeur* through the promotion of liberal order in Africa. This is clearly evident in Ivory Coast, where intervention policy may have changed along with developments on the ground, but was consistently justified according to liberal principles. The move to multilateralism and greater emphasis on the UN after the Cold War, the view that the EU can be a power multiplier for France, the restructuring of security policy in Africa toward liberal norms of order, the recent move back into NATO, and the leading role in the 2011 bombing of Libya, are all indicative of tactical shifts by France to maximize its power and influence in the world to maintain a meaningful sense of *grandeur*.

## The Prestige Motive

Prestige is the conceptual linkage with three 'tendrils' that connects these large and diffuse conditional factors into a concrete policy of armed intervention in the periphery to restore order in 'failed' states. To explain this, it is useful to first disaggregate the concept of motive across three dimensions: the normative, instrumental and emotional. These dimensions of motive correspond with the conceptual foundations of the interpretive framework outlined above: international order (normative), distribution of capabilities (instrumental) and ontological security (emotional).

### *Norms, Instrumentality and Emotions*

Joseph Schumpeter (1951: 43) observed in the 1919 essay, *The Sociology of Imperialism* that 'human motivation is always infinitely complex, and we are never aware of all its elements'. The ascription of motives is, however, central to both explanation and understanding in the social sciences. This book takes a Weberian sociological approach in considering motives as reflective 'reasons' for action, rather than 'forces' or 'drives' that impel motion. Jeremy Bentham (1996: 98) theorized that a motive must be both previous to an act; a motive in prospect, while in order for action to be directed by such a motive, the actor must also 'look beyond that event which is called his action … to the consequences of it': a motive in *esse*. Any account of motives will incorporate a before and after component. The latter is the anticipated consequences or outcomes of the action concerned. For clarity, the term 'motive' will be used throughout the book's case studies to refer to before-the-fact reasons for action. The word 'objectives' is used to describe the anticipated outcomes of such action, which may be distinct from its motives.

Both cognitive (rational) and emotional (non-rational) elements will shape motive formulation in small group contexts (Weber 1947: 48–9). I maintain the distinction here that emotional motives are 'non-rational' in that their object is to satisfy subjective sensibilities, or to produce gratifying feelings that inhere in the performance of an act regardless of its utility function or whether it is compatible with social norms. The rational side of the motives equation can be further broken down into normative, or rules-based conduct, on the one hand, and the instrumental pursuit of interests on the other. Normative ideas are rational but non-instrumental (Jackson 1993: 112–13). Instrumental action is contingent, future-oriented and concerned with outcomes. Norm-based actions, by contrast, are relatively rigid and process-oriented. While norms and their relationship to interests have been heavily theorized in IR since the constructivist 'turn' in the 1990s, the relationship between emotions and norms is underdeveloped. In what follows, I show that the interplay between norms and emotion is crucial to understanding the prestige motive.

A number of scholars have made the case that norms are variously constituted, sustained, strengthened or at least mediated by emotions (e.g., Jeffery 2011, Mercer 2006, 2010, Ross 2006). In this sense, emotions are analytically prior to norms as motives for moral or rules-based action. Crawford (2000: 128–9), however, suggests that emotions are socially constructed, learned by reference to the cultural beliefs and moral values of the community. In this sense, cultural norms and sensibilities condition emotional responses. While the direction of the relationship between norms and emotions remains contested, it seems clear that the social value of norms, whether explicit or tacit, is best identified in the 'breach' by the types of emotions that are expressed. Elster (1990: 864) argues that '[f]or norms to be social, they must be shared by other people and sustained by their approval and disapproval'. This pattern is reinforced by emotions. An almost certain way of determining the social value of norms is via the negative emotions observed when they are violated and the positive emotions associated with their validation (see Steele 2010: 91, Alkopher 2007: 11, Fattah and Fierke 2009: 70).

As discussed above, for status quo actors order is both functional, in that it provides for regulative norms of behaviour, and constitutive in that beliefs about the right principles of order are extremely important. These beliefs are emotional and reflected in a normative language of values and standards. Prevailing orders are path-dependent and status quo-oriented. Normative threats give rise to negative emotions such as frustration, fear and anger because of the betrayal of expectations and the generation of uncertainty about the future. In considering normative threats, two of the emotional expressions that Creppell (2011: 481–2) identifies are the 'affront' and 'indignation' felt at an intolerable challenge to an actor's status within a social order. The following section applies these three dimensions of motive, and the dynamics between them, to the concept of prestige in international relations.

### *Prestige as Instrumentality*

Traditionally in International Relations, prestige has been considered instrumentally (e.g., Morgenthau 1978: 77–91, Gilpin 1981: 30–31). It serves international considerations and is equivalent with 'credibility'. Demonstrations or assertions of prestige, it is calculated by policy-makers, will bolster a state's credibility and thereby prevent challenges to its present and future interests. Prestige in this sense is a positive reputation for power and resolve. The positive character of prestige differentiates it from reputation: 'Reputations can be positive or negative, whereas prestige always grows out of a positive reputation' (Wylie 2009: 113). I argue below that prestige can also be thought of in a normative, relational sense as a positive reputation for maintaining international order. An adequate discussion of prestige cannot end here, however, because our imagining of the opinion others hold of us can deeply affect how we feel about ourselves.

### *International Reputation, Self-Respect and National Honour*

In *A Cultural Theory of International Relations*, Richard Ned Lebow (2008: 63) notes that the classical notion of 'spirit' dropped out of use with modernity because of its unpalatable association with aristocracy. 'Spirit' has since become invested in feelings of self-esteem, which Lebow defines as 'a subjective sense of one's honor and standing'. Spirit seeks to 'gain the respect and esteem of people who matter', by fulfilling the normative obligations of honour, so we can 'feel good about ourselves' (Lebow 2008: 15). Those who matter are peers in an honour group, suggesting that satisfying the needs of spirit must be external and relational. Lebow's formulation also seems to indicate, though, that while the relational aspect is necessary, the ultimate ends of spirited action are subjective and emotional: to feel good about ourselves.

I suggest that this external concept of honour used by Lebow is equivalent with 'reputation' as commonly understood; a directly relational concept compared with self-respect, which is internal and subjective. This distinction is supported by Frank Henderson Stewart (1994: 18), who distinguishes between 'inner honor' and 'outer honor as reputation'. In international relations, I argue that this distinction can be understood on the one hand as 'national honour', which is about feelings of self-respect within the domestic polity, and is ultimately emotional. On the other hand, outer, or external honour, is relational and normative. It refers to a state's reputation in the international society for upholding its responsibilities. For a status quo great power, this means responsibility for international order in areas considered to be in their spheres of influence. Reputation is clearly implicated in Lebow's (2008: 67) statement that '[e]xternal honor must be conferred by others and can only be gained through deeds they regard as honourable'. Reputation is associated with fulfilling normative expectations.

An actor's sense of internal honour is not the same as its external reputation. Self-respect is an imaginative and persuasive act. We look from the outside-in and persuade ourselves of what we think others will find honourable in us (Welsh 2008: 11). This will necessarily be coloured by our biographical narrative. Steele (2008: 245) concurs that '[h]onor exists in a constitutive relationship with a nation's self-identity'. National honour is about the internal perception of what the state considers its true worth; what qualities and responsibilities entitle it to a right to respect in the international arena (Stewart 1994: 44). Because of this, incongruence between an actor's 'virtuous words' and its deeds in the face of normative threats will be potentially humiliating and therefore a strong motive for action. Normative threats that challenge national honour will arouse emotions such as frustration, anger and fear. These are available to observers through discursive statements or social expressions of affront, insult and humiliation. It is this internal dimension of prestige; that of national honour, which is most closely tied to emotions, and least concerned with prudential calculation because of its resonance with identity-affirmation.

### *Normative Threats and the Emotional Dimension of Prestige*

In considering prestige emotionally, it is useful to divide the concept into negative and positive emotions. A challenge to an actor's reputation will damage internal self-respect. Disruptions to reputational norms, or 'normative threats', are an affront to a status quo power's national honour and will produce the negative emotional expressions of insult and humiliation, followed by a desire for retribution (Saurette 2006: 506–7, Welsh 2008: 14–15). Disproportionate behaviour that appears motivated by revenge will highlight how intensely something is felt as a humiliation, and therefore the social value of the norm. Revenge is intensely emotional, because it has an object to which it is directed and is defined by the pleasure experienced at the suffering of another (Löwenheim and Heimann 2008: 686–7). The goal of revenge inheres in the feelings experienced in the act of vengeance itself. Actors 'first and foremost want to come to terms with their past by transforming the emotions they have towards it', from humiliation back to self-respect (Löwenheim and Heimann 2008: 691–2).

Positive feelings expressed as pride, self-aggrandizement and glory may be evident when norms are re-validated and national honour restored. Or as Saurette (2006: 519) puts it, when the insulted party publicly highlights 'their re-respected status'. While reputation is relational, and at least in part, other-regarding, national honour 'is grounded in an obligation to oneself rather than a duty to others'. Honour motivates normative behaviour 'because of the pleasure of self-respect that it produces' (Krause 2002: 4–5). Glory is the subjective emotional prize associated with certain positive relational accomplishments, whether instrumental or normative (Slomp 2000: 34, Zmora 2007: 452). An important point is that glory is not felt or expressed because we have some particular power or accomplishment. Rather, the 'aptitudes' or accomplishments 'we have give us glory because we take them to mean something deeper', more meaningful about ourselves (Hampton 1999: 81). It is this sense of meaning that resonates with a state's identity narrative.

## Prestige and Intervention in the Periphery

To summarize, I argue that normative threats to status quo great powers in areas where they see themselves as the purveyors of international order, are experienced as a challenge to their reputation, and consequently, to their self-respect and national honour. Normative threats from failed states on the periphery are experienced as an affront, insult and potential humiliation because the reputation of status quo powers is heavily invested in the prevailing pattern of international order, which is a meaningful part of their self-identity narrative. It is this element of insult and humiliation that engages the emotional desire for retribution and instrumental concerns for credibility in other areas. The prestige motive, as conceptualized here, is the thread that draws together international order, the distribution of capabilities and ontological security to understand state failure and intervention in the periphery.

A number of recent studies have sought to explain the reasons for such interventions. Jeffrey Taliaferro (2004a: 3) makes the argument that it is 'the aversion of senior officials to perceived losses – in terms of their state's relative power, international status, or prestige – [that] drives great power intervention in peripheral regions'. This can only be a partial explanation, however, because Taliaferro's 'balance-of-risk' theory is strictly cognitive and instrumental. It draws on prospect theory, 'a psychological model of decision-making under conditions of risk' (Taliaferro 2004a: 16). Prestige is defined simply as 'a state's reputation for having material capabilities or status and using those commodities to achieve its desired aims' (Taliaferro 2004a: 40). Norms and emotions play little part, when the preceding discussion suggests that they are necessary dimensions of the prestige motive.

From a normative perspective, the argument advanced here also challenges Martha Finnemore's thesis in the influential 2003 book, *The Purpose of Intervention*. I agree with Finnemore's claim that armed interventions are the most visible way of enforcing standards of conduct in international society (Finnemore 2003: 2–3). But Finnemore seems to discount prestige-based motives altogether in stating that 'glory acquired by success at arms is no longer a prominent goal of powerful states nor a justification for military intervention that is accepted by other states or mass publics' (Finnemore 2003: 6). This is contradicted by the evidence, even in the current period. The evidence presented below suggests that with varying degrees of emphasis, the three dimensions of the prestige motive analysed above remain present in this context across different historical periods.

Closest to my position here, Oded Löwenheim (2007: 3) uses a comparative historical study to argue that the policies of great powers towards harmful transnational actors 'depends not solely on the material consequences' of their activities, but more importantly, 'on the level of threat' this harm poses to great power 'authority'. Weak or 'failed' states provide ungoverned political spaces in which harmful transnational actors can flourish. But because pirates and terrorists are elusive, great powers instead punish the peripheral states that host them. Such interventions serve to reproduce the role identity of great powers by punishing challenges to their authority. Authority is predicated on the 'regulation and institutionalization of transborder violence' (Löwenheim 2007: 22). This may be sought for a number of reasons including the material advantages it may confer, but also for self-esteem, prestige and identity-affirmation (Löwenheim 2007: 24, 29–30).

This argument has a number of flaws. Historically, it is status quo great powers, rather than all great powers, that are most concerned to regulate transborder violence. Revisionist great powers have periodically sought to violently transcend the international society. In qualifying this, Löwenheim (2007: 25) makes the disputable claim that 'irresponsible' states such as Napoleonic France and Nazi Germany lacked legitimacy and therefore were not genuine great powers. The characterization of transnational actors is also very narrow. The focus is on materially harmful groups, such as pirates and terrorists. This runs counter to the authoritative definition of transnational activity as 'the movement of tangible or intangible items across state boundaries when at least one actor is not an agent of a government' (Nye and Keohane 1972: xii). Löwenheim would seem to rule out normative threats from the periphery that lack tangible, physical consequences.

Löwenheim (2007: 47) also excludes other non-state actors that may engage in transnational activity but do not ultimately seek to 'violate the containing function of sovereignty'. This would rule out regional insurgent or revolutionary movements seeking to capture a peripheral state, which may be a more acute threat to a great power's authority, and therefore to its prestige, than the type of transnational actor Löwenheim considers. The case studies in Chapters 4, 5 and 6 demonstrate that great powers intervene in the periphery when a normative threat to international order engages their prestige concerns. International order involves a much greater range of responsibilities than the regulation of transborder violence. These responsibilities also change over time.

Not all states and their leaders will seek prestige in the same way due to their different values, positions and roles in the international system (Markey 1999: 150). Rising powers may seek to have their status recognized by others commensurate with their growing power and influence (Schweller 1999: 55). Prestige may also play out in the foreign policies of smaller or weaker states. Hymans (2006) argues in this context that the decision to acquire nuclear weapons by a certain type of political leader is a self-expressive, emotional act to satisfy national pride. Generally, however, small states are externally-constrained rule takers (Hey 2003). Humiliation is more readily internalized by subordinate actors because they lack responsibility and the capacity to respond (Lindner 2006: 11–22).

What both revisionist and weak states lack, is the deep sense of responsibility for the prevailing order of things; which, as theorized above, carries great meaning in a state's identity narrative. From the perspective of status quo great powers, this heavy burden of responsibility entitles them to a special and heightened respect in the international society (Jackson 2000: 173). They will therefore be more sensitive to perceived insults and humiliation than other categories of state. Lebow (2008: 69) argues that such powers become 'enraged' if slighted by actors perceived as lacking 'the standing to challenge or insult' them. Using the interpretive framework developed in this chapter, the remainder of the book examines three case studies of state failure and intervention in the periphery to support these arguments.

# Chapter 4
# British Intervention in Egypt, 1882

This chapter examines the book's first case study of state failure and intervention to restore order on the periphery of the European international society of the late-nineteenth century.[1] The British intervention in Egypt from July 1882 can be understood as a response to a normative threat to international order in the sensitive strategic location of the Near East. The primary British interest in the area was to protect the short routes to India and the Empire in Asia by keeping the other Powers, with the partial exception of France, out of Egypt. At the time, Egypt was a de facto independent state but remained under the legal suzerainty of the Ottoman Empire and subject to Anglo-French administrative guidance. The normative threat presented by the proto-nationalist revolt in Egypt disrupted British expectations for stability in the area. It generated uncertainty about Egypt's ambiguous status within the Ottoman Empire and the possibility of interference by the other Powers. These adverse developments were a challenge to the reputation of Britain as the primary arbiter of international order in the Near East. Being a source of international order is a meaningful part of the identity narrative and ontological security of status quo great powers. Challenges to the reputation of such powers threaten their credibility and also affects the way they see themselves – their sense of national honour.

The flow of events in the Egypt crisis shows that it was a normative threat to the European standard of civilization that first engaged British prestige concerns. The Egyptian military revolt led by Colonel Ahmed Urabi first threatened international treaty commitments by circumventing the legitimate government recognized by the international society, and then by overturning the Anglo-French control over Egyptian finances. This was an insult to Britain as the leading status quo power with important interests in the area. According to the late-nineteenth century standard of civilization, state failure in Egypt was characterized as 'anarchy', 'misgovernment' and 'revolution'. The situation further deteriorated from governmental disorder to violent anti-Christian and anti-European civil unrest as Britain and France applied greater external pressure in the form of a naval demonstration and an ultimatum to the nationalist regime. This turn of events was perceived in London as a tangible threat to British lives and property in Egypt, the most fundamental breach of international order. These fears were realized with the Alexandria massacre of 11 June 1882. The emotional dimension of national honour hence becomes more explicit. The massacre was deeply humiliating to British national honour,

1 An earlier version of the research in this chapter has been published in Halvorson (2010b).

provoking anger and the desire for retribution. It also damaged British imperial credibility on which the Empire in India, with its large Muslim population, was believed to rest. The chapter shows that restoration of British prestige across its three dimensions was the primary motive for the intervention.

The reinterpretation of the Egypt intervention that I advance in this chapter is a challenge to dominant historical accounts of this episode. Historians such as David Steele (1983: 1–3) and M.E. Yapp (1987: 81–2, 227–8) have previously noted the theme of prestige with respect to India in the Egypt crisis. However, this line of thinking has remained underdeveloped in the context of the events and decision-making examined in this chapter. The pushing forward of turbulent frontiers by local British administrators, thereby reluctantly drawing in the metropole, is also an important theme in explaining British imperialism that has some resonance here (e.g., Galbraith 1960). But the scholarship of recent decades is dominated by two interpretations, both grounded in broader theories of British imperialism. P.J. Cain and A.G. Hopkins' (2002) 'gentlemanly capitalist' thesis posits a metropolitan drive to imperial expansion emanating from the financial and service sectors of the City of London. The 1882 occupation was the result of a 'conscious and sustained defence of Britain's expanding economic interests in Egypt' (Hopkins 1986: 385). Ronald Robinson and John Gallagher's 'official mind' (1961) thesis sees a status quo-oriented Victorian metropole reacting to peripheral disorder in a crucial geographical location. The proto-nationalist revolt in Egypt (1879–82) posed a strategic threat to the Suez Canal route to India.

The primary source evidence presented below strongly implies that Egypt's international financial obligations, and the safety of the Suez Canal, the threat to which was doubtful even at the time, could have been secured by making terms with Urabi. Neither are plausible motives for military intervention. For example, Prime Minister Gladstone (Public Records Office [PRO]: 30/29/126), Ferdinand de Lesseps, Chairman of the Suez Canal Company (*The Pall Mall Gazette* 1882l: 11), and rebel leader Colonel Urabi himself (*The Times* 1882k: 5, *The Daily News* 1882i: 5), all stated that the Suez Canal would only come under genuine threat from the rebels *if* provoked by an external intervention. The nationalist regime only defaulted on Egypt's debt repayments after Britain engaged in gunboat diplomacy in July 1882.

In the historiography of the British Empire, the economic imperialism thesis is sometimes advanced as a structural cause that to some degree unconsciously shaped and directed the more immediate motives of policy-makers in dealing with crises on the periphery. This is to explain the absence in the primary source documentation for economic motivations relative to other explanations. For example, Eric Stokes (1975: 413–14) argues that

> as a sociological phenomenon imperialism has to be read much more widely to embrace not merely political action but the whole range of activities by which an intrusive advanced society impinges upon another less advanced. It must include not merely the metropolitan and local agencies of modern commerce

> but also the sub-imperialist elements of the settler and trader as well as the local 'collaborators' of the indigenous society … who have partly escaped metropolitan control. To demonstrate that metropolitan governments were pulled into the periphery for non-economic reasons against their inclination does not in this larger context dispose of economic imperialism.

A similar defence of economic imperialism is put forward by Anthony Hopkins (1986) based on the distinction between 'objective causes' and the 'subjective motives' of policy-makers.

The existence of these large, structural economic factors is beyond dispute. But if British financial interests could have been secured by making terms with the nationalist regime in Egypt, armed intervention cannot be directly attributed to this cause. And rather than some unconscious structural force, politicians were quite cognisant of economic pressures. For example, in debates on Egypt, government ministers repeatedly denied that they would intervene with military force in support of the 'bondholders' interest' (see *Hansard's Parliamentary Debates* 1882c: 774, 1882d: 173, 1800). Any advantage to private interests was incidental to the principle that the Egyptian government must fulfil its international obligations (*Hansard* 1882e: 1942–3). By late June 1882, the Continental Powers were treating the Urabi regime as an accomplished fact. For Britain to also follow this course of action would have been consistent with the Gladstonian foreign policy principles laid out in the Midlothian election campaign of 1879, which, as counter to Disraeli-Toryism, stressed the equality of nations and respect for the will of 'civilized' Europe (Gladstone 1971: 115–17, 123). The adamant British refusals to treat with Urabi, in opposition to the other Powers and contrary to Liberal principles, suggest that other motives were at play at the height of the Egyptian crisis.

There was, however, a very high threshold for permissible intervention in Egypt consistent with a pluralist international order. In the post-Napoleonic period, the Great Powers of the European Concert could only directly intervene in other member states of the international society to restore 'legitimate' governments in the event of revolutionary activity. The British were even less willing than the Continental Powers to interfere in the internal affairs of other states (Owen 2002: 385–7). In addition, any armed action in Egypt was also heavily constrained by multipolar strategic competition. To assuage these normative obligations *and* prudential constraints, the Gladstone Cabinet first sought the intervention of Turkey as legitimate suzerain. Failing this, the matter was referred to a European Conference for a mandated intervention. When this proved ineffectual, joint intervention with France and Italy was explored. Only after all options were exhausted was a unilateral British intervention undertaken. While failing to confer multilateral legitimation, this process did eventually gain grudging acquiescence from the Continental Powers for a unilateral and temporary British ground intervention in August 1882. The objectives of the intervention were consistent with the pattern of order in the international society: the restoration of the legitimate authority of the

Khedive, sound financial governance to ensure Egypt's international obligations would be met and the prudent development of self-governing institutions.

But there was a fundamental inconsistency in British intervention policy. The limited nature of the intervention's objectives was a function of the pattern of international order, whereas its temporary duration was due to strategic concerns. Multipolar competition resulted in continual attempts by the Continental Powers to erode the perceived relative gain of Britain's position in Egypt. The interference of the other Powers in areas of international jurisdiction, and their intransigence in permitting any change to these arrangements, served only to undermine the achievement of the intervention's objectives, and therefore to ensure its prolongation. Despite the Gladstone government's repeated commitment to withdraw as soon as possible, the British intervention in Egypt lasted for seventy years. The case study proceeds by first providing some brief historical background and a chronological overview to orient the reader.

## Historical Background and Case Overview

The Ottoman Empire was in terminal decline in the second half of the nineteenth century. Territory was lost in the Balkans and North Africa, and after 1875, Constantinople was subject to intrusive surveillance of its financial affairs. The disintegration of centuries of Turkish control in the Near East gave rise to the seemingly insoluble 'Eastern Question', which dominated the affairs of the European Powers between 1821 and 1914 (Clayton 1971: 9). The Ottoman Empire had gained the protection of the public law of Europe and tentative acceptance as a member of the international society by the Treaty of Paris in 1856 that settled the Crimean War. The signatories to the Treaty mutually recognized that the 'independence and integrity of the Ottoman Empire were necessary for the peace of Europe' (Gong 1984: 113). This assumption had been the cornerstone of British policy in the area since the 1830s; the main purpose of which was to protect the short routes 'to India by maintaining a Turkish state sufficiently strong and extensive to withstand Russian military and political influence' (Medlicott 1968: 25).

Despite this international guarantee, Russia and France were active in supporting nationalist movements in the Ottoman Empire's Balkan provinces (Shaw and Shaw 1977: 141). The Eastern Question entered an acute phase with the Russo-Turkish War of 1877–78, prompted by a series of rebellions in Bosnia and Herzegovina, Bulgaria, and in Serbia and Montenegro (1875–76) fomented in part by Russian pan-Slavism (Anderson 1966: 184). The inability of Turkey to maintain order on the Empire's peripheries or to effect modernizing administrative reforms raised the continual ire and frustration of European statesmen (Gong 1984: 114).

From the British perspective taken in this case study, the strategic implications and turbulent domestic political effects of Turkish decline were brought home by the war scare of 1878, in which the Mediterranean fleet had to be despatched to the Straits to check a Russian advance on Constantinople. Turkish atrocities reported during the Balkan conflict, such as the highly publicized 'Bulgarian Horrors' (Gladstone 1876), served also to affront British liberal opinion and offend the European pattern of international order. Turkey defaulted on its public debt in 1875 in a further affront to Victorian principles of good government, and by 1881, was under international financial control. Thereafter, British expectations of meaningful reform at Constantinople became deeply pessimistic and Ottoman claims to its remaining territorial integrity and membership of international society came under increasing question (e.g., Freeman 1880: 974, Lathbury 1880: 204–5).

The Egyptian Question was derivative of the broader problem of Ottoman decline and remained a European question, subject to the scrutiny and interference of all the Powers. The Treaty of Berlin (1878) temporarily eased tensions in the Balkans and during the 1880s the focus of the Eastern Question shifted to the breakdown of order in Egypt. France and Britain had paramount interests in Egypt, intensifying after the opening of the French-constructed Suez Canal in 1869. France held longstanding cultural and financial interests, and viewed Egypt as part of a wider sphere of influence in North Africa. Britain also had important trade and financial ties with Egypt, but its primary interest was to ensure the short Suez Canal route to India remained open to British shipping in both peace and war (Temple 1882: 507). Facing insolvency in 1875, Egypt's Khedive Isma'il (1863–79) sold his shares in the Suez Canal to Britain under Disraeli's Conservative government (1874–80).

Anglo-French dominance compounded Egypt's ambiguous political status within the Ottoman Empire. Since the 1820s, Egypt's Turko-Circassian ruling aristocracy had wrested increasing political concessions from Constantinople to the point of de facto statehood under nominal Ottoman suzerainty by 1873. But as Egypt's political autonomy increased, so too did its penetration by European debt finance. The sale of the Canal shares staved off bankruptcy for only one year. From 1876, the Khedivate was progressively placed under international financial supervision. Formal settlement of Egypt's debt was made by the international Law of Liquidation of 1880, alterable only by the consent of all European creditor Powers. Already by 1877 it had become clear that the new arrangements were unable to rein in government expenditures. A damning report on Isma'il's administration was released in 1878 and a new Ministry was installed under pressure from the European Powers (Richmond 1977: 119). In February 1879, the first of a series of military revolts took place which gained support from both nationalist and Islamic sentiment in the country. Nationalism and liberal-constitutionalism became focused in the Chamber of Notables, a deliberative assembly established in 1866. The Arabic press and Muslim landowners whose fiscal privileges were threatened by international administration were at the centre of anti-European and anti-Christian sentiment.

In response to these pressures, the Khedive ousted the pro-European Ministry in April 1879, replacing it with a native Egyptian one and advanced a financial proposal that reduced the rate of interest on the public debt. The French and British governments viewed this as a veritable coup d'état, and in July, Isma'il was deposed as Khedive by the Turkish Sultan in favour of his son, Tawfiq (1879–92), under whose authority the Law of Liquidation was decreed. The Law separated the debt and administrative budgets of the state with priority assigned to the former. Shortfalls in revenues assigned for debt-service had to be extracted from the administrative budget. In 1879, British and French representatives were appointed to Egypt's executive Council of Ministers, which was responsible only to the Khedive, as 'Controllers-General', to supervise state revenues and expenditures. Unquestioned at the time was the assumption 'that loans to a foreign government carried with them political control' (McLean 1976: 292). The Anglo-French 'Dual Control' was based on an explicitly political rather than economic rationale: neither state would 'tolerate the establishment in Egypt of political influence on the part of any other European Power in competition with that of England and France' (*Parliamentary Papers* 1884: no. 10).

Another pro-European Ministry survived from September 1879 to September 1881 when smouldering discontent resurfaced. The crisis entered its acute phase on 9 September 1881 when Egyptian military officers led by Colonel Ahmed Urabi forced the dismissal of the Khedive's Prime Minister and demanded the convocation of the Chamber of Notables and a Constitution on their own, rather than the Khedive's authority. The Notables were initially moderate, but reserved the right to control the portion of the state budget not assigned to the debt, in defiance of the Controllers-General who opposed any local discretion over finances.

France had established a protectorate over Tunis in May 1881, and the new government of Léon Gambetta formed in November of that year favoured a 'forward' policy in North Africa. With the political situation at Cairo deteriorating in the face of perceived Arab 'fanaticism', the French and British governments issued a strongly-worded Joint Note on 8 January 1882, pledging to defend the Khedival regime as the legitimate government in Egypt. The Note sought to reinforce order by adherence to the principle that statehood could only be considered legitimate if recognized as such under European international law. The Note produced the opposite of its intended effect, however, becoming catalyst for a serious escalation of the crisis in which the Khedive was marginalized and effectively removed from power by the formation of a nationalist Council of Ministers with Urabi as Minister for War on 5 February 1882.

As a status quo power, the response from London to developments in Egypt was reactive until the early months of 1882. The Earl of Granville, Foreign Secretary in Gladstone's second Liberal government (1880–85), was obliged to take the lead in the Egyptian crisis due to the fall of Gambetta's government in Paris on 26 January 1882. Refugees fled Cairo and the interior of Egypt for Alexandria in the following months as violent anti-Christian and anti-European persecution mounted. On 15 May, British and French naval squadrons were sent to Alexandria. The joint naval demonstration failed to quell the crisis. Fifty Europeans were allegedly murdered by local mobs on the streets of Alexandria on 11 June and the rebel

Egyptian army fortified positions around the harbour. A conference of the Powers was convened at Constantinople to deal with the crisis, but proved ineffectual. Sultan Abdul Hamid II (1876–1909), who, it was anticipated by the British, would furnish a Turkish intervention force to operate under Anglo-French supervision, declined to participate. Agreement also failed to be reached on the second option of a joint Anglo-French intervention as mandatories of Europe. To the frustration of the British, France remained vehemently opposed to any Turkish intervention in North Africa, while none of the other Powers held much hope of its effectiveness in any case.

The British naval squadron bombarded Alexandria on 11 July 1882 without the participation of France after an ultimatum to surrender the fortifications passed unheeded. Rebel Egyptian forces withdrew from Alexandria and Urabi was left in control at Cairo. In early August, British and Indian troops led by General Wolseley landed at Suez, Port Said, and Alexandria, decisively defeating Urabi's forces at Tel-el-Kebir on 13 September 1882. Cairo was occupied and Urabi captured two days later, bringing to an end the overtly military aspect of the British intervention.

The post-intervention British position in Egypt was 'uneasy, complex and obscure' (Anderson 1966: 145–6). As part of the Eastern Question and subject to the European balance of power, the annexation of Egypt or the declaration of a protectorate could not be considered (Cromer 1908: 93). The Dual Control with France was quickly abandoned but the plethora of international obligations that bound Egyptian finance remained in force. The intervention aroused the deep hostility of France and received no support from the other Continental Powers. Gladstone's Liberal government undertook to withdraw British forces as soon as possible.

In August 1883, it was announced that British troops would withdraw to Alexandria where a small force would be temporarily maintained. This was impeded by the failure of the European Powers to reach agreement on Egypt's untenable financial arrangements and also by military disasters in the Sudan, where the Mahdist movement had routed Egyptian forces. The subsequent decision of the Khedive, under British advice, to evacuate the Sudan to a defensible frontier was deeply unpopular at Cairo, precipitating the fall of another Ministry, and plunging the country into renewed crisis. Britain could not withdraw from Egypt until there was a stable and solvent pro-British regime in Cairo. In attempting to achieve this after 1883, the onus increasingly fell on the small group of British officials, led by Agent and Consul-General, Sir Evelyn Baring (later Earl of Cromer), which 'advised' the Egyptian government.

In negotiations with France prior to a general Conference on Egyptian Finance in June 1884, agreement was reached that Britain would withdraw in three years if the Khedival government was stable. At the Conference, however, the French, unopposed by the other Powers, rejected all British proposals to achieve a more sustainable debt position for Egypt. Granville continued to press for a solution to Egypt's financial difficulties, and after another series of torturous negotiations, the London Convention was finally signed in March 1885. By the end of the 1880s,

Egypt's fiscal position had improved significantly under British administration, thereby reducing the main point of international leverage against the ongoing political intervention (Richmond 1977: 141).

Under renewed tension with Russia over Afghanistan in 1885–87, Britain sought to revive the liberal *entente* with France by again engaging Turkey in a solution to the Egyptian imbroglio. An Anglo-Turkish Convention was signed on 22 May 1887 providing for a British withdrawal in three years unless the security of Egypt came under internal or external threat. A right of re-entry was granted for both Britain and Turkey in the event of misgovernment or external invasion. The Convention seemingly institutionalized Britain's leading position in Egypt and was opposed by France and Russia. The British plenipotentiary left Constantinople without Turkish ratification on 15 July 1887.

Since late 1882, Britain had attempted in vain to leave Egypt. The 'veiled' protectorate in Egypt was considered indefinite with the failure of the 1887 Convention. Subsequent British governments rebuffed French, Russian and Turkish overtures for a settlement between 1888 and 1894. The Sudan was reconquered in 1898. The formal Anglo-French entente of 1904 eliminated further French interference and abolished residual international controls. A formal protectorate was finally declared on the eve of the Great War in 1914. In 1922, the British unilaterally declared Egypt independent reserving rights to re-entry. A bilateral Anglo-Egyptian Treaty to similar effect was signed in 1936. The last British troops withdrew only months before the Suez Crisis of July 1956.

## The Threat to Civilized Order in Egypt

This section shows how British officials came to view events in Egypt as a normative threat to international order and the negative emotional expressions that this evoked. The meaning of state failure in this case was the administrative 'anarchy' and governmental 'breakdown' that would occur if European influence was removed. This normative threat was a challenge to the reputation of Britain as the primary arbiter of international order in the Near East. Challenges to the reputation of status quo powers also affect the way they see themselves – their sense of national honour. The negative emotions expressed by British officials and foreign correspondents demonstrate the importance attached to the norm that international obligations must be kept. It is important to note that newspaper correspondents in this period worked very closely with British representatives abroad, and in some cases were one and the same. For example, Sir Auckland Colvin, the British Controller-General of finances at Cairo, was also the Egypt correspondent for *The Pall Mall Gazette*, Prime Minister Gladstone's preferred daily newspaper. The material reported by foreign correspondents was therefore not disinterested and closely reflected the views of British officials (see Chamberlain 1981: 14–16, Hopkins 1986: 383). The language used in describing the rebellion from September 1881 and the removal of European political control indicates affront and disrespect at the hands of a low status actor.

Press correspondents at Alexandria viewed the political instability fostered by the 'ignorant soldiery' as threatening the entire fabric of Egyptian governance (*The Times* 1881b: 5). It was intolerable that the rebels could repeatedly defy the Khedive and damage the prestige of the Anglo-French Control. The greatest risk was the complete breakdown that would result if the army, subject to nothing but force, became 'recognized as a distinct and separate power in the State', representing Arab Muslims against the civilian government 'under the control of Europeans' (*The Times* 1881c: 10). For his part, Colvin seemed shocked that the rebel officers 'spoke like men convinced that they would be allowed to settle their own disputes with the Government; that Europe had neither the right nor the wish to interfere' (Foreign Office Records [FO] 1881: 407/18/50).

The hundreds of Europeans staffing the Egyptian Civil Service and international financial administrations were a major source of Arab nationalist and Islamic resentment (Osborn 1882: 29). The pan-Islamic thrust of the vernacular press became more pointed from September 1881. European administrators were attacked as the agents of Muslim oppression (FO 1881: 407/18/85). The tone of diplomatic despatches and news reports suggests a mounting combination of trepidation, indignation and fear. This was more than a simple soldier's mutiny. For example, *The Times* (1881e: 4) reported on 6 October 1881 that local sentiment behind the rebellion was that the 'army represented Egypt as against Europe – Moslem as against Christian'.

In the wake of this unrest, the public reiteration of British policy on 4 November 1881 was consistent with the pattern of international order. Granville said that Britain sought to retain Egypt's administrative independence, and continued that the government of

> England would run counter to the most cherished traditions of national history were it to entertain a desire to diminish that liberty or to tamper with the institutions to which it has given birth … The only circumstance which could force us to depart from the course of conduct which I have above indicated would be the occurrence in Egypt of a state of anarchy. (FO 1881: 407/18/257)

On the same day, *The Times* (1881f: 8) correspondent at Alexandria warned ominously that 'public order in Egypt was never so imminently threatened … The Ministry stands or falls precisely so long as it acts in accordance with the views of its electors, the rioters'.

This was seemingly an accurate assessment. British Agent and Consul-General at Cairo, Sir Edward Malet, reported on 26 December 1881 that the movement would soon make the nationalist Ministry responsible to the Chamber rather than the Khedive, thereby giving them control of the budget (Cabinet Office Records [CAB] 1881: 37/7/4). The normative threat in this development was twofold: it demonstrated 'first, a disposition to ignore or modify the engagements by which

Egypt is bound.' Second, it would remove foreign control of state financial administration, the only guarantee of good government. A memorandum from Colvin, which was circulated to the British Cabinet, concluded that direct Anglo-French 'financial control over the country' was essential to the preservation of international order in the Near East. It was 'the main safeguard against the recurrence of an "Egyptian question"' (CAB 1881: 37/7/4). Granville advised Prime Minister Gladstone on 15 January 1882 that the situation in Egypt was contrary to international Treaty engagements, a core criterion of the European standard of civilization, and therefore unacceptable (PRO 1882: 30/29/125).

This message was communicated to the Egyptian national movement on 16 January 1882. These events at the political level were accompanied by the first reports of civil unrest and danger to the security of Europeans. Despatches reported that of Muslims had 'assumed an attitude of a very insulting and threatening character towards the Christian population' (FO 1882: 407/19/123). The crisis escalated on 5 February 1882, as predicted by British representatives on the ground, with the formation of a Council of Ministers responsible only to the Chamber of Notables with Urabi as War Minister. This development coincided also with reports that the rebel Egyptian military had begun to upgrade its coastal fortifications around the harbour at Alexandria (FO 1882: 407/19/162, 166). Soon after, a new Organic Law was introduced allowing the Chamber to control the state budget. This removed the Anglo-French 'Control' over Egypt's finances. The European Controllers were subsequently excluded from Ministerial meetings.

Malet reported to London on 17 February 1882 that the rebellion was a much more fundamental threat to international order than the assertion of local control over government finances. Overturning the Control was symbolic of wider 'revolutionary feeling, of which anti-Europeanism is the real base' (FO 1882: 407/19/259). Press correspondents reported that 'whatever the present Ministry's programme may declare, it is distinctly anti-European … its sympathies are Mahommedan' (*The Pall Mall Gazette* 1882c: 2). The true object of the national movement was the removal of Europeans from government altogether, thereby destroying 'honest and enlightened administration' (*The Pall Mall Gazette* 1882d: 1). Writing in March 1882, Colvin was certain that the point of state failure had been reached: 'the country is at this moment without an efficient government and in imminent danger of disorder' (FO 1882: 407/19/411). In the view of the British Cabinet, Egypt's descent into anarchy was complete when Urabi, 'casting off the mask' of constitutionality, assumed arbitrary rule on 11 May 1882, responsible to nothing but force (*Hansard* 1882d: 1581–2). Executive power in Egypt now rested in an illegitimate, unaccountable and hostile sub-state actor. This was a gross breach of British expectations in Egypt and a severe challenge to its reputation as primary arbiter of international order in the Eastern Mediterranean. In response to this, British officials expressed a sense of affront and insult at such a challenge from an insubordinate actor. This began to shift toward trepidation and fear as the seriousness of the situation became evident. The emotion of anger and the desire for retribution became more overt as the political revolt deteriorated into violent civil unrest threatening the lives and property of British subjects.

## The Strategic Ramifications of the Egypt Crisis

This section canvasses the strategic concerns inherent in the Egypt crisis. I first show how the damage to Britain's reputation from the revolt in Egypt came to be viewed through the lens of imperial credibility in India. I then demonstrate that despite the urgency of the normative threat the British Cabinet's decision-making toward armed intervention in Egypt was heavily constrained by multipolar strategic competition. In the context of mounting tension at Cairo in 1881, the French occupation of Tunis in May of that year had prompted a re-assessment of Britain's Egyptian interests. The evidence clearly demonstrates the sensitive strategic location of Egypt in the multipolar system. For Britain, Egypt's strategic significance was indelibly linked with its imperial interests in India in two ways. India Secretary Lord Hartington (in Gwynn and Tuckwell 1917: 450–51) instructed Undersecretary for Foreign Affairs, Sir Charles Dilke, to consider how we now '"stood with reference to the despatch of troops through Egypt in the event of (1) a rising in India, (2) an invasion of India by Russia"'.

The most dangerous threat to British imperial authority in the nineteenth century had been the Indian Mutiny of 1857–59. The origins of the Mutiny were complex, but it involved a civil-military uprising in North-Central India focused on the Muslim Dynasty of the Mogul King of Delhi, which was once the dominant political force on the subcontinent. Since then, Britain had viewed 'fanatical' Islamic movements as the most acute risk to European influence and control in the Orient (Steele 1983: 2). The pan-Islamic subtext to the Egyptian revolt played on these existing fears, which were apparently well founded. In March 1879, for example, the High Sheriff of Mecca wrote to then Foreign Secretary, Lord Salisbury, that the

> state of Mussulman feeling in India, throughout Asia, and in Egypt, is such that a slight event might create wars and raise revolt in all Mahommedan countries. Suspicion, mistrust, doubt, and irritation have taken deep root in the hearts of Mussulmans, and these sentiments … can only gradually be eradicated and confidence restored by the exercise of great prudence and delicacy, and by avoiding any and every measure which may excite fanaticism. (CAB 1879: 37/1/8)

Concerns for the maintenance of stability and order in Egypt were not simply about protecting the Suez Canal or the interests of British investors. The revolt in Egypt and its mobilization of Islamic sentiment carried much wider Empire ramifications for British policy-makers. The credibility of the British position in India was deeply implicated in its handling of the Egypt crisis. It also began to play on British ontological security needs of peace, economy and prestige, which are addressed below. Parts of the world deemed essential to the prosperity and prestige of the Empire, such as Egypt, and even more importantly, India, needed to be seen to be orderly and safe.

France was also extremely sensitive to pan-Islamic influences undermining its sphere of influence in North Africa. In differing from the British, however, French concerns focused more on a renewal of Muslim influence in North Africa promoted by the Turkish Sultan in the role of Islamic Caliph. It was for this reason that Paris vehemently opposed any sign of Turkish intervention in Egypt throughout the entire episode (Cromer 1908: 201). The alternative of joint Anglo-French action in Egypt, was, however, regarded in London as deeply problematic. The Foreign Office analysis was unequivocal:

> If we let the French … into Egypt we shall never get them out again without war … The proper authority to put down a rebellion in Egypt is the Sultan & we should be careful how we derogate from this principle. Under no circumstances should we admit the entrance of French troops into Egypt. (PRO 1881: 30/29/121)

The British press also made clear the dangerous linkages between Egyptian disorder and French expansion in North Africa, while reiterating that Britain's 'Imperial interest in Egypt is beyond and above that of all other countries put together' (*The Times* 1881d: 4).

The worsening of the political situation at Cairo in September 1881 only exacerbated the simmering Anglo-French rivalry and raised mutual suspicions. The other Powers also promptly declared their interest. On 17 September 1881, for example, Granville rebuffed a proposal 'to admit Italian intervention in Egyptian affairs on the same footing as England and France' (FO 1881: 407/18/44). Lord Dufferin reported from Constantinople that Germany and Russia were also insisting 'upon a right of interference in Egyptian affairs' (FO 1882 407/18/44). The British were of the opinion that if armed intervention was necessary this must be the responsibility of the Turkish Sultan as legitimate suzerain, but under strict supervision. This was consistent with international order and the major British interest in the Near East of keeping the other Powers out of Egypt, but was irreconcilable with its core European interest of 'steady concert with France' (PRO 1881: 30/29/124).

The irreconcilable conflict between the strategic imperatives of keeping the Continental Powers out of Egypt, while maintaining the liberal alliance with France was quickly apparent. This dilemma was further compounded for the Foreign Office by the fact that any Turkish intervention in Egypt as legal suzerain would only serve to reopen the Eastern Question:

> If the Porte [the seat of Ottoman government] were to intervene in any manner in Egypt, the question would thereby become a European one. The Great Powers … would not fail to claim their proper share in the settlement of the matter.

> France and England would of necessity lose the exclusive patronage of Egypt which they enjoyed at this moment; Egyptian questions would be subject to the decision of seven Powers instead of two, and it was impossible to say what might be the result. (FO 1881: 407/18/72)

British Ambassador at Berlin, Lord Ampthill, was 'informed that Prince Bismarck is not unfavourable to a Turkish occupation of Egypt'. This was apparently supported by both Russia and Austria-Hungary (FO 1881: 407/18/89).

The options of either a Turkish or Anglo-French military intervention were both unpalatable from the British perspective. But on balance, a Turkish intervention would be less likely to inflame pan-Islamic sentiment across the Orient, while interference from the Continental Powers would not be in the form of troops on the ground. The unattractiveness of both alternatives is evident in Granville's restatement of British policy on 4 October 1881. The statement indicates the status quo nature of Britain's engagement, its expectations for stability on the existing arrangements, and its claim to be the primary arbiter of order in Egypt. Granville told the Turkish Ambassador to London that the British Cabinet had

> no desire to take any steps toward an English occupation or annexation of the country; still less did we wish to see it occupied or annexed by any other Power. We were anxious to maintain the present *status quo*, and to uphold the Sultan's rights; but we should object to any attempt to extend those rights, or to use them for the purpose of diminishing the autonomy of Egypt, and interfering in its internal administration. (FO 1881: 407/18/106)

By the end of January 1882, the evidence suggests that a settlement involving the other Powers, which a Turkish intervention would certainly bring, was deemed preferable by the British Cabinet over the possibility of any French military occupation of Egypt, joint or otherwise (PRO 1882: 30/29/125, Gwynn and Tuckwell 1917: 454–5). An important conclusion to draw from this was that British imperial interests in Egypt, and by extension, India, were considered more important than the alliance with France in Europe. This is important in understanding why concerns for imperial credibility were so powerfully engaged by threats to the lives and property of Europeans as the Egyptian crisis worsened during 1882.

During December 1881, the diplomatic despatches from Egypt brought the alarming assessment that the Chamber of Notables, supported by the army, was insisting on control of the budget as a precursor to taking full control of state finances. There was no local remedy, according to Colvin and Malet, for this administrative 'anarchy' (see FO 1882: 407/19/78, 87, 127). On 15 January 1882, Granville wrote to Gladstone that this would reopen the Egyptian question and could not be allowed (PRO 1882: 30/29/125). Gladstone replied on 31 January that, as to the Anglo-French Control 'and internationally sanctioned laws we withhold it bodily from the Notables' (PRO 1882: 30/29/125). The evidence makes clear that British representatives at Cairo and decision-makers in London felt that the political situation in Egypt had become untenable by the end of January 1882. It was not until 11 May, however, that the Cabinet came to the view that an external intervention was unavoidable.

The long delay in the face of these grave threats to international order was due to the ominous rumblings from the Continent that grew louder as the situation in Egypt deteriorated, raising unavoidable prudential concerns for Britain in the multipolar system. Russia continued to bluntly assert that Egypt was part of the broader Eastern Question and Britain could not take unilateral action (e.g., *The Daily News* 1882a: 5). On 2 February 1882, Russia, Italy, Austria, and Germany made the unequivocal joint statement that the status quo in Egypt 'could not be modified except by an accord between the Great Powers and the Suzerain Power' (FO 1882: 407/19/149). The constraints of multipolar competition on British decision-makers were pervasive and unavoidable. Prudential concerns virtually guaranteed that a matter as sensitive as the Egypt crisis be placed under the jurisdiction of a European Concert, carrying with it profound constraints on British action.

## National Honour and Imperial Credibility: Britain Responds

This section shows how the disorder in Egypt and challenge to Britain's reputation began to engage the national honour dimension of the prestige motive and instrumental concerns for imperial credibility in India. Strong negative emotions were expressed as the Egypt crisis escalated and began to resonate as a British national honour concern at home. Prior to the advent of opinion polling, the temper of public sentiment was difficult to gauge. In the late-Victorian era, perceptions of public opinion were mediated into Cabinet decision-making by the views of parliamentarians, but more importantly, by the tone and disposition of the mass-circulation press, which, however erroneously, was considered synonymous with public opinion (Kennedy 1981: 51, Lowe 1969: 11). Cabinet decision-makers felt public opinion to be a policy constraint on action or inaction only in particular, highly publicized cases (Lowe 1969: 12). It was not a positive factor driving foreign policy.

The substance of the anxiety felt by the domestic polity in this period was resonant with the British identity narrative of peace, economy and prestige. Threats to the lives and property of Britons abroad, the prosperity and prestige of the Empire, and insults to national honour, were the main themes in newspaper coverage of the Egypt crisis. This was in addition, of course, to the constant, underlying risk of Great Power conflict precipitated by disorder in the strategic regions of the Balkans, Near East and Central Asia (Thornton 1966: 42–3, Clayton 1971: 124–5). The most recent 'war scare' with Russia had been only a few years previously in 1878.

The tenor of press opinion became more alarmist and sympathetic to intervention with the formation of the military-backed, nationalist Ministry at Cairo in February 1882. *The Pall Mall Gazette* (1882a: 1) argued that 'the representative Assembly is being compelled to do the bidding of a military adventurer'. This impudence was precipitating an 'exceedingly critical' situation calling 'for decisions on the part of the Powers fraught with the gravest issues as to European peace'. The government's referral of the Egyptian Question to a European Concert prompted the conservative *Standard* to accuse the Cabinet of pursuing a policy of vacillation and inactivity out of fear to offend anyone while surrendering the country's special interests in Egypt (in *The Pall Mall Gazette* 1882b: 12). Questions were also raised in the press as to what guarantees for the Suez Canal could be expected from the Egyptian national movement, especially in the event of another Muslim uprising in India. The lack of public order and security for Europeans in Egypt due to the 'appearance of armed bands of lawless men', and 'the increase in the temper of the Moslem mob' became prominent elements of the coverage from February 1882 onwards (*The Pall Mall Gazette* 1882d: 1). The escalating levels of hysteria in the daily press created a backdrop of urgency to Cabinet decision-making that could not be ignored.

By March 1882, *The Pall Mall Gazette* (1882d: 1) held that 'collapse' in Egypt did 'not seem very far off'. Britain was 'confronted with the alarming possibility that we may have to intervene in Egypt to restore order at any moment'. War was being 'openly declared against all Europeans in official functions' (*The Pall Mall Gazette* 1882e: 7). *The Daily News* (1882b: 5) argued that while Urabi's national movement may not yet have formally breached Egypt's international obligations, it had succeeded in breaking the Anglo-French Control. The Control not only represented the 'superiority of the interests and the rights of France and England over those of any other Power' (FO 1882: 407/19/292). It also represented the prestige of Britain, and more generally, of Europe, in the Muslim world. Considerations of British national honour and imperial credibility became increasingly salient as the political disorder in Egypt developed into physical violence and civil unrest threatening the lives and property of Europeans. Matters came to a head when a conspiracy to kill Urabi was uncovered on 20 April 1882. In the subsequent political turmoil, British representatives claimed that Urabi was about to depose the Khedivate for a military dictatorship (FO 1882: 407/20/173). This was a gross breach of the standard of civilization. There could be no reliable assurance that Egypt's international obligations would be met. The political situation was thus of 'an absolutely revolutionary character' (FO 1882: 407/20/188).

The first act in response was the despatch, at the instigation of Paris, of British and French warships to Alexandria on 15 May 1882. The other Powers were informed that this was 'to strengthen the authority of the Khedive, and to safeguard the legal state of things in Egypt which has been recognized by Europe'. To placate the French, Granville also advised the Turkish Sultan to, at least for the present, 'abstain from all intervention and all interference in Egypt' (FO 1882: 407/20/230). Northbrook, First Lord of the Admiralty, was suspicious of the proposal for a naval demonstration. It would further weaken the position of the Khedive and without an effective landing force would only endanger Europeans. Northbrook thought the French were trying to provoke disorder with 'this futile naval demonstration' to precipitate Anglo-French intervention over that of Turkey (PRO 1882: 30/29/138). The outlook from St. Petersburg and Vienna was not favourable. Germany was assuming 'an attitude of extreme reserve' (FO 1882: 407/20/338). The Italian press was accusing its government of bringing 'Italy to the "lowest depths of humiliation" by her present exclusion' from the joint action of the Western Powers (FO 1882: 407/20/479).

The situation in Egypt deteriorated further with the presence of the ships. The tempo of local military preparations increased and anti-European sentiment only intensified (FO 1882: 407/20/505). From around mid-May 1882, the relatively passive British disposition of reacting to events moved towards a policy of trying to gain control of the situation. In conjunction with the naval demonstration, an ultimatum was to be delivered by the British and French Consuls to the military regime on 25 May demanding its resignation and exile (FO 1882: 407/20/537). This prospect was rejected in advance by Urabi on the humiliating grounds that Britain and France had 'no authority' to 'interfere in such a question' (FO 1882: 407/20/505). Army and police officers in Alexandria refused to guarantee public order unless the Ministry was officially and symbolically reinstated by the Khedive. This duly occurred on 28 May after intense pressure from Christian and Jewish leaders fearing communal violence in the event of a refusal (*The Standard* 1882a: 5).

In the following days the British Cabinet decided that Turkey must intervene under strict Anglo-French supervision. Northbrook articulated the growing concerns for British prestige in complaining that French intransigence about Turkish intervention was bringing 'risk and discredit' on the British government (PRO 1882: 30/29/138). For Britain in this case, concerns for imperial credibility followed the normative threat to international order and its attendant humiliation. This was reinforced by the press, with clear prestige-based statements referring both to the domestic sense of national honour and to international credibility. For example, *The Daily Telegraph* (1882a: 5) claimed that at stake in the Egyptian crisis was 'the fate of England and France as first-class Powers' and 'their future rank amongst the nations of the world'.

The build-up of excitement and outrage in the popular press signalled by the ultimatum to Urabi's Ministry on 25 May 1882, and its immediate rejection, was deflated by the announcement on 1 June of a Conference of the Powers at Constantinople to deal with the Egypt question. By this time, even liberal opinion had turned toward a unilateral British intervention. Two immediate objections to the Conference were raised: the delay it would entail 'in circumstances where delay may be fatal; and secondly, the opportunity which it affords of reopening the whole of the Egyptian question' (*The Pall Mall Gazette* 1882f: 1). The Conservative Opposition pressed these points harder. Lord Salisbury argued that no European

Concert could diminish the burden of British responsibilities in Egypt. The crisis did not brook delay (*Hansard* 1882a: 1773–4).

The submission of the Egyptian problem to Europe also immediately raised questions in the press as to the damage to Britain's reputation, especially in the eyes of Germany, and therefore to its sense of national honour. It was argued that any international settlement would remove forever 'England's preponderating influence on the banks of the Nile'. *The Daily Telegraph* (1882a: 5) complained that 'every day the tone of the two German Powers is getting firmer and more peremptory'. Diplomatic despatches warned of growing fear and panic among the British population. Correspondents reported that Europeans were in a state of 'gloom and humiliation' because of the 'repeated victories' of Urabi (*The Daily News* 1882c: 5). The tabloid press focused on the threat to the lives and dignity of British subjects in Egypt, which, according to *The Evening News* (1882a: 3) 'were not worth a days purchase'. *The News of the World* (1882a: 2) reported that in the villages, British 'lives are openly threatened by the natives, excited by the success of Arabi Pasha'. The defiance of the rebel Egyptian military in continuing their fortifications at Alexandria was 'accompanied with verbal insolence ... scarcely possible to believe' (*The News of the World* 1882b: 4). These statements clearly indicate the feeling of disrespect and corresponding damage to national honour.

Admiral Seymour, commander of the British naval squadron, advised London on 29 May 1882 that Urabi's military party now controlled Alexandria. There was much panic among European expatriates at Cairo and Alexandria, and British subjects were demanding to be evacuated (FO 1882: 407/20/621). Reports from the interior were claiming that 'fanatical anti-Christian' sentiment was being mobilized. Europeans and Egyptian Christians were fleeing in great numbers (FO 1882: 407/20/623). News of serious rioting at Alexandria reached London three days later. Vice-Consul Calvert telegraphed that there were many wounded, including the British Consul. A British naval engineer had been murdered as Egyptian police looked on. European property had been plundered by the mob (FO 1882: 407/20/884, 885). The following day Calvert confirmed that 'about fifty Europeans were killed and only three Arabs ... Nearly all the Europeans killed or wounded have been clubbed ... Vessels in port are crowded with European fugitives' (FO 1882: 407/20/903). *The Times* (1882h: 7) correspondent at Alexandria reported that an 'exodus of all the Christians, Syrians, Jews, and Europeans has set in with increasing volume'. Urabi reportedly declared a Holy War on 14 June, raising the risk of pan-Islamic uprisings elsewhere in the Orient. According to *The Daily News* (1882d: 5), the Arabic language press was urging the 'extermination of the Europeans'.

As greater external pressure was applied to Egypt, what had essentially been a governmental crisis was transformed into wider and violent anti-European and anti-Christian unrest. It has since been argued by a number of historians that British representatives and press correspondents in Egypt grossly exaggerated this to encourage an intervention (see Galbraith and Al-Sayyid-Marsot 1978: 483, Cole 1989: 121–8, Schölch 1976). Nonetheless, the impression created in London was of an acute threat to British lives and property, which was the most fundamental breach of the standard of civilization. This was also critical to considerations of imperial credibility, especially in India, and to feelings of national honour.

## The Alexandria Massacre and British Retribution

The crisis in Egypt was now seen to be in full breach of the most basic tenet of international order: the security of Europeans abroad. The motive of retribution becomes prominent after the Alexandria massacre. This can be considered emotionally, as an end in itself that restores national self-respect for a past humiliation. It can also be considered instrumentally, as asserting imperial credibility with respect to India and the Empire in the 'East'. There is substantial primary source evidence to support this prestige-based interpretation.

For example, in its emotional dimension, Dilke (in Gwynn and Tuckwell 1917: 460) wrote on 13 June 'that "there is an overwhelming public opinion here for very strong measures; that the great majority of the Cabinet share that view ..."' His diary entry the following day records, '"Our side in the Commons is very Jingo about Egypt. They badly want to kill someone"'. Northbrook commented on 18 June that Britain may now have to take unilateral action because the question 'involves the honour of England and the lives and property of British subjects ...' (PRO 1882: 30/29/138). Dilke threatened to resign from Cabinet if a decision to remove Urabi was not taken. He later softened his stance somewhat in agreeing to a joint Anglo-French intervention provided he was given '"startling reparation for the murders and insult to our Consul at Alexandria"' (in Gwynn and Tuckwell 1917: 462). In Parliament, the Opposition argued that the humiliation of being 'compelled to beg Arabi to protect European life and property, especially after the presentation of the Ultimatum demanding his exile' was intolerable (*The Standard* 1882b: 5). The Opposition continued to hammer the point over the succeeding days that Britain 'had lost the prestige and power which it formerly possessed' in the East because of the government's inability to enforce the ill-judged ultimatum it had made to Urabi (*Hansard* 1882b: 1725). According to both Dilke and Hartington, by the end of June, the majority of the governing Liberal Party was now demanding some form of British armed intervention (PRO 1882: 30/29/132, *The Pall Mall Gazette* 1882i: 11).

On the diplomatic front, Granville informed the German Ambassador on 27 June 1882 that Britain was now prepared to take any necessary steps with regard to Egypt (FO 1882: 407/20/1504). The Italians were similarly told that preparations were 'ready for every contingency'. Rome was informed in a language of retribution that Britain 'had an account to settle with Egyptians for the massacres and losses inflicted on the Queen's officers and subjects' (FO 1882: 407/20/1508). In Paris, Lord Lyons confirmed the British position that the 'question of national honour, and of the safety of European residents in Egypt and other Mussulman countries' was now an immediately pressing matter. The Urabi regime must be removed (FO 1882: 407/21/1).

Considerations of British imperial credibility also acquired an urgency that increased in parallel with the delay and ineffectiveness of the Conference of the Powers convened at Constantinople in June 1882 to deal with the Egypt problem. For example, Hartington complained to Granville that 'the state of things is getting worse and more discreditable to us' (PRO 1882: 30/29/132). Despatches from 16 June brought the news that the marginalized Khedive was now making terms with the Urabi regime (FO 1882: 407/20/1115; 1121), thus disregarding the ultimatum of 25 May and gaining impunity for the massacre of 11 June. This was both a grievous insult to British national honour and damaging to imperial credibility. Hartington wrote that even if the other Powers were able to compromise; 'it is not possible for us' (PRO 1882: 30/29/132). *The Pall Mall Gazette* (1882g: 11) captured this sentiment succinctly in pointing out that holding an expansive Empire that had been won

> in the past by force through the exercise to-day of patience, meekness, longanimity, and every saintly virtue, is the most extraordinary delusion that ever intruded into the politics of any land. It cannot hold sway in England for even half a year; no Ministry can retain power and practically apply it.

Bismarck was informed that Britain could not acquiesce to 'any arrangements in Egypt, especially after the late massacre at Alexandria, which would destroy, not only the influence and credit of this country, but also of Europe, in the East' (FO 1882: 407/20/1182).

This reasoning was articulated most explicitly by former British Controller-General in Egypt and then Suez Canal Director, Sir Rivers Wilson (in *The Pall Mall Gazette* 1882j: 10), who argued that, while Britain's interest in Egypt was primarily as the highway to India,

> there is more than this. We govern India by means of our prestige, some 60,000 British troops, and by the people's implicit belief in the resolution, determination, and strength of the British Empire. Without these qualities, and a confidence in them, it is not 60,000 men we should need to hold India, but an incalculably larger number; therefore, destroy that prestige and our difficulties in retaining India would enormously increase. Now when it becomes known in India ... that Englishmen have been outraged and insulted, the Indian population will anxiously look to see what reparation is demanded and exacted for [the] outrages ... It will, therefore, depend very much on the result of our present action whether our prestige is increased or weakened in India.

This was reinforced by the Colonial Secretary, Lord Kimberley (in *The Pall Mall Gazette* 1882j: 11), who said that while the government was '"acting wisely in inviting the advice and concert of the European Powers"', it was '"resolved to defend the interests and honour of the nation 'come what may"'. These statements clearly indicate that British intervention was now felt necessary to restore imperial credibility in India as well as national honour at home.

French founder and Chairman of the Suez Canal Company, Ferdinand de Lesseps, accurately claimed that the main motive of British military preparations was not to defend the Canal, which was not under any genuine threat, but to enforce the ultimatum of 25 May 1882. All that was required to secure the Canal was to come to an agreement with Urabi as the other Powers had already done (*The Pall Mall Gazette* 1882l: 11, Farnie 1969: 284–5). This shows that an alternative interest-based policy was available to the British Cabinet, but it was discounted for prestige-based reasons. Gladstone even agreed on 16 July that the Canal would not come under any serious threat unless Urabi was provoked by an intervention. But the Prime Minister clearly indicated, however, that the British government could not treat with Urabi (PRO 1882: 30/29/126).

An acceptance by Cabinet that a break with France over Turkish intervention might not be avoided was evident by the end of May 1882. The archival evidence clearly indicates that British military contingencies were also being considered in secrecy by this time. For example, Granville wrote to War Secretary, Hugh Childers, on 29 May that 'things do not look pleasant at Paris or Cairo – I trust that we shall not have to break with the French, but there is a possibility of it. I believe I rightly understood that you had privately considered at the War Office, all contingencies' (PRO 1882: 30/29/118). Actual military preparations in Britain for an expeditionary force were initiated on 16 June. Preparations for troops from India appear to have been made a few days prior to this (see Childers 1901: 88–9, PRO 1882: 30/29/138). This suggests that at least among some British Cabinet members a Turkish intervention was considered an unlikely prospect prior to the first sitting of the European Conference on 17 June. It was certain that the majority preference of the Conference would be to sanction the intervention of Turkey as the legitimate suzerain. But to complicate matters, Germany had refused in advance the strict British terms for a supervised Turkish intervention. The French remained opposed to any form of Turkish involvement (FO 1882: 407/20/1096, 1212).

From around 17 June 1882 then, it would seem that the British Cabinet could have held little expectation that the Conference would produce any effective outcome, and that there would have to be some form of British military intervention. The continuing British pressure thereafter for Turkish intervention appears to have been disingenuous, serving the prudential function of being seen to consult, while in the background military preparations were carried on. Dufferin was issued new instructions to take to the Conference on 21 June. The new Ministry in Egypt could not be accepted. The Powers were to be asked 'to provide or sanction a military intervention, other than Turkish, under their authority' (FO 1882: 407/20/1339). Dufferin thought that France, Italy and possibly Russia, would not acquiesce in any final settlement that included Urabi, in opposition to Germany and Austria, who appeared to accept the new situation on the ground. France 'appeared to prefer any amount of delay' to ensure that Turkish intervention was averted, while the Italians felt the deliberations of the Conference would last many months (FO 1882: 407/20/1460, 1461).

While secret military preparations had been taking place at the War Office and Admiralty since the end of May, reports in the press on 24 June 1882 from sources 'close to government', that a 'large force' was being put in readiness 'for immediate deployment in Egypt', suggests that the pressures of national honour were starting to be felt (*The Pall Mall Gazette* 1882h: 8, see also *The Times* 1882i: 9). That serious military preparation was taking place concurrently with the Conference, which was almost universally seen to be ineffectual, supports the proposition made earlier that the Cabinet's intent in pursuing it by this time was prudential. The delay inherent in the Conference, and the perception of vacillation it projected onto the government, had to be balanced against managing the risk of Great Power conflict. The French belatedly acquiesced in principle to Turkish intervention at the next meeting of the Conference on 3 July (FO 1882: 407/21/59). By this time it was too late. Turkish intervention had been ruled out in London.

Also on 3 July 1882, the British naval squadron was instructed to prevent the further arming of harbour fortifications at Alexandria. The tone of the reporting of the subsequent naval bombardment of 11 July indicates the positive emotion of glory at restoring national honour by taking revenge on the Egyptians. For example, *The Times* (1882j: 5) emphasized that 'the prestige of England … which had been gradually sinking … will have risen again to zenith height'. According to the excerpts published in the British press, the German and Austrian papers were, indeed impressed that Britain would '"not allow Europeans to be massacred by ruthless barbarians, and the trade and commerce of civilized countries to be interrupted"' (*The Daily News* 1882e: 5).

After the bombardment Urabi's forces withdrew, reportedly leaving Alexandria at the mercy of mob violence. Recent research by R.T. Harrison (1995), however, convincingly makes the case that the wholesale destruction of large sections of the city and up to 2,000 casualties was the result of the ten-hour, 3,000-shell British naval barrage, more so than any local rioting. The disproportionate nature of this attack, ostensibly to disable artillery placed around the harbour, demonstrates the authenticity of the revenge motive. This sentiment was well-summarized in *The Daily News* (1882f: 5): 'The 11th July has avenged the 11th June. The cruel massacre and the subsequent insults have been punished …' Although a little more circumspect, Dilke admitted the revenge motive in commenting that 'reparation at Alexandria was being virtually extracted by the bombardment' (Gwynn and Tuckwell, 1917: 468).

In Parliament, both Gladstone and Dilke defended the action primarily on the grounds of prestige. Their statements were also consistent with British identity and ontological security needs. The Prime Minister argued that the effect that the unavenged Alexandria massacre 'would have had upon the security, not only of all Englishmen and all British subjects, but of all European people throughout the whole East' was inestimable (*Hansard* 1882d: 177). Dilke followed by saying

> it must be perfectly clear that, by massacres of this kind, European life throughout the whole of the East is endangered, and the effect of any such massacre being passed over without redress, would be to put the lives of Europeans throughout the East absolutely at the mercy of a fanatical mob of Mahomedans. We ought to remember not only the enormous number of British subjects who live in Egypt and abroad, but the immense interests which our country possesses, and which were protected during late years by the sanctity of European life observed throughout the East'. (*Hansard* 1882d: 190–91)

The tempo and intensity of the press coverage of the alleged atrocities committed against Europeans after the bombardment served to reinforce Cabinet decision-making toward unilateral intervention at the same time as the internal contradictions of the Conference played themselves out to a standstill. The content of newspaper headlines and lead stories revolved around the horrible atrocities and brutal massacres inflicted on Europeans and other Christians in Alexandria (e.g., *The Pall Mall Gazette* 1882m: 8, *The Evening News* 1882b: 3, *The Morning Post* 1882: 5). *The Daily Telegraph* (1882b: 5) luridly recounted that 'the Arabs' had killed 'all the Christians they could find'. The scene at Alexandria was a ghastly catastrophe, with the ancient city in flame and ruins, pillaged by Egyptian soldiers and Arab mobs (see *The Daily News* 1882g: 5, *The Evening News* 1882c: 3, *The News of the World* 1882c: 2). Fanatical mobs had forced their way into nearly every European home, plundering and murdering at will (*The Daily News* 1882h: 5).

## The Case for Military Intervention

The evidence suggests that Gladstone agreed to a British military intervention sometime between the bombardment of Alexandria on 11 July and 20 July 1882. In a despatch ostensibly to Dufferin dated 11 July but released publicly on 20 July as a *Parliamentary Paper*, Granville stated the official Cabinet position that only force could now put an end to the intolerable state of affairs in Egypt. This was justified by reference to international order norms and British imperial credibility. British objectives were

> that the navigation of the Suez Canal should be maintained open and unrestricted, that Egypt should be well and quietly governed, free from predominating influence on the part of any single power, that international engagements shall be observed, and that those British commercial and industrial interests which have been so largely developed in Egypt shall receive due protection, and shall not be exposed to outrage; – a principle which is not applicable only in Egypt, but is essential for our national interests in all parts of the world. (*Parliamentary Papers* 1882: no. 10)

Granville said that 'in accordance with general principles of international law and usage'; the force that should be employed was that of the sovereign power, Turkey. But if this method was to 'prove impracticable', it would 'become necessary to devise other measures' (*Parliamentary Papers* 1882: no. 10).

The case for the British intervention was made before both Houses of Parliament over a number of sittings from 24 to 27 July 1882. On 24 July, Gladstone defended the Cabinet's policy on the grounds of international order and liberal foreign policy principles. He described the situation in Egypt 'as one of lawless military violence ... aggravated by cruel and wanton crime' (*Hansard* 1882d: 1576). Such violence and disorder was incompatible with the growth of freedom. The Prime Minister indicated that the situation in Egypt was now within the grounds of permissible intervention under international law. Gladstone said that 'the Egyptian Question, under its present conditions, lies entirely outside the general question of non-intervention'. Britain was bound by contractual international engagements, which had been 'imperatively regulative of the government's conduct' (*Hansard* 1882d: 1579). The government had first sought the intervention of Turkey as legal suzerain. Failing this, the government had appealed to the authority of Europe, of which 'there is nothing more important for the future of civilization' (*Hansard* 1882d: 1584).

Consistent with the British variant of the European standard, the objectives for the intervention would be limited to settling Egyptian affairs based on the maintenance of existing international obligations, restoring the legitimate authority of the Khedival state by suppressing the rebellion, and 'within the limits of reason, to favour popular liberty' (*Hansard* 1882d: 1589–90). Dilke similarly elaborated that the objectives of the intervention would be 'the due observance of international engagements' without interfering beyond what was strictly necessary 'in the internal administration of the country' (*Hansard* 1882d: 1722).

In the House of Lords, Granville confirmed that in Egypt's present anarchical state, 'force must be applied. The question is how that force should be applied, and by whom'. A supervised Turkish intervention was preferable, but the crisis did 'not admit of indefinite delay' (*Hansard* 1882d: 1493). Granville said that no final response had been received from France, but it seemed clear that Paris would not cooperate in an armed intervention. Neither would the other Powers give a formal mandate, but according to Granville's somewhat disingenuous assessment, the Cabinet had their good will and moral support (*Hansard* 1882d: 1493). Granville also made two crucial points. The first was that of prudence with respect to the other Powers in multipolar context. The second clearly indicated the perceived British responsibility to manage the disorder in Egypt. Granville was 'not at all sure' that

> confidence would have been felt either by France or by the other powers if, three or four months ago, by a precipitate course, we had taken sole action upon ourselves. At this moment, however, Europe is entirely prepared for such a contingency ... but not the less does it leave upon us an immense burden and

> a great responsibility … I also believe that your Lordships, and the House of Commons, and the country at large, do not wish that we should shrink from the fulfilment of the obligation. (*Hansard* 1882d: 1493–4)

On the following day in the House of Commons, both Dilke and Joseph Chamberlain asserted that the primary motive for restoring order in Egypt was the maintenance of British prestige in the East. Dilke argued again that it was impossible to 'acquiesce in any arrangement in Egypt, especially after the massacre at Alexandria on the 11th of June, which would destroy, not only the influence and credit of this country, but of all Europe in the East' (*Hansard* 1882d: 1721). Chamberlain said that he could not 'conceive anything more dangerous to the security of our people and to the security of our Possessions that an idea should get abroad that we could be set at defiance with impunity' (*Hansard* 1882d: 1801).

### The Drift into Permanence

This section argues that post-intervention British policy in Egypt contained a fundamental inconsistency. While the limited objectives of the intervention were a function of the pattern of order, as represented by the British variant of the European standard of civilization, the intended temporary duration of the intervention was in large part due to multipolar strategic competition. As part of the Eastern Question it was necessary that the British Cabinet eschew any perception of an indefinite or permanent position in Egypt, much less annexation or a formal protectorate (Reid 1884: 200). France remained opposed to the Egyptian occupation until 1904, while Russia opposed British policy in all spheres of mutual interest. The consent of all Powers was also needed to modify Egypt's international financial arrangements (Taylor 1954: 290).

This internal contradiction in the British position gave rise to an insoluble political situation in Egypt. The informal and undefined status of the intervention allowed the continued interference of the Continental Powers in areas of international jurisdiction and was accompanied by constant affirmations of withdrawal by British Liberal Ministers. The uncertainty over the status and duration of the intervention proved 'fatal to security and enterprise', according to Colvin (1906: 114), therefore serving to undermine the achievement of the intervention's objectives. One of Granville's final despatches as Foreign Secretary in June 1885 explained how the multipolar system had thwarted the temporary nature of the intervention. Granville noted that both France and Britain desired the same thing: an early British withdrawal from Egypt, but that every obstacle put in the way by the Powers, which sought to erode Britain's position in Egypt, could only serve to extend the longevity of the intervention (FO 1885: 407/65/301).

The first objective of the intervention was achieved swiftly and effectively, fulfilling the government's prestige requirements across all three dimensions. Urabi's forces were decisively defeated on 13 September 1882 and the country quickly pacified. The Khedival autocracy was reinstated at Cairo on 25 September, with British officials appointed in a 'consultative' function as ministerial advisors and provincial inspectors. Because of the limited objectives and temporary duration of the intervention, decisive British control was exercised only in the War, Public Works and Finance Ministries. Other branches of administration, such as the Interior, Justice, Health and Education Ministries were subject to sporadic and varying levels of guidance by British officials until 1887, but remained largely staffed and directed by Egyptians in anticipation of an early British withdrawal (Tignor 1966: 92, 146).

Three phases can be identified in the post-intervention period prior to the abandonment of any serious commitment to withdraw in 1887 under Prime Minister Salisbury. The first phase encompassed the immediate aftermath of the intervention and included Lord Dufferin's mission to establish the detailed reform program for the targeted parts of Egyptian administration. The second phase, which marked a two-year period of crisis, began with the arrival of Sir Evelyn Baring as new Agent and Consul-General in September 1883. Baring's arrival coincided with the collapse of the Anglo-Egyptian position in the Sudan soon followed by the failure of the 1884 London Conference on Egyptian finances. An international settlement and guaranteed loan of March 1885, which successfully modified the 1880 Law of Liquidation, marked the end of the second post-intervention phase. The third phase encompassed the election of a Conservative government in Britain in July 1885 with Lord Salisbury as Prime Minister and Foreign Secretary, the stabilization of Egypt's financial position, and the Drummond-Wolff mission to conclude a final settlement with Turkey, which was abandoned on 15 July 1887. This period was interrupted by the brief tenure of a third Gladstone Liberal government from February to August 1886.

In a message to Lord Lyons in Paris a few days after the failure of the 1887 Anglo-Turkish Convention, Salisbury made the famous observation that British policy would now be 'to sit still and drift awhile' (in Cecil 1932: 48). The Convention had served to finally define Britain's rights, responsibilities and status in Egypt. The commitment to withdraw, consistent since 1882, had been offered and accepted by the only state with legal standing in the territorial aspect of the matter. It had been withdrawn by Constantinople after threats by the other Powers which in themselves justified the conditions which Britain had reserved for itself in the Treaty (Cecil 1932: 49). It became clear to subsequent British governments that the main objective of the intervention, on which international order depended, the maintenance of the authority of the Khedive, could not be sustained without continued military occupation and administrative guidance. In a self-perpetuating cycle, the Khedivate only became weaker and less sustainable as Baring exerted greater control over Egyptian administration into the 1890s (Lowe 1969: 52). Under this logic, the intervention solidified into a permanent British presence lasting until the upheavals of two World Wars transformed international relations into the postcolonial pattern of order and bipolar Cold War structure examined in the case study to follow. The British presence in Egypt was finally forced out only in the Suez Crisis of 1956.

## Conclusion

My purpose in this chapter was to reinterpret a case of peripheral disorder and intervention in the pluralistic international order of the late-nineteenth century through the framework developed in Chapter 3. The evidence presented and findings of the primary source analysis support the book's arguments to a convincing degree. The interpretation in May 1882 that Egypt was a state 'failure' requiring an external intervention can be understood as a normative threat to British expectations for international order in the sensitive location of the Near East. Urabi's nationalist rebellion first breached the normative principles of order by removing the legitimate government of Egypt recognized under international law, thereby risking the repudiation of Egypt's international treaty obligations. The subsequent deterioration of the situation from financial to physical disorder that threatened the lives of British subjects and other Europeans, however much exaggerated, was shown to be a further and most intolerable breach of the standard of civilization. The threshold for state failure and intervention in this case was found to be quite high, consistent with the theoretical propositions made earlier in the book about pluralist international orders. The Egyptian rebels removed the legitimate government under international law in a 'revolutionary' capture of the state. This met the permissible requirements for armed intervention in the nineteenth century pluralist international society. This was noted explicitly by Prime Minister Gladstone in his justification of the intervention before the House of Commons on 24 July 1882.

The analysis also found that while British representatives on the ground appeared convinced that the Khedival state had 'failed' by the end of January 1882; the Cabinet did not reach this decision until 11 May even with a further series of intense provocations in the interim. This was due primarily to prudential concerns in the European multipolar system. Britain first sought the intervention of Turkey as the legitimate suzerain power. When this proved ineffectual, the matter was referred to a European Conference for a mandated intervention. When this failed, further options of a joint intervention with France and Italy were explored. It was only after all options were exhausted that a unilateral British intervention was undertaken. This supports the observation made in Chapter 1 that status quo powers only undertake interventions in the periphery reluctantly. The impetus for unilateral intervention became much stronger as the crisis escalated in June 1882 and began to strongly engage with British prestige concerns.

The chapter has also demonstrated that each theoretical dimension of the prestige motive was evident to varying but convincing degrees. For Britain, it was the normative threat to the standard of civilization in Egypt that engaged its reputational concerns as the primary arbiter of international order in the Near East.

Urabi's rebellion broke international treaty commitments, removed the legitimate government recognized by Europe and threatened the lives and property of British subjects. Being a source of international order is integral to the identity narrative of great powers and the meaning they draw from this. Challenges to their reputation threaten their credibility in other areas of the world and also impinge on their sense of national honour. The disorder in Egypt was increasingly viewed by policy-makers as an insult to Britain's reputation as the leading status quo power with important interests in the area. In this it represented a lack of due respect from a lower status actor. As greater external pressure was applied, risks to the physical safety of Europeans increased and the emotional dimension of prestige became explicit.

Fears for the safety of British subjects were realized with the Alexandria massacre of 11 June 1882 that took place under the guns of the ineffectual Anglo-French naval demonstration sent to intimidate the Egyptian rebels. Compounding the earlier humiliation of the failed ultimatum to Urabi's regime, this profoundly damaged Britain's sense of national honour as evidenced by the strong emotional expressions of insult and the vengeance that was acted out. The disproportionate nature of the bombardment of Alexandria, justified openly in a language of retribution and 'accounts to settle', supports the argument that revenge as an emotional motive was taken as an end in itself. There is, however, little evidence that Gladstone's Liberal government openly pursued glory from their actions in Egypt, although the British press certainly emphasized this aspect of national honour for the domestic audience.

Finally, prestige considered in its instrumental dimension as credibility is very clear in this case study. The British Cabinet came to firmly believe that armed intervention in Egypt was necessary to maintain British imperial credibility abroad, particularly to forestall any challenges to its authority and control in India. The maintenance of prestige, as reputation for power and resolve, is also implicated in statements that allowing a massacre of this sort to go unpunished would endanger the safety of Europeans around the world more broadly. Indeed, as the tempo of British action increased with the bombardment of Alexandria, the prestige-based motive of maintaining imperial credibility in India and the East was explicitly stated as the primary motive for the ground intervention.

As with all the case studies in the book, the objectives of the intervention were consistent with international order norms and the values of the intervening power. The British, as a status quo great power, sought the maintenance of international order through the restoration of the legitimate authority of the Khedive, sound financial governance to ensure Egypt's international obligations would be met and the 'prudent development' in Egypt of self-governing institutions. While the documentary evidence suggests that British representatives in Cairo and Alexandria were reasonably well informed about local social, cultural and political issues, there was little attempt in London to understand the complex dynamics of a changing Egyptian society, or to try and genuinely address the root causes of the state weakness that gave rise to the rebellion. This supports the above claim made in Chapters 1 and 2 that interpretations of state failure are made in large part by reference to factors other than the empirical conditions within weak states.

Despite the undertaking to withdraw from Egypt as soon as possible, British post-intervention policy was plagued by problems partly due to the multipolar strategic context. From London's perspective, the intervention could not be withdrawn until a stable and solvent pro-British government was securely in place at Cairo and was able to control the country. However, multipolar competition resulted in continual attempts by the Continental Powers to erode Britain's position in Egypt. This involved pernicious interference in areas of international jurisdiction and intransigence in permitting any change to these arrangements. This undermined the achievement of the objectives of the intervention and ensured its indefinite prolongation. As tighter British control was exerted to secure the intervention's policy objectives, the Khedival state could only become weaker and less sustainable. As I argued in Chapter 2, not all polities can be socialized to dominant international norms of appropriate statehood at any given time. There could be no guarantee for Britain under the prevailing international order and distribution of capabilities that if the intervention was withdrawn, the inherently weak state would not succumb to the same depredations that had resulted in its failure in 1882.

# Chapter 5
# United States' Intervention in South Vietnam, 1965

This chapter examines the book's second case study of US armed intervention in 1965 to prevent the state 'collapse' of South Vietnam. The Vietnam intervention took place in the postcolonial pattern of order and bipolar international system of the Cold War. The direct US combat intervention in Vietnam, beginning with air operations from February 1965, and with ground forces from July 1965, can be understood as a response to a normative threat to Washington's expectations for international order in a sensitive strategic location. By early 1965, the impending collapse of the Republic of Vietnam (RVN) in the south of the country was a fundamental breach of Washington's requirements for a stable, non-communist 'free world' order in the postcolonial periphery.

The US identity narrative held that preponderant American power bestowed on Washington a special burden of responsibility to preserve a pluralistic liberal world order by containing communist expansion. Developments in Indochina in the 1960s were a direct challenge to the US responsibility for preserving freedom in the world and therefore to its ontological security needs. As mentioned in Chapter 3, in the Cold War climate of zero-sum ideological and strategic bipolarity, international order requirements and the distribution of capabilities were tightly interlocked. The collapse of South Vietnam was considered by most policy-makers as a profound strategic risk in the tense early-1960s Cold War climate even though it presented no direct security threat to the United States. The domino analogy entrenched in 1954 by President Eisenhower placed great emphasis on the transmission of peripheral threats to the North Atlantic core (Snyder 1991: 3).

US reputation for resolve in resisting communist aggression was believed to be damaged by adverse developments anywhere on the globe that challenged its role as the guarantor of 'free world' order. However from Washington's point of view in the early 1960s, state weakness in areas within operational reach of the strategic adversary, particularly along the Asian rim of the communist bloc, but also close to home in Central America, was believed to be more threatening and hold greater reputational consequences than other areas (see Kennedy 1963: 298–9, Hilsman 1963: 44, McNamara 1964: 895). From the vantage point of US policy elites, communist gains in Southeast Asia would erode America's reputation for maintaining an anti-communist international order in the region. This would also challenge Washington's global credibility, thereby risking a 'free world' collapse elsewhere in the postcolonial periphery. Reputational challenges to status quo powers also affect the way they feel about themselves by damaging their sense of national honour. In this case, elite policy-makers, especially President Johnson, were highly sensitive to the potential humiliation of 'losing' South Vietnam to communism (Steinberg 1996). The prestige-based motivations of maintaining reputation and strategic credibility, and avoiding humiliation, overrode alternative interest-based arguments against the intervention.

The analysis to follow shows that in the face of the National Liberation Front (NLF) insurgency in South Vietnam, the steadily deteriorating effectiveness of the RVN government from 1960 was an acute normative threat to US requirements for 'free world' order in postcolonial Southeast Asia. In the early years of the 1960s, this increasingly engaged with Washington's prestige concerns across all three dimensions: the normative, instrumental and emotional. More so than in the previous nineteenth century case study, domestic politics was also critical to understanding the timing and nature of the policy of direct military intervention in Vietnam. Mindful of public opinion, President Johnson was not prepared during 1964 to either 'lose' South Vietnam or get the country into a 'war' in an election year. According to most observers, South Vietnam had been without organized government and on the verge of collapse for at least a year when in February 1965 the President was finally convinced that there was no possibility of establishing a viable state without direct US intervention.

The early part of the US intervention from February 1965 centred on a limited bombing campaign against North Vietnam to coerce Hanoi into calling a halt to NLF activities. This proved ineffective in arresting the insurgency in South Vietnam or in shoring up the Saigon regime. Continuing perceptions of imminent collapse throughout the first half of 1965 combined with reports of increasing NLF strength and effectiveness prompted the policy change in July to a ground combat intervention. Johnson was convinced that the intervention must be kept low-key with graduated escalations and incremental troop deployments to avoid damaging public perceptions of a large war reminiscent of Korea.

In addition to domestic political constraints, the normative threshold for permissible intervention under the postcolonial international order emerging after 1945 was the most stringent of the three case studies considered in the book. The UN Charter explicitly provided for a pluralist international order with foundational principles of self-determination and non-interference in states' internal affairs. Armed intervention was only permissible in international law in the event of overt external aggression. In public statements, US policy-makers were always careful to emphasize that Saigon's chronic state weakness was not due to internal political conflict and social disaffection but a consequence of the NLF insurgency instigated and sponsored externally by the aggression of Hanoi and Beijing. Similar to the British case study in Chapter 4, the US intervention was also heavily constrained in the bipolar system by strategic competition. Decision-makers in Washington had to balance the imperatives of demonstrating the credibility of America's global commitments by preventing the collapse of South Vietnam, while also avoiding a wider war with China as in Korea, or a general war with the Soviet Union.

I argue in this chapter that the primary motive for the intervention was to maintain US prestige in Cold War context by protecting South Vietnam from external communist aggression. This would maintain Washington's reputation as the indispensable source of free world order and also bolster US credibility against communist challenges in other parts of the world. It would also meet the Johnson administration's requirements to show 'strength' in standing up to the communists, thereby avoiding humiliation and satisfying national honour in the domestic political sphere by living up to the country's identity narrative. The objectives of the intervention were consistent with the pluralist international order: to preserve a free, independent and stable South Vietnam, consistent with the provisions of the 1954 Geneva Accords and the UN Charter.

There were two fundamental inconsistencies in US policy that denied the intervention success in achieving its objectives. The first was that the indefinite duration of the intervention was incompatible with the constraints of domestic politics: there could be no protracted and inconclusive ground war in Asia. The second contradiction was that Hanoi would not curtail the NLF insurgency in the South unless faced with the aerial obliteration of its industrial and population centres. Cold War competition precluded this option. A threat to Hanoi's survival was considered to be one of the triggers for Chinese and possibly Soviet intervention. Johnson's middle-ground policy of graduated escalation by ground and air was therefore never likely to achieve the intervention's objectives, while also prolonging it indefinitely. Domestic dissatisfaction with Johnson's Vietnam policy then increased in almost direct proportion to increases in the application of force until the President signalled de-escalation in March 1968.

## Historical Background and Case Overview

The US intervention in South Vietnam cannot be understood outside the all-encompassing context of the Cold War, arguably at its most intense in the early 1960s.[1] The intervention was a product of the values, interests and policies that had defined Washington's approach to the bipolar world since the Korean War (1950–53). The more fluid formative period of the Cold War (1946–50) had by the early 1950s solidified into a rigid anti-communist consensus and ideology of containment (MacDonald 1991: 112–13). For the United States, the period of peak Cold War insecurity began with the Soviet launch of *Sputnik* in 1957, subsequent perceptions of a dangerous 'missile-gap', repeated crises over Berlin in 1958–59 and 1961, and culminating in October 1962 with the Cuban missile crisis. Opinion polls in the early 1960s indicated that a majority of the American public believed that there would be another world war within five years. In such a war hydrogen bombs would be dropped on the United States with respondent's holding little

1 Unless otherwise noted, the material in this background and overview section is drawn from Kahin (1986) and Herring (1979).

chance for their survival (Levering 1978: 112). Nuclear insecurity coincided also with the perception of Soviet and Chinese bellicosity in fomenting Third World revolution. Direct nuclear tension with the Soviet Union eased after the Cuban crisis, but fears remained that limited wars could escalate. The belief was widespread that any civil conflict in the 'free world' periphery must be supported by the Soviet or Chinese communists.

France had been comprehensively defeated in Indochina by Ho Chi Minh's communist-led Viet Minh in May 1954, bringing to an end the First Indochina War (1946–54). In July of that year, the Geneva Conference partitioned Vietnam at the seventeenth parallel. French forces were to be withdrawn completely from the country and Viet Minh guerrillas from South Vietnam. The United States and South Vietnam did not sign the Geneva Accords but Washington supported its major provisions. The communist Democratic Republic of Vietnam (DRV) was established at Hanoi, and from Paris, Emperor Bao Dai appointed Catholic mandarin, Ngo Dinh Diem, as Prime Minister of the State of Vietnam (SVN) at Saigon. Diem deposed the Emperor and assumed Presidency of the Republic of Vietnam (RVN) in 1955.

The prospects for a stable, non-communist RVN looked favourable in 1955. Diem had shown considerable resolve in suppressing the South's criminal organizations and religious sect militias. However, attempts to establish control over the southern countryside in 1956 involved the persecution and murder of former Viet Minh cadres and others accused of communist affiliation. Diem, an urban aristocrat, had little understanding of rural life. His officials were notoriously corrupt, his security forces heavy handed, and land reform lagged well behind Viet Minh arrangements (Bergerud 1991: 12–15). By 1959, Diem had failed to gain legitimacy in rural South Vietnam. Government control was effective only in Saigon and major urban areas. Washington's optimistic outlook on the viability of the South Vietnamese regime eroded as a renewed insurgency into the 1960s risked its survival as an independent non-communist state.

In May 1959, the Vietnamese Worker's Party (VWP) in Hanoi authorized the formation of armed units for self-defence in the South but insisted the movement remain political and not attempt to overthrow Diem by force. In the latter months of 1959, it became apparent that the Southern organization was acting in advance of Hanoi's directives by attacking Army of the Republic of Vietnam (ARVN) bases. Forced to catch up with events, the third VWP Congress of 5–10 September 1960 authorized the armed liberation of the South. The National Liberation Front (NLF) was formed on 20 December. The NLF was referred to in a pejorative sense as the 'Viet Cong' by US personnel.

At the time of John F. Kennedy's election in November 1960, the Diem regime had survived a first military coup, lacked political legitimacy, had little effective control over rural areas, and faced a committed insurgency. In early 1961 the new US President was unwilling to risk a full-scale military commitment but also unwilling to pursue a negotiated settlement. Kennedy instead chose a middle course of expanding indirect US military aid and advisory involvement.

The Military Assistance Advisory Group (MAAG) established in 1955 by the Eisenhower administration was enlarged and adopted a counter-insurgency training role. The ARVN went on the offensive in 1962 in a serious attempt to contain the insurgency. In conjunction, the strategic hamlet program, modelled after the British experience in Malaya, was also implemented. The larger US Military Assistance Command Vietnam (MACV) superseded the MAAG. These initiatives met with little success. The ARVN suffered heavy losses. ARVN commanders became less discriminating, killing many ordinary villagers and delivering regular propaganda victories to the NLF. The strategic hamlets did not incorporate adequate land reform and were hastily and poorly implemented. Most of the settlements were quickly infiltrated or overrun.

Relations between the Kennedy administration and the Diem regime became increasingly strained in 1963. Tensions were exacerbated in May when Buddhist protests against Diem's repression culminated in the highly publicized self-immolation of a monk in Saigon on 11 June. Diem and his brother, security chief Ngo Dinh Nhu, were executed in the aftermath of a military coup on 1 November, only three weeks before Kennedy's assassination. The NLF exploited the political turmoil. Infiltration from the North was increased and the NLF tightened its hold on the countryside. President Johnson was advised in late December 1963 that unless this trend was reversed, the RVN would be lost. The ineffectual military junta that had overthrown Diem was itself removed on 29 January 1964 in a second coup led by Major-General Nguyen Khanh.

The escalating crisis in South Vietnam was deeply unwelcome to the new Johnson administration. Johnson retained the Kennedy commitment to Vietnam and most of the former President's advisors. He was convinced that fighting the insurgency was essential to the containment of Chinese communism in East Asia. US withdrawal and neutralization of the RVN were rejected as policy options in early 1964. Johnson was, however, reluctant to commit ground forces, especially in an election year. Throughout 1964, the numbers of US advisors was increased and covert operations were introduced. Most of Johnson's key advisors favoured a strategy of graduated pressure against the North to compel it to halt its support for the NLF and thereby prevent the collapse of the RVN. The Tonkin Gulf incidents of early August 1964, in which DRV gunboats allegedly attacked American warships, cleared the way for reprisal air strikes, which garnered high levels of Congressional and public support.

Reprisal bombings of North Vietnam failed to provide the catalyst for political stability in Saigon. Khanh was forced to resign in August 1964, and in January 1965 another coup brought Vice Air Marshal Nguyen Cao Ky and General Nguyen Chanh Thi to the leadership of an unstable military-civilian government. A major attack by the NLF on a US army barracks and airbase at Pleiku on 6 February 1965 prompted Johnson to introduce an ongoing program of graduated air strikes against North Vietnam known as Rolling Thunder. Intelligence reports predicting the imminent collapse of the RVN generated pressures to expand the air campaign and commit ground troops to direct combat. By early 1965, government control in the South had been further reduced to a series of islands surrounding the provincial capitals.

On 8 March 1965 the first combat deployment of Marines landed at Danang on Vietnam's Central Coast to protect the enlarged air commitment. It was evident by mid-March that the bombing campaign had failed to produce immediate results. Little alternative existed to a major American ground intervention. This was further reinforced by another coup in Saigon in the same month, which installed the longer-lived regime of Ky and General Nguyen Van Thieu. The use of B-52s for bombing NLF strongholds in the South was authorized as the air intervention was extended to cover much of Vietnam and the Ho Chi Minh trail in Laos, with the exception of areas close to the Chinese border. In July 1965, Johnson approved the first major deployment of 50,000 US combat troops with further increases before the end of the year.

Two years later, half a million American troops were in Vietnam, $2 billion a month was being spent, and more tonnage of munitions had been expended than in World War II. Yet the NLF was still effective and Hanoi had not been persuaded to halt its 'aggression'. All major targets in North Vietnam had been destroyed by 1967 with no appreciable effect on the ground in the South. Massive US economic aid and military force had not built a viable, independent South Vietnamese state. The Johnson administration continued to believe that the war must be kept limited to avoid provoking Chinese intervention. Domestic opposition within the United States mounted as the conflict dragged on and American casualties increased. By the end of 1967, US forces had prevented a South Vietnamese collapse, but General Westmoreland's tactics of aerial bombardment followed by search-and-destroy operations had produced only a frustrating military stalemate.

Domestic support for the US effort in Vietnam declined in 1967. It turned into widespread protest in 1968 after the shock of the Tet Offensive of 30 January. The NLF suffered debilitating and irreversible losses in the series of coordinated attacks, but Tet was a political and psychological victory for the Vietnamese communists. Johnson rejected requests from commanders for more troops, and on 31 March 1968 announced that he would not stand for re-election and focus on pursuing a negotiated settlement. This decision marked the end of US escalation, but Washington refused to accept any settlement that did not preserve the RVN as an independent non-communist state. The change of direction reduced the intensity of US operations and introduced the concept of 'Vietnamization'. Formal peace talks opened on 13 May but Johnson left office without securing a resolution to the conflict.

The Nixon administration (1969–74) came to office convinced the United States must extricate itself from Vietnam. President Nixon and National Security Advisor, Henry Kissinger (1969–73), maintained, however, that an American withdrawal must be free from the taint of humiliating defeat and that the RVN's independence must be ensured. In 1971, peace talks remained deadlocked and large anti-war protests resumed in the United States. Hanoi launched a major offensive in March 1972. Nixon responded with a drastic escalation, including further massive aerial bombardments and a naval blockade. The deadlock was broken with the Paris Peace Accords of January 1973. Remaining US forces were quickly withdrawn and Congress severely restricted further aid to South Vietnam. The RVN collapsed and communist forces captured Saigon in April 1975.

## South Vietnam and the Threat to Free World Order

This section demonstrates how the deterioration of the Diem regime in South Vietnam between 1961 and 1963 came to be viewed by Washington as a threat to 'free world' order. Public statements by the new Kennedy administration in 1961 were forthright in articulating Washington's vision of international order and the threat of communist expansionism in the Third World. The flow of information into the decision-making process in Washington clearly portrays the deteriorating effectiveness of the RVN under Diem, and the political vacuum that followed his removal, as an acute threat to Washington's expectation for a stable, anti-communist regime in South Vietnam. In the zero-sum ideological and strategic bipolarity of the Cold War, adverse developments in Vietnam were damaging to Washington's reputation for resisting communism and also to US credibility in maintaining the 'free world' position in Southeast Asia and by extension, East Asia and the Pacific, and the world.

The intellectual framework, bureaucratic processes and policy objectives that underpinned the Vietnam episode until March 1968 were established during the first year of Kennedy's administration. On taking office in January 1961, the situation in Indochina inherited by Kennedy was evaluated according to the normative criteria of international order elaborated in Chapter 3. Developments in South Vietnam in the previous year had been 'adverse to the stability and effectiveness' of Diem's government. NLF success was in large part due to 'political discontent with the Diem government', which had been prevalent for some time. However, the immediate threat to the viability of the South Vietnamese state was the increasing intensity of the communist insurgency. It was imperative that the RVN immediately undertake 'extraordinary action to regain popular support and to correct the organizational and procedural weaknesses which contribute to the growth of Viet Cong power' (*FRUS* 1961, vol. 1: doc. 1).

The new President's inaugural address of 20 January 1961 set the tone for his administration's vision of international order. Kennedy (1961b: 1) first recognized the revolutionary character of the modernization process: 'The world is very different now … man holds in his mortal hands the power to abolish all forms of human poverty and all forms of human life'. Yet in continuity with the American liberal tradition, 'the same revolutionary beliefs for which our forefathers fought are still at issue around the globe – the belief that the rights of man come not from the generosity of the state but from the hand of God'. Synthesizing these themes with decolonization in the Third World, Kennedy pledged 'to those new states whom we welcome to the ranks of the free, we pledge our word that one form of colonial control shall not have passed away merely to be replaced by a far more iron tyranny'.

The Kennedy and Johnson administrations were deeply imbued with the assumptions of modernization theory. The problems and needs of the postcolonial periphery could be comparatively analysed and objectively ascertained by scientific techniques. The building of infrastructure, diffusion of American technology and training, and tutelage in politics and government would promote progress and development, and therefore reduce and eventually eliminate the threat of communism. The Third World was seen as a crucial theatre in the Cold War struggle after Khrushchev's 1961 pledge to support wars of 'national liberation'. Modernization theory appeared to provide practical solutions to the spate of Third World crises that seemed to beset the Kennedy administration in 1961 (Latham 2000).

Kennedy (1961e: 205) reiterated to Congress on 22 March 1961 that communist subversion in the Third Word was a dangerous symptom of the emerging postcolonial order, but that decolonization was an inevitable part of the modernization process. The President pointed out that 'we live at a very special moment in history'. The 'whole southern half of the world' was 'caught up in the adventures of asserting their independence and modernizing their old ways of life'. These new nations needed 'aid in loans and technical assistance', but they also needed help for the special reason that they were under external communist pressure. This was direct military pressure in some cases. But in others, it took 'the form of intense subversive activity designed to supersede and break down the new – often frail – modern institutions they have thus far built' (Kennedy 1961e: 205). Major statements by President Kennedy, such as these, clearly demonstrate Washington's requirements for international order, and how the communist challenge had shifted away from direct superpower confrontation to Third World subversion and insurgency.

Because order and power were tightly interlocked during the Cold War, communist pressure in Indochina was also indelibly linked to the Cold War distribution of capabilities from the outset. In early 1961, US documents described the situation in Vietnam as a 'communist-inspired insurgency … designed ultimately to absorb SVN [South Vietnam] into the Communist bloc'. The Kennedy White House ranked the defence of South Vietnam from communist aggression among its highest foreign policy priorities (*FRUS* 1961, vol. 1: doc. 1). Vietnam was a prime test-case for the Democratic administration's new strategic-level Cold War policy known as 'flexible response'. In a message to Congress on 28 March 1961, Kennedy (1961f: 236) declared that

> the Free World's security can be endangered not only by a nuclear attack, but also by being slowly nibbled away at the periphery, regardless of our strategic power, by forces of subversion, infiltration, intimidation, indirect or non-overt aggression, internal revolution, diplomatic blackmail, guerrilla warfare or a series of limited wars.

In his State of the Union address of 30 January, Kennedy (1961a: 23) expressed this tight connection between the pattern of international order and the distribution of capabilities by directly associating the state weaknesses of the 'struggling' nations of Asia with the 'relentless pressures' of the Chinese strategic 'menace'.

Reflecting these comments, an intelligence estimate circulated on 28 March 1961 indicated serious problems of postcolonial state effectiveness. Most Southeast Asian states were experiencing 'serious political crises arising out of foreign intervention, domestic strains, or a complex of factors attributable to their basically unstable and unhealthy political, social, and economic structure'. One of the most serious problems was the 'precarious governmental situation in South Vietnam' (*FRUS* 1961, vol. 1: doc. 22). Diem's difficulties were attributed to his autocratic, familial rule and a lack of modern institutions. After returning from Saigon, the President's military advisor General Taylor advised that nepotism and corruption might have been acceptable if combined with efficiency and progress but when accompanied by 'administrative paralysis and steady deterioration', the situation was becoming intolerable (*FRUS* 1961, vol. 1: doc. 210, Appendix C).

Despite these internal problems, the US military establishment tended to view the insurgency in South Vietnam as almost exclusively driven externally by Hanoi and backed by Beijing. In August 1961, the Joint Chiefs of Staff (JCS) advised Defense Secretary Robert McNamara that 'a large proportion of the support for communist aggression in all of Southeast Asia passes through North Vietnam'. This judgement informed the US military's preoccupation throughout the entire episode with interdicting NLF supply lines from the DRV through Laos, Cambodia and by sea; and by the punitive bombing of North Vietnam to compel Hanoi to cease its support (*FRUS* 1961, vol. 1: doc. 123).

The Defense Department held that 'the fall of South Vietnam ... would lead to the fairly rapid extension of Communist control, or complete accommodation to Communism, in the rest of mainland Southeast Asia and in Indonesia'. The clear objective was therefore to prevent the collapse of South Vietnam, by military means if necessary (*FRUS* 1961, vol. 1: doc. 227). The President's Special Assistant for National Security Affairs, McGeorge Bundy, concurred with this assessment. Kennedy, however, rejected committing US combat forces on 15 November 1961, based on the principles of international order. The NLF insurgency was not a clear-cut case of cross-border external aggression as in the Korean War. Unlike Korea, the President said, the conflict in South Vietnam was 'more obscure and less flagrant'. Any overt military intervention would attract international opprobrium and therefore be damaging rather than reinforcing of Washington's reputation (*FRUS* 1961, vol. 1: doc. 254).

The Country Team in Saigon, and many State Department officials, by contrast to the Defense Department and military establishment, tended to see the sources of the communist insurgency as mostly indigenous to South Vietnam, precipitated by Diem's unresponsive and autocratic regime (e.g., *FRUS* 1961, vol. 1: doc. 152, 155, 1963, vol. 3: doc. 52). The answer to the problem was an effective non-communist government in the South that was responsive to the needs of the people in providing security and public goods. While the successful interdiction of external support would be helpful, it was no substitute for building state capacity and political legitimacy (*FRUS* 1961, vol. 1: doc. 170). These tensions between the JCS and Defense, on the one hand, and the State Department and Country Team on the other, were accommodated in the overall strategy which prevailed with little substantive change until 1968: the graduated escalation of air-naval harassment of the DRV while suppressing the insurgency in the South by building the military and civil capacity of the Diem and successor military regimes. The only changes were of means, through the injection of major US combat forces from July 1965, not ends.

A major initiative to strengthen the Saigon regime and better provide security was the 'strategic hamlet' program introduced on 2 February 1962 (see *FRUS* 1962, vol. 2: doc. 42). The plan, authored by Kennedy's Chair of the Special Group for Counterinsurgency, Roger Hilsman, sought to create 'strategic villages' by regrouping existing smaller hamlets into compact, more easily defended areas. The lack of success in putting this into effect only highlighted the weakness and ineffectiveness of Diem's government. Problems with the policy's implementation were evident after only a month of its operation. Diem's brother and head of the internal security apparatus, Nhu, had in an 'overhasty, ill-advised' manner ordered the program to be completed as soon as possible (*FRUS* 1962, vol. 2: doc. 125). Many Vietnamese engaged in constructing the hamlets were foregoing work on their own crops having been promised payment in either money or food, which was not being made. There was genuine social distress as a result of the program, hardly conducive to its success (*FRUS* 1962, vol. 2: doc. 127).

Robert H. Johnson of the State Department's Policy Planning Staff wrote on 16 October 1962 that 'the strategic hamlet program is mostly pure façade'. This debacle was the direct result of US pressures for responsiveness and quick results foisted on the ineffective RVN bureaucracy (*FRUS* 1962, vol. 2: doc. 303). Blame was unequivocally sheeted home to the Diem regime. It was neither efficient nor popular. It offered no hope of breaking the vicious cycle or winning the support of villagers. There was little chance that the Strategic Hamlet program could be implemented. Moreover, there seemed to be little hope of altering Diem and Nhu's methods of governing (*FRUS* 1962, vol. 2: doc. 268).

Consistent with the pluralist pattern of international order, Washington's public statements in 1962 and 1963 downplayed the Diem regime's lack of effectiveness and repeatedly attributed blame for the insurgency to Hanoi until the Buddhist crisis erupted in South Vietnam in May 1963 (e.g., US comments on Report of Control Commission for Vietnam 1962: 109, Rusk 1963: 729). The collapse of the Diem regime commenced with the Buddhist uprising at Hue on 8 May after which civil unrest continued for several months. Diem and Nhu were eventually removed from power and then summarily executed in the US-supported military coup of 1 November 1963.

President Kennedy's instructions to the Country Team in Saigon after the coup were to help the 'new government to be effective in every way that we can'.

Reasons for the withdrawal of support for Diem were based on US requirements for international order, and the now rapidly increasing concerns for global credibility should South Vietnam be 'lost' to communism. It was, according to Kennedy, 'ineffectiveness, loss of popular confidence, and the prospect of defeat that were decisive in shaping our relations to the Diem regime' (*FRUS* 1963, vol. 4: doc. 304). The new Johnson administration was even more rigid in its insistence that the source of South Vietnam's weakness was external. Reflecting UN Charter principles, Johnson's first National Security Action Memorandum (NSAM) on the issue on 26 November 1963 stated that it remained a central objective of the United States to help South Vietnam 'win their contest against the externally directed and supported Communist conspiracy' (*FRUS* 1963, vol. 4: doc. 331).

## A Failing State in South Vietnam and the Constraints on US Action

This section first establishes that most high level US policy-makers throughout 1964 came to the conclusion that South Vietnam was effectively ungoverned in a political sense. It was a country with a US-backed army but with little social basis or political community for nation-statehood. Without any change in external circumstances, it was believed to be only a matter of time before the country was lost to communism. This was profoundly damaging to Washington's reputation for maintaining free world order and was also perceived as an acute risk to US global credibility in an instrumental sense. Emotions of fear at the potential humiliation of losing Vietnam and frustration at the failure of existing policy also became more explicit during 1964. Johnson's fears of humiliation were directly informed by his past political experiences of Truman's 'loss' of China and the stalemate of the Korean War. Despite the gravity of the situation, this section also shows that the Johnson administration had to manage both strategic and domestic political constraints in formulating a policy of direct armed intervention in Vietnam.

Johnson maintained a high degree of continuity with Kennedy's policies and personnel. The concentration of policymaking in the White House was accelerated during Johnson's tenure (Nathan and Oliver 1994: 32–3). As the consummate domestic political operator, Johnson instinctively sought middle-ground, consensus positions (Barrett 1993: 172–3). This is clearly evident in his decision-making on Vietnam. The key advisors in developing the intervention policy in the first half of 1965 were Bundy, McNamara and Secretary of State, Dean Rusk, along with Under Secretary of State, George Ball and William P. Bundy, Assistant Secretary of State for Far Eastern Affairs (Herring 1979: 8). Johnson also routinely consulted prominent Senators that opposed the ground combat intervention such as Foreign Relations Committee Chairman, J. William Fulbright and Democratic Majority Leader, Mike Mansfield (Barrett 1993: 164–5, Herring 1979: 14–15). Ball was the most prominent critic within the administration, making his case against the deployment of ground forces a number of times in the lead up to the intervention in July 1965.

Johnson had rarely been involved in Vietnam policy as Vice-President and lacked a politico-cultural framework for understanding nation-building in South Vietnam. In foreign affairs, Johnson lacked the nuance and sense of practical possibilities that characterized his mastery of congressional politics. Johnson appeared to believe uncritically that American values were universal; its intentions benign and altruistic. Political differences were always amenable to persuasion and bargaining (Taylor 1993: 114–15, Kearns 1976). The President reportedly agonized over every increment of military force applied in Vietnam, becoming frustrated and incredulous at the communists' lack of responsiveness. Johnson came to the presidency with huge self-imposed demands to achieve great things in the domestic sphere. He bitterly resented the distraction of Vietnam, but was convinced that its 'loss' to communism would undermine his Great Society Program and 'destroy' his presidency (Herring 1979: 17).

McNamara visited Saigon on 19 and 20 December 1963. He began his report to President Johnson with the grim observation that 'current trends, unless reversed in the next 2–3 months, will lead to neutralization at best and more likely to a Communist-controlled state'. The new Saigon regime was 'indecisive and drifting'. The Generals that had replaced Diem had little experience in political administration and no talent for it. The provinces were receiving little or no direction. The NLF now controlled 'very high proportions of the people in certain key provinces' (*FRUS* 1963, vol. 4: doc. 374). CIA Director John McCone concurred with McNamara: there was 'no organized government in South Vietnam at this time' (*FRUS* 1963, vol. 4: doc. 375).

The ineffectual post-Diem government was ousted at the end of January 1964 in a second coup. In the wake of this further political turmoil, an intelligence estimate on 12 February warned that South Vietnam was 'on the verge of collapse' (*FRUS* 1964, vol. 1: doc. 42). In early 1964, the possibility of direct military action against North Vietnam to prop up the government in the South began to be seriously canvassed but was fraught with concerns over the possible Chinese reaction. A JCS analysis on 14 February held that 'the threat of large-scale intervention by ChiCom military forces will continue behind the [Vietnamese] communist's activities'. It was, however, deemed extremely unlikely that China would directly commit its forces unless its own territory was attacked or if US troops approached its borders as they had done in the Korean War (*FRUS* 1964, vol. 1: doc. 12). The Soviets, for their part, would be cautious and concerned that the conflict did not expand. The JCS concluded 'that Moscow would initiate no action which, in the Soviet judgment, would increase the likelihood of nuclear war' (*FRUS* 1964, vol. 1: doc. 66). These strategic considerations informed all subsequent US policy aimed at reducing the pressures on the RVN by compelling Hanoi to cease infiltration.

Taylor and McNamara were again despatched to South Vietnam in March 1964. The situation had grown even worse. Large segments of the population were apathetic and indifferent. There were high rates of desertion from the ARVN. The governance structure from Saigon out to the hamlets had completely disappeared following the coup against Diem. Power vacuums in rural areas had resulted in confusion and disorder. The viability of the current Khanh regime was uncertain (*FRUS* 1964, vol. 1: doc. 84). A CIA assessment on 15 May stated that 'the over-all situation in South Vietnam remains extremely fragile' (*FRUS* 1964, vol. 1: 159).

Kennedy's counterinsurgency policy in Indochina had not involved direct combat by US forces. It was left to Johnson to manage the domestic politics of combat intervention in Vietnam. In approaching the issue, Johnson was keenly aware of the humiliating political legacy of Truman's 'loss' of China. He was also heavily influenced by the Chinese intervention and frustrating military stalemate in Korea, but was resolved that communist expansionism in Asia would be contained in Vietnam (Galluci 1975: 2–3). Some of the President's emotional reactions are able to be gauged from transcripts of the *Johnson White House Tapes*. In a telephone conversation with John S. Knight, editor of the *Miami Herald* on 3 February 1964, for example, Johnson (in Beschloss 1997: 213–14) said that one of the things he could do was 'run and let the dominoes start falling over. And God Almighty, what they said about us leaving China would be just warming up, compared to what they'd say now'. Johnson was very concerned that a humiliating US failure in Vietnam could derail his election campaign later in the year in November: Republican frontrunners Richard Nixon and Barry Goldwater were already 'raising hell about it'.

The JCS record of Johnson's intentions in early March 1964 stated that 'the President accepted the need for punishing Hanoi without debate', but pointed to his political difficulties. It was apparent that he did 'not want to lose South Vietnam before next November nor does he want to get the country into war' (*FRUS* 1964, vol.1: doc. 70). That any ground combat intervention was dependent on election timing was clearly recognized by Washington's decision-makers. US troops would remain in an advisory role. Air operations would continue to be undertaken by RVN-marked and piloted aircraft.

It did not take long before renewed tensions about what to do in Vietnam were again evident among US policy-makers. In May 1964 McNamara appeared increasingly frustrated in arguing that even where US policy was being carried out, 'we are continuing to lose. Nothing we are now doing will win'. The situation in the provinces was 'much worse' than in January. McNamara felt that the current measures would 'not substitute for the use of force against North Vietnam'. By contrast, and citing the strategic constraints involved, Rusk held that 'a better situation in Saigon is a supporting requirement to a decision to go north' (*FRUS* 1964, vol. 1: doc. 172). Despite Rusk's sentiment, a perceptible shift toward the Defense Department and JCS position is evident from late May. For example, on 25 May Bundy recommended that a presidential decision be made to 'use selected and carefully graduated military force against North Vietnam' (*FRUS* 1964, vol. 1: doc. 173).

Contrary to Defense, JCS and CIA estimates, all of which unanimously held that the risks of a land war with China, or a general nuclear war with the USSR, were very small, leading State Department officials Rusk and Ball were less convinced, a position more in line with that of Congressional leaders. Rusk, personally, seemed convinced that the United States would go to war, if necessary, against both the DRV and China 'to keep Laos and South Vietnam from being overrun by the Communists'. Washington was therefore obliged to take all possible measures 'to strengthen South Vietnam because the alternative is the use of force' with all its attendant risks of major war (*FRUS* 1964, vol. 1: doc. 172).

For his part, Johnson also maintained an enduring fear that China would intervene, reflecting how deeply the experience of the Korean War had permeated his thinking. This was despite consistent intelligence estimates that this scenario was extremely unlikely. For example, Johnson (in Beschloss 1997: 370) said to Bundy on 27 May 1964 that

> it looks to me like we're getting into another Korea. It just worries the hell out of me. I don't see what we can ever hope to get out of there with, once we're committed. I believe that the Chinese Communists are coming into it. I don't think that we can fight them ten thousand miles away from home … I don't think it's worth fighting for and I don't think that we can get out.

Bundy (in Beschloss 1997: 370) agreed that South Vietnam, in itself, was not worth fighting for, but making the link to Cold War credibility, added that it was 'what the rest of that half of the world is going to think if this thing comes apart on us. That's the dilemma'.

Input into the elite decision-making process from Congress tended to mirror Rusk's view rather than that of the JCS and Defense Department. In a conversation with Chair of the Senate Armed Services Committee, Richard Russell, Johnson (in Beschloss 1997: 364–5) said most of his advisors did not believe 'that the Chinese Communists will come into this thing. But they don't know and nobody can really be sure'. Russell replied that he did not see how the administration could get out of this mess 'without fighting a major war with the Chinese'. Johnson said the American people were not ready for such a war: 'I don't think the people of the country know much about Vietnam and I think they care a hell of a lot less'. The conversation turned to the hawkish Republican position. Johnson (in Beschloss 1997: 369) commented that 'all the Senators, Nixon and Rockefeller and Goldwater [were] all saying let's move, let's go into the North'. The President concluded by observing that 'practically everyone' was saying he had to go in.

## National Honour and Credibility in Vietnam

This section shows that the commitment to direct military intervention after the November presidential election was decisively formed in the second half of 1964. This was due predominantly to three factors. The first was the strong engagement of the emotional dimension of the prestige motive with Johnson's increasing fear of humiliation at 'losing' Vietnam. During campaign speeches for the 1964 election, Johnson also framed US involvement in Vietnam in terms of national honour in living up to the country's identity narrative of preserving freedom by containing communism. These speeches also reflected the motifs of strength and peace that were evident in public opinion polling. Appeals to national honour were also made in private meetings available in the documentary record, suggesting these statements were more than just campaign rhetoric. Second, with the Gulf of Tonkin attacks of August 1964, the communist side had directly breached the norms of international order thereby clearing the way for the first direct US air strikes against North Vietnam. While this represented the crossing of a major psychological barrier, it did not affect the situation on the ground in South Vietnam, which only worsened. Third, the continuing bad news from the south reinforced the emerging view that the United States would have to take direct responsibility for the defence of South Vietnam to maintain its global credibility.

The President's opinion that little alternative existed to some direct form of military intervention after the election seems to have firmed in the first half of 1964. This was based in large part on Johnson's personal fears of humiliation. Both Democratic administrations of the 1960s operated in a foreign policy milieu in which regional issues were viewed in broader Cold War context as tests of strength between the United States and the USSR or China (Levering 1978: 111). They also operated under the domestic legacy of McCarthyism, and both Kennedy and Johnson exhibited deep fears of being seen as personally weak in national security affairs (Gaddis 1982: 212, 242, Dean 1998, Steinberg 1996: 79). Playing on these presidential fears of humiliation was the perception in the early 1960s of Soviet dynamism under Khrushchev, a fanatical China on the march in Asia; that while competing nationalisms were at play, the communists remained monolithic in their hostility toward America, and that the domino theory was valid, especially in Southeast Asia (Thomson 1988: 206, Gaddis 1982: 211).

For example, in another conversation with Senator Russell about Vietnam on 11 June 1964, Johnson (in Beschloss 1997: 401–3) said he did not 'believe the American people ever want me to run. If I lose it, I think they'll say *I've* lost … At the same time, I don't want to commit us to a war'. Russell said, 'as a practical matter, we're in there and I don't know how the hell you can tell the American people you're coming out … They'll think that you've just been whipped, you've been ruined, you're scared. It'd be disastrous'. Johnson replied that he would have to say to the public, 'I didn't get you in there, but we're in here by treaty and our national honor's at stake'.

A few days later on 16 June 1964, Johnson spoke to McNamara about a meeting he attended the previous evening with influential columnist, Joseph Alsop, and lawyer Clark Clifford, later to replace McNamara as Defense Secretary. With regard to Vietnam, Johnson said 'they think we're about to lose the greatest race the United States has ever lost'. It would 'be the first time that we've ever turned tail and then shoved out of a place'. McNamara replied 'I just don't believe we *can* be pushed out of there, Mr. President. We just can't *allow* it to be done. You wouldn't want to go down in history as having …' Johnson cut McNamara off at this point by saying 'not at all' (in Beschloss 1997: 410–11). These statements suggest that avoiding the humiliation that the 'loss' of Vietnam to communism would bring, not only in domestic politics, but also as a historical legacy, was uppermost in the mind of policy-makers in Johnson's administration.

The Gulf of Tonkin incidents of 2 to 4 August 1964 provided the means by which the normative and strategic constraints felt by decision-makers in Washington could be lifted. It has become generally accepted that the second attack did not occur, although it was widely believed that it did at the time. Johnson authorized the first direct air strikes against North Vietnam on 4 August. In Saigon, new Ambassador General Taylor did not think that the incident should bring forward plans for sustained air attacks against the DRV, which were postponed until after the November election. Taylor maintained that Washington should not 'get involved militarily with North Viet Nam and possibly with Red China if our base in South Viet Nam is insecure' (*FRUS* 1964, vol.1: doc. 319). After the Tonkin Gulf incident, General Khanh made a clumsy attempt to centralize his authority and improve governmental effectiveness in the South. This precipitated renewed political disaffection.

Serious anti-American and anti-Khanh demonstrations by dissident Buddhists and students along with NLF political involvement erupted in the major South Vietnamese cities of Hue, Danang and Saigon on 23 August 1964. According to Taylor, it was now possible that Saigon might move towards some sort of 'popular front' government susceptible to accommodation with the NLF. Washington could passively acquiesce to this, or actively assume 'responsibility for the outcome' based on 'the limited viability of any South Vietnamese government'. Taylor argued that US credibility ruled out the first option: 'If we leave Vietnam with our tail between our legs, the consequences of this defeat in the rest of Asia, Africa and Latin America would be disastrous'. There was little choice but to take on the full responsibility for the defence of South Vietnam (*FRUS* 1964, vol. 1: doc. 339).

Taylor attended a meeting in Washington on 9 September 1964. The President asked whether anyone doubted Vietnam was worth the effort. All present agreed it was, based on US credibility. Taylor repeated that 'we could not afford to let Hanoi win, in terms of our overall position in the area and in the world'. New JCS Chairman General Earle Wheeler reported the 'unanimous view of the Joint Chiefs that if we should lose in South Vietnam, we would lose Southeast Asia'. After that, 'country after country on the periphery would give way and look toward Communist China as the rising power of the area'. McCone and Rusk agreed (*FRUS* 1964, vol. 1: doc. 343). A CIA assessment on 28 September concluded that 'the signs of deterioration' in the RVN 'are so many and so clear … that the odds now favour a continuing decay of South Vietnamese will and effectiveness in coming weeks, sufficient to imperil the political base for present US policy and objectives in South Vietnam' (*FRUS* 1964, vol. 1: doc. 365). It seems clear that by the end of October 1964, both the intelligence and military establishments thought that US combat intervention was unavoidable.

President Johnson made a succession of speeches and public comments explaining Washington's involvement in Vietnam in the weeks following the Tonkin Gulf episode and during the 1964 election campaign. These appealed to US national honour in living up to the nation's identity narrative of preserving freedom in the world. Johnson evoked the theme of strength in resisting communism, but also emphasized peace in avoiding a major ground war in Asia. In preserving freedom, the administration's actions in Vietnam were located firmly within the narrative of Cold War containment policy from Greece and Turkey through Berlin, Korea, the Taiwan Straits, Lebanon, and the Cuban Missile Crisis (e.g., Johnson 1964a: 1161–5, 1964b: 1391, 1964c: 1242).

Johnson won the 3 November 1964 election in a landslide, one of the largest in US history. The Election Year Survey found that 46 per cent of respondents now favoured the escalation of US military action in Vietnam with only 13 per cent supporting withdrawal (Lunch and Sperlich 1979: 27). A further series of opinion polls in January and February 1965 lent support to a policy of intensifying the limited actions. The January American Institute of Public Opinion (AIPO) poll had 50 per cent support for continued US involvement. The February AIPO poll recorded 66 per cent support for present efforts, while a *LA Times* national poll had 40 per cent support for preventing a communist takeover (Mueller 1973: 54, 82). Newly elected, Johnson could be reasonably confident to carry public opinion with him in a limited combat intervention in Vietnam provided it did not escalate to a wider war with China or the Soviet Union.

## The Dynamics of State Failure in South Vietnam

This section shows that by early 1965, the South Vietnamese state had failed to maintain even minimal levels of administrative competence and territorial control or to carry out its rural pacification program. This was an unacceptable breach of Washington's expectations for a stable, non-communist international order in Southeast Asia. As shown in the previous sections, the collapse of the RVN to communism was seen by Washington as a disastrous defeat for US credibility in bipolar context that would imperil the free world strategic position not only in Southeast Asia, but right across the global periphery. In early 1965, most US policy-makers came the view that there was no prospect for South Vietnamese viability until the 'external' communist pressure could be eased. All initiatives at capacity building and improving government cohesiveness had failed.

Ambassador Taylor arrived in Washington for post-election talks on 26 November 1964. He reported that more important than the deteriorating situation in the countryside was 'the continued weakness of the central government', because this was 'the prime cause'. It was 'impossible to foresee a stable and effective government under any name in anything like the near future'. Washington was 'playing a losing game'. Given the insurgency had now progressed this far, Taylor conceded that regardless of the prospects for South

Vietnam's political stability, 'we will not succeed in the end unless we drive the DRV out of its reinforcing role' (*FRUS* 1964, vol. 1: doc. 426). From this point the Country Team dropped its recommendation that a viable Saigon government was a prerequisite for attacking North Vietnam. This marked a convergence with the Defense, military, and intelligence viewpoint that attacks on the North would have the effect of consolidating and galvanising the South.

Taylor returned to Saigon in December 1964 with instructions from President Johnson that a last ditch effort be made to achieve some minimal performance benchmarks (*FRUS* 1964, vol. 1: doc. 435). These became academic with further coups in December 1964 and January 1965. The latter installed an opaque alliance of General Khanh and the Buddhist Institute leadership. This was particularly ominous for Washington as the Buddhist Institute was known to have connections with the NLF. Reports on 3 February 1965 suggested that the new government might seek US disengagement (*FRUS* 1965, vol. 2: doc. 41, 58, 59). Bundy wrote to the President after the latest coup that in his and McNamara's opinion now, hoping for a stable government can now 'lead only to disastrous defeat' (*FRUS* 1965, vol. 2: doc. 42).

Taylor commented on 6 January 1965 that before the original 1963 coup against Diem, no one could have 'appreciated the magnitude of the centrifugal political forces which had been kept under control'. He then made the explicit point that it was the deficiencies in South Vietnam's political culture that led to state ineffectiveness and institutional failure, and that Washington could not change these in the short term. The basic factors responsible for the endemic political turmoil were chronic factionalism, civilian-military distrust and lack of experience in modern administration. In addition and compounding this were the intangible factors: an 'absence of national spirit and motivation', and a 'lack of cohesion in the social structure' (*FRUS* 1965, vol. 2: doc. 9).

These observations from Taylor clearly imply the inadequacy of the instrumental view of the state posited by modernization theories, and calls into question whether a South Vietnamese state was a viable proposition at all. Taylor concluded that 'some things we clearly cannot do – change national characteristics, create leadership where it does not exist, raise large additional GVN [government of Vietnam] forces or seal porous frontiers to infiltration'. About the only realistic thing that Washington could do was a 'program of graduated air attacks directed against the will of the DRV' (*FRUS* 1965, vol. 2: doc. 9). Taylor's memorandum demonstrates the acute contradictions inherent in a postcolonial pattern of order overlaid by the Cold War distribution of capabilities. Unviable states created through the rights-based model of postcolonial sovereignty could not in strategic areas be left to their own devices due to the pressures of bipolar competition. The RVN was a double contradiction: an unviable postcolonial state created purely by virtue of the bipolar distribution of capabilities.

On 6 February 1965 an attack on a US airfield and army barracks at Pleiku in Vietnam's Central Highlands resulted in seven deaths and 109 wounded. This attack on top of the chronic instability in Saigon seemed to mark the final threshold for

Johnson who subsequently dropped altogether any concerns for stable government in Saigon before attacking the DRV. From this point, the RVN, by most reports on the verge of collapse since early 1964 was judged to be a state failure requiring a direct US military intervention to preserve free world order. This interpretation is supported by Kenneth T. Young (1967: 509) who argued in 1967 that decision-makers perceived a 'likely imminent collapse of South Vietnam' in the winter of 1964-1965. From 6 February, the content of policy discourse shifted from whether or not to intervene in Vietnam to the form such intervention would take.

## Rolling Thunder and the Logic of Ground Intervention

This section examines the initial phase of the US intervention in Vietnam, which was dedicated to air attacks against the North to compel Hanoi to cease its support for the NLF and therefore to shore up the Saigon regime. I show that, constrained by the distribution of capabilities, the bombing of North Vietnam was ineffective in arresting the disorder in the South. Continuing indications of the imminent collapse of South Vietnam combined with assessments of increasing NLF strength continued to threaten US requirements for a stable anti-communist international order in Southeast Asia. This prompted the change of course to a direct ground combat intervention. The intensifying US military involvement was justified publicly by President Johnson according to the pattern of international order and on the prestige-based grounds of national honour and Cold War credibility.

The intervention phase opened with a restatement of the stakes for Washington. The US managerial responsibility for international order, its reputation and strategic credibility were all believed to be on the line in Vietnam. Bundy argued on 7 February 1965 that direct US intervention to prevent the collapse of South Vietnam was a necessity:

> the stakes in Vietnam are extremely high. The American investment is very large, and American responsibility is a fact of life … The international prestige of the United States, and a substantial part of our influence, are directly at risk in Vietnam. There is no way of unloading the burden on the Vietnamese themselves, and there is no way of negotiating ourselves out of Vietnam which offers any serious promise at present. (*FRUS* 1965, vol. 2: doc. 84)

The JCS proposed a program of direct air strikes on North Vietnam code named Rolling Thunder on 11 February 1965. It was assessed that neither the Soviet Union nor China would become directly involved but would provide increased materiel support to Hanoi (*FRUS* 1965, vol. 2: doc. 109). Johnson approved the first strikes on 24 February. The following day Rusk (1965: 365) acknowledged the administration's deep concern about 'the essential unity and solidarity of the Government in Saigon'. The point was then made that, consistent with the pluralist international order, US involvement was to be based solely on the 'external aspect of the matter' (Rusk 1965: 366). Rusk (1965: 368) argued that 'the pacification of the country would be easy if the external aggression were stopped'. Taylor reported similarly on 7 March that infiltration from North Vietnam continued as the core of the problem. Given that the RVN's frontiers could not be closed from the inside, the purpose of the bombing campaign should be to 'get Hanoi to order it to stop' (*FRUS* 1965, vol. 2: doc. 186). This was the purpose of Rolling Thunder.

Ball disputed these assessments. He wrote to Johnson on 13 February 1965 that short of the sort of catastrophic defeat that would likely trigger Chinese intervention, Hanoi would not abandon the NLF campaign in South Vietnam (*FRUS* 1965, vol. 2: doc. 113). Senior Democratic Party leaders also began to voice concerns about the administration's policy direction in Vietnam with the commencement of the bombing campaign. As mentioned above, Johnson's decision-making was heavily informed by his past political experiences of the 'loss' of China under Truman, McCarthyism and Korea. He failed to appreciate powerful new sources of domestic opposition emerging from the left of the political spectrum. Vice-President Hubert Humphrey outlined his concerns with the direction Vietnam policy was taking on 17 February. Humphrey reminded Johnson of the difficult domestic politics for Democrats in going into Vietnam. As in Korea, the Republicans would attack 'either for failure to use our military power to "win" a total victory, or alternatively for losing the country to the Communists'. Humphrey argued that 'involvement in a full scale war with North Vietnam would not make sense to the majority of the American people'. The public would not 'understand why we would run grave risks to support a country which is totally unable to put its own house in order'. Humphrey accurately predicted that US air bombardments across an international border in response to 'elusive, small-scale terror which has been going on for 10 years in what looks like a civil war' would not be sustainable in public opinion (*FRUS* 1965, vol. 2: doc. 134).

The logic of committing ground forces to protect the expanded air commitment against NLF attacks quickly became apparent. The preliminary elements of two Marine battalions arrived at Danang on Vietnam's Central Coast on 8 March 1965. These were the first US combat troops deployed to South Vietnam. The CIA reported that there was no sign of a military response from either the DRV or China. The Soviet Union seemed 'more worried about the dangers of escalation and anxious to reassure itself of the limited character of US military action' (*FRUS* 1965, vol. 2: doc. 190).

Despite Humphrey's concerns, opinion polling in March 1965 showed reasonable levels of support for the administration's policy. The *LA Times* national poll indicated 46 per cent support for 'holding the line' in Vietnam, while 35 per cent advocated negotiating a settlement. An AIPO poll found 66 per cent of respondents favouring a continuation of the 'present effort' with only 19 per cent in favour of withdrawal (Mueller 1973: 83). CIA Director McCone viewed these figures as soft and wrote to the President on 2 April that public approval would erode if the present level of bombing failed to have any effect, as was likely. McCone argued that the bombing must be heavy enough to break Hanoi's will and bring it to a negotiating position before public opinion started to turn. McCone thought that domestic pressure to stop the bombing would only intensify with a slowly ascending tempo of air strikes (*FRUS* 1965, vol. 2: doc. 234).

Johnson did not share McCone or Humphrey's opinions. The President appeared convinced that to avoid the domestic problems that had plagued Truman over China and Korea, the Vietnam intervention had to be managed with two fundamental considerations in mind. The first was that it must be kept limited to the extent that it avoided any risk at all of a broader war. Second, increases in the operational tempo must take place gradually so as to avoid politically damaging public perceptions of a large war similar to Korea. All developments were to be announced simply as incremental changes to existing methods in achieving longstanding American goals (*FRUS* 1965: doc. 239, 242). There was no major speech, for example, by the President marking the commencement of the Rolling Thunder bombing campaign even though it signalled a profound change in operational policy.

After some initial optimism, it was deemed questionable by 16 March 1965 that air operations alone would compel Hanoi to stop infiltration or order the NLF to observe a ceasefire. Bundy argued that Washington's bargaining position in future negotiations could only be enhanced with greater numbers of ground forces (*FRUS* 1965, vol. 2: doc. 200). The JCS recommended that 'US land forces should be introduced in a combatant role, in such strengths as to achieve an effective margin of combat power' (*FRUS* 1965, vol. 2: 208). On 1 April, the President approved two additional Marine battalions and an increase in existing US force levels by 18–20,000 personnel, largely to fill out existing advisory and support deployments. Most crucially, however, the US mission in Vietnam was modified with ground forces now authorized to engage in direct counterinsurgency operations at MACV commander, General Westmoreland's discretion. A gradually increasing tempo of air operations was also approved, although staying out of range of Hanoi's Soviet-supplied air defences (*FRUS* 1965, vol. 2: doc. 230, 242).

Johnson explained the changes to the prosecution of Vietnam policy in a major speech at Johns Hopkins University on 7 April 1965, some two months after the decision was taken. The reasons for the air campaign and Marine deployments were consistent with UN Charter principles. Johnson (1965a: 606–7) stated that 'North Viet-Nam has attacked the independent nation of South Vietnam. Its object is total conquest'. The President conceded that 'some of the people of South Viet-Nam are participating in attack on their own government. But trained men and supplies, orders and arms, flow in a constant stream from North to South'. The President also linked the conflict directly to the distribution of capabilities in East Asia. Hovering over the war, 'and all of Asia', was 'the deepening shadow of Communist China' (Johnson 1965a: 607).

The objectives for the intensified US actions were given in a normative language of international order and were also resonant with the US identity narrative of preserving freedom. Johnson (1965a: 606) stated that 'tonight Americans and Asians are dying for a world where each people may choose its own path to change'. The United States was joining the fight because this was a necessity 'if we are to live in a world where every country can shape its own destiny, and only in such a world will our own freedom be finally secure'. The only reasonable path to a settlement was consistent with the pluralist pattern of order: an independent South Vietnam, securely guaranteed and freely able to shape its own relationships, free from external interference, and tied to no alliance (Johnson 1965a: 608). The air attacks on North Vietnam were not a change of purpose, but 'a change in what we believe that purpose requires' (Johnson 1965a: 607).

Each dimension of the prestige motive is evident in this speech. The United States was involved in Vietnam to 'strengthen world order', on which Washington's reputation for keeping its word and its commitments depended (Johnson 1965a: 606). In appealing to national honour, the President emphasized strength in resisting Chinese and North Vietnamese aggression. Strength was invoked in the phrases 'we will not be defeated'; 'we will not grow tired'; 'we will not withdraw, either openly or under the cloak of a meaningless agreement'. National honour was invoked in the statement that the United States was in Vietnam 'because we have a promise to keep' (Johnson 1965a: 606). Since 1954, all Presidents had offered support to South Vietnam to help defend its independence. Johnson said he intended to keep that promise. Credibility was invoked in that the result of abandoning South Vietnam would 'be increased unrest and instability and even wider war'. The President also drew on the Munich analogy and its connotations of shame and dishonour that 'the central lesson of our time is that the appetite for aggression is never satisfied. To withdraw from one battlefield means only to prepare for the next'. America's Cold War 'responsibility' for the defence of freedom in Asia was the same as that of Europe in World War II (Johnson 1965a: 607).

## The Case for Ground Intervention and its Critics

This section examines the final phase of decision-making from April to July 1965. During this time, the governance situation in South Vietnam continued to deteriorate. This prompted the change in Washington's Vietnam policy to a ground combat intervention. This decision was supported by consistent reports from US intelligence agencies and direct contacts with both Beijing and Moscow that allayed prudential concerns. A wider war was deemed highly unlikely if US military actions remained geographically limited to Indochina; did not threaten the survival of the DRV; did not attack Chinese planes or shipping; and that ground forces did not approach Chinese borders. This consensus was disputed by leading figures in the Democratic Party and within the administration by Ball and McCone. President Johnson gave consideration to these criticisms and alternative courses of action, but on 27 July 1965 decided to deploy the first 50,000 of an eventual half-million combat troops to South Vietnam. The decision was made on the grounds of US responsibility for free world order, national honour and Cold War credibility.

McNamara returned from the annual Honolulu meeting with Commander-in-Chief Pacific, Admiral Sharp, Ambassador Taylor and MACV commander, General Westmoreland, with the view that North Vietnam would not capitulate or come to terms in the near future. Any settlement with Hanoi would more likely come as a result of a NLF failure on the ground than the bombing campaign. This meeting indicates a break in the consensus that had built since early 1964 that bombing the North was the key to maintaining the position in the South. The strategy emerging from this meeting was to 'break the will' of the NLF-DRV by 'denying them victory' on the ground (*FRUS* 1965, vol. 2: doc. 265). Johnson was advised of the outcome of the meeting on 20 April 1965.

Bundy pointed out that this marked quite a difference in US policy, while both Ball and McCone were critical for different reasons. Ball argued that room for negotiation with Hanoi was greater than most people thought, and maintained that a ground campaign carried serious risks of escalation with the Chinese and Soviets. McCone felt bombing at the current levels could be no more than an inconvenience to Hanoi, and would certainly not halt infiltration. The administration seemed to be drifting into a ground 'combat situation where victory would be dubious and from which we could not extricate ourselves' (*FRUS* 1965, vol. 2: doc. 266). Ball advocated a negotiated settlement, if only a tactical one, in the near future. He argued that intervention under the current circumstances was likely to diminish US prestige rather than enhance it. Continued bombing and the opening of a ground war without any moves toward a political settlement would erode both the United States' international reputation and the administration's domestic position (*FRUS* 1965, vol. 2: doc. 267).

On 31 May 1965 a message from the People's Republic of China (PRC) was delivered through the British Embassy in Beijing. It indicated that China 'would take direct part in the conflict only "if the war was expanded to Chinese territory"' (*FRUS* 1965, vol. 2: doc. 321). From Moscow, US Ambassador Bohlen advised on 2 June that even if the United States attacked Soviet-supplied and supported aircraft in North Vietnam, the USSR would not respond militarily in Europe or Asia (*FRUS* 1965, vol. 2: doc. 325). On 21 July, Averell Harriman, Johnson's Ambassador at Large, met with Soviet Premier Kosygin. Kosygin communicated that Moscow envisaged any political settlement as retaining the strategic status quo and existing boundary between North and South Vietnam (*FRUS* 1965, vol. 3: doc. 68). There was no warning or indication that the Soviet Union would oppose intervention in South Vietnam on the limited terms under consideration by Washington. These direct contacts were consistent with most intelligence estimates and would have appeared to ease prudential concerns that the proposed combat intervention could escalate.

Also by early June 1965, further political turmoil in Saigon and a series of major ARVN defeats in the field eroded any residual optimism about the success of the bombing campaign and initial troop deployments. Captured documents indicated an imminent NLF summer offensive that would be a further serious challenge to the South. Morale in the ARVN had dropped precipitately after being temporarily boosted by the US air campaign. Desertion rates were high. The Country Team argued that currently 'the cumulative psychological impact of a series of significant ARVN defeats could lead to a collapse', despite the increased US presence in the conflict (*FRUS* 1965, vol. 2: doc. 332).

The State Department confirmed publicly on 8 June 1965 that Westmoreland now had authorization to commit US ground forces to combat in support of the ARVN as appropriate. Critics of this development in Vietnam policy began to voice their opinions. For example, Senator Mansfield wrote to Johnson that this

> formal delegation of authority to Westmoreland to commit American combat troops comes at a time when the last semblance of constituted government … in Saigon is disappearing. As I understand it, Westmoreland will respond to requests from the Vietnamese military not the Vietnamese government. This underscores the fact that there is not a government to speak of in Saigon. In short we are now at the point where we are no longer dealing with anyone who represents anybody in a political sense. (*FRUS* 1965, vol. 2: doc. 341)

Ball also dissented against the drift toward a combat intervention. He argued on 18 June that since 1961 Washington had met with successive disappointments in South Vietnam. Administrations had underestimated the NLF. The United States had 'been unable to bring about the creation of a stable political base in Saigon'. Consistent with Mansfield, Ball also pointed out that 'the Saigon Government is becoming more and more a fiction – in real terms South Viet-Nam has an army but no government'. Ball continued that the more combat forces the US deployed in Vietnam, 'the harder we shall find it to extricate ourselves without unacceptable costs if the war goes badly'. Once large combat forces were committed, 'failure to turn the tide will generate pressures to escalate' (*FRUS* 1965, vol. 3: doc. 7).

Ball's opinion is given much play in the *FRUS* document series on which this case study is based, but represented a minority view among decision-makers within the administration. Johnson's biographer Doris Kearns (1976: 261–2) points out, for example, that 'the policy of escalation was advocated by every individual at the highest level of responsibility for actions related to national security'. Bundy laid out the majority position to the President on 30 June 1965 by reference to the pattern of international order. The United States was 'responding to the call of a people under Communist assault, a people undergoing a non-Communist national revolution' (*FRUS* 1965, vol. 3: doc. 33).

The final stages of the decision-making process began on 1 July 1965. The 'July decisions' are regarded as marking the definitive change in Vietnam policy from indirect advisory involvement to direct ground combat intervention (Herring 1979: 142). Bundy presented President Johnson with four policy recommendations from Rusk, Ball, McNamara and William P. Bundy, with respect to intensifying the bombing campaign and introducing the first of the 175,000 combat troops requested by Westmoreland in an offensive role.

Rusk advanced the rationale that Washington should not be concerned with what Saigon would do if it was left alone. America was involved 'in South Viet-Nam only because of the aggression of Hanoi'. Rusk linked the US response to South Vietnam's failure directly to Washington's reputation for resolve rather than the internal situation in the country: 'the integrity of the US commitment is the principal pillar of peace throughout the world'. He wrote that if that commitment became unreliable, 'the communist world would draw conclusions that would lead to our ruin and almost certainly to a catastrophic war' (*FRUS* 1965, vol. 3: doc. 39). Rusk's recommendation was to concentrate maximum effort in South Vietnam through air attacks and ground intervention by the proposed 34 US battalions augmented by 10 battalions from South Korea, Australia and New Zealand. Rusk argued that the air war in North Vietnam was supplementary (*FRUS* 1965, vol. 3: doc. 39). This contradicted the earlier CIA position under McCone, which held that Hanoi was unlikely to desist without massive aerial bombardment of its industrial and population centres.

Reflecting his previous position papers, Ball argued that most evidence suggested the RVN was a lost cause. He accurately predicted that the outcome of present proposals would be 'a protracted war involving an open-ended commitment of US forces, mounting US casualties, no assurance of a satisfactory solution, and a serious danger of escalation'. Ball stressed the urgency of coming to a compromise solution now. He offered an alternative interest-based way to proceed. No further troops should be deployed. Bombing should continue in its current limited form without attacking the Hanoi area and staying clear of China. In conjunction with this 'holding pattern', serious diplomatic feelers should be sent indicating a genuine willingness to compromise rather than simply demanding Hanoi's capitulation (*FRUS* 1965, vol. 3: doc. 40).

Johnson's Deputy Special Assistant for National Security Affairs, Francis M. Bator (2008: 315), wrote with the benefit of hindsight in 2008 that the administration could have

> stopped where we were in early June 1965. There were then about 75,000 American soldiers in place to train and advise the South Vietnamese army, 20,000 of them in combat echelons to help protect Saigon and the bases from which we bombed the southern parts of North Vietnam. With U.S. casualties kept very low, there would have been no American war in Vietnam as we came to know it.

Recent historical work also suggests that US policy-makers knew enough about the broader context to events in Vietnam, some quite favourable, to have given them more serious pause about a ground intervention. For example, it was highly likely that a unified Vietnam would encourage a rivalry of influence between Moscow and Beijing, further opening up the Sino-Soviet split and weakening international communism to Washington's overall advantage (Oliver 2004: 772). Rational, interest-based alternatives to a ground intervention were repeatedly rejected for intangible, prestige-based reasons as demonstrated below.

In sharp contrast to Ball, McNamara began by stating that 'our objective is to create conditions for a favourable settlement by demonstrating to the VC/DRV that the odds are against their winning'. McNamara laid out the expanded military plan for a proposed ground combat intervention. The deployments would be augmented by intense air attacks on NLF positions in the South. The aerial bombardment of North Vietnam would be intensified to strike all infrastructure related to the war effort, including communications and supply lines between the DRV and China. McNamara felt that a negotiated settlement would become a realistic option only after the tide had turned in the United States' favour. McNamara assessed that the Soviet and Chinese reaction would be limited to the provision of aid and equipment to Hanoi. Greater overt involvement by the People's Army of North Vietnam (PAVN) was conceded as a serious possibility when the tide began to turn against the NLF (*FRUS* 1965, vol. 3: doc. 38).

The fourth recommendation from William Bundy was a middle-ground proposal. Its main thrust was that maximum air power should be used against the NLF in the South. Bundy also advocated an increase in troop levels to only 85,000. Troops would act offensively only 'where a battle has been or can be joined and US military advantages are greatest' but 'not in general countryside operations'. Bundy also recommended stepping up the bombing of the North while avoiding the Hanoi-Haiphong and Chinese border areas. Every effort should continue to be made to consolidate the Saigon government. Discreet contacts should also be made with Hanoi and the NLF for opening channels and playing on historic Vietnamese fears of Chinese domination (*FRUS* 1965, vol. 3: doc. 41).

The President made no immediate decision but sent McNamara to Saigon for further reporting. McNamara delivered his latest report on 20 July 1965. It started by reiterating the familiar characteristics of state failure in South Vietnam. The situation was 'worse than a year ago (when it was worse than a year before that)'. The tempo of the war was now quickening with a 'hard VC push'. The economy was in free fall. The odds were 'less than even that the Ky government will last out the year'. Rural pacification was 'making little progress'. Estimated force ratios between the RVN and NLF were almost at parity (*FRUS* 1965, vol. 3: doc. 67). McNamara elucidated nine outcomes that US policy must achieve based on the pattern of international order. These were the clearest statement of the objectives of the US intervention. They were to (1) stop NLF attacks and greatly reduce terrorism and sabotage; to (2) reduce infiltration from the DRV 'to a trickle'; a (3) cessation of the bombing of North Vietnam; the (4) maintenance of the RVN's independence; a (5) Republic of Vietnam capable of exercising governmental functions over substantially all of its territory; the (6) communists remaining quiescent in Laos and Thailand; the (7) withdrawal of North Vietnamese personnel from the South; the (8) transformation of the NLF into a purely political organization; and the (9) withdrawal of US combat forces, although not aid workers or military advisors. McNamara argued that his proposed course of action 'would stave off defeat in the short run and offer a good chance of producing a favorable settlement in the longer run' (*FRUS* 1965, vol. 3: doc. 67).

A high level meeting to discuss the McNamara report was held on the morning of Wednesday 21 July 1965. The President wanted to know what had changed in the last month that required this decision to commit such an increase in forces. McNamara and new CIA Director Vice-Admiral William F. Raborn outlined the deteriorating situation (*FRUS* 1965, vol. 3: doc. 72). The President then asked 'is there another course in the national interest that is better than the McNamara course?' Ball answered that 'there is no course that will allow us to cut our losses. If we get bogged down, our cost might be substantially greater'. The President asked again, 'what other road can I go?' Ball again replied that the United States could take what precautions it could, let the RVN fall apart, negotiate a settlement, and then watch the country probably be taken over by the communists (*FRUS* 1965, vol. 3: doc. 71).

Another meeting was held at 2.30pm on the same day. The President asked Ball to again reiterate his doubts. Ball repeated his previous arguments and also emphasized that Washington was underestimating the terminal condition of the RVN. He also felt that a prolonged counter-insurgency war would disclose the weaknesses rather than the strengths of the United States. Johnson asked that in the event of a US withdrawal, 'wouldn't all those countries say Uncle Sam is a paper tiger – wouldn't we lose credibility breaking the word of three presidents … It would seem to be an irreparable blow'. Ball replied by saying that intervention in Vietnam would likely damage US prestige rather than enhance it. A 'worse blow' than withdrawal 'would be that the mightiest power in the world is unable to defeat guerrillas'. He added that it might be different if we were 'helping a country with a stable, viable government' (*FRUS* 1965, vol. 3: doc. 71).

Bundy entered the debate arguing that 'if the Communist world finds out we will not pursue our commitment to the end, I don't know where they will stay their hand'. It was clear that 'we are not going to be thrown out', so domestic public opinion would also be alarmed if Washington withdrew of its own accord. Reappointed Ambassador to Saigon, Henry Cabot Lodge, Jr. argued that withdrawal would be akin to Munich in 1938, a disgrace to national honour (*FRUS* 1965, vol. 3: doc. 71). The country was in no mood to accept such grim news as a US withdrawal in the face of communist pressure (*FRUS* 1965, vol. 3: doc. 72). The President did not make a final decision on combat troop deployments until the NSC meeting of 27 July 1965.

At this meeting, Johnson acknowledged the grim situation in South Vietnam and laid out five choices as he saw it. These were to use massive air power 'to bring the enemy to his knees'. Only a small minority were advocating this option. The second choice was simply to withdraw, but Johnson said this was also a minority position: most Americans felt that national honour was at stake and commitments must be kept. The third choice was to keep forces and activities at the present level and continue to lose slowly. No one was advocating this. The fourth choice was to 'ask for everything we might desire from Congress – money, authority to call up the reserves, acceptance of the deployment of more combat battalions'. Many favoured this course, but it was only likely to prompt greater Chinese and Soviet aid to the DRV. Johnson said the administration would embark on a fifth choice: to do what was necessary to meet the present situation, without being 'unnecessarily provocative to either the Russians or the Communist Chinese. We will give the commanders the men they say they need and, out of existing materiel in the US, we will give them the materiel they say they need'. The policy was not opposed by anyone at the meeting. Later in the day after a meeting with the joint congressional leadership, Johnson said 'he was giving Westmoreland what he needed' (*FRUS* 1965, vol. 3: doc. 93).

Johnson held a press conference on 28 July 1965 to explain that US involvement in Vietnam was being expanded and intensified. His speech made reference to each of the three background conditions for state failure and intervention outlined in Chapter 3. The situation in South Vietnam was attributed to external aggression, a clear breach of UN Charter principles, and therefore a permissible reason for intervention in the postcolonial international order. Johnson said that the 'central fact' of the conflict in South Vietnam was that it was 'guided by North Viet-Nam, and it is spurred by Communist China' (Johnson 1965d: 262). This was a threat to US requirements for a stable, non-communist international order in the postcolonial periphery. Johnson said that the goal of the aggression against Saigon was 'to conquer the South, to defeat American power, and to extend the Asiatic dominion of communism' (Johnson 1965d: 262–3). Momentous stakes were in the balance. This reflected the tightly interlocked nature of international order and the distribution of capabilities in the bipolar world. Johnson (1965d: 263) argued that an Asia threatened by communist domination 'would certainly imperil the security of the United States itself'.

Much of the speech focused on the US identity narrative and ontological security needs. Johnson presented the fight against communist aggression in South Vietnam as the responsibility of the United States comparable to its defence of 'freedom' in World War II. Three times in the President's 'lifetime, in two world wars and in Korea', Americans had 'gone to far lands to fight for freedom' (Johnson 1965d: 262). This was what had brought America to Vietnam. National honour was invoked in placing the intervention within the narrative of Cold War containment policy. Johnson (1965d: 263) placed himself firmly in the legacy of the Vietnam policy commitments of two former Presidents over the previous eleven years. The United States could not dishonour its word, abandon its commitment, or leave those that had trusted it to the terror, repression and murder that would surely follow a communist victory. Defeating the insurgency without engaging in a wider war would satisfy the country's national honour requirements and also Johnson's emotional need to avoid humiliation and show personal strength on national security issues.

The President invoked 'strength' and US credibility in again referring to the Munich analogy that a withdrawal from South Vietnam would simply mean a renewal of conflicts from country to country. The primary motive for the intervention in South Vietnam was prestige-based: to 'convince the communists that we cannot be defeated by force of arms or superior power' (Johnson 1965d: 263). The administration did not, however, 'want an expanding struggle with consequences that no one can perceive, nor will we bluster or bully or flaunt our power, but we will not surrender and we will not retreat'. The President would meet all Westmoreland's needs. These measures were designed to 'bring an end to aggression and a peaceful settlement' (Johnson 1965d: 264).

## Limited War, Stalemate and De-escalation

This section shows that US intervention policy contained two inconsistencies that denied it success in achieving its objectives. The first was that the indefinite duration of the intervention was incompatible with the constraints of domestic politics since Korea: there could be no protracted, inconclusive ground war in Asia. Johnson stated on a number of occasions that the intervention would be indefinite. For example, on 17 April 1965, the President said that the United States would 'remain as long as is necessary' (Johnson 1965b: 429). In questions at the 28 July press conference, Johnson (1965c: 799) would not predict whether the intervention would take months, years or decades. Always mindful of domestic opinion, however, it is inconceivable that Johnson was referring to the combat phase as being indefinite (Small 2005: 54–5). Most US officials felt that after a brief period of stiff resistance, the NLF-DRV would quickly give way (e.g., *FRUS* 1965, vol. 2: doc. 107, 110).

Unlike the previous case study where a decisive British military intervention quickly restored physical security, the core objective of defending South Vietnam from 'external' aggression was never achieved. This was an indispensable condition for the fulfilment of all other US objectives. The second contradiction in US policy, as recognized above by McCone and Ball, was that Hanoi would not curtail infiltration or pressure the NLF to abandon the insurgency unless faced with the aerial obliteration of its industrial and population centres. Given the elusive transnational nature of the NLF insurgency in the South, with its sanctuaries in Laos and Cambodia, this was the only way to quickly end the external 'aggression'. The constraints of the Cold War precluded this option, however. A threat to the survival of the DRV was considered to be one of the triggers for Chinese and possibly Soviet intervention (e.g., *FRUS* 1965, vol. 2: doc. 214, 222, 1966, vol. 4: doc. 41, 1967, vol. 5: doc. 169). The policy of graduated escalation by ground and air, without threatening Hanoi's survival, was therefore never likely to achieve the administration's objectives, while also prolonging the intervention. And as predicted by Vice-President Humphrey, deep dissatisfaction with Johnson's conduct of Vietnam policy within influential segments of public opinion then increased in almost direct proportion to graduated increases in the application of force. This was almost the precise opposite of Johnson's assumptions about the management of public opinion.

The relative optimism that accompanied the initial ground combat intervention in the second half of 1965, had, by mid-1967, given way to deep frustration. US troop numbers peaked at around 525,000 in 1968. The injection of major American forces, had, by the close of 1966, staved off the collapse that appeared imminent in 1964 and early 1965, but Westmoreland's search-and-destroy and attrition tactics had only produced a frustrating stalemate. Johnson was faced by mid-1967 with the irresolvable dilemma of being unable to end the war by military means, and also unable to force the NLF-DRV to the negotiating table without a humiliating back-down on his stated objectives for the intervention.

The direct commitment of major US combat forces and infrastructure meant the short-term imperative for RVN state effectiveness lost much of its urgency thereby eroding one of the intervention's main objectives. Attempts to build a viable state in South Vietnam, had, of necessity, to be pursued concurrently with escalating military operations. The stability of the Saigon government actually improved during the combat intervention, but rural pacification was a near complete failure. The NLF remained effective and there was scant evidence that bombing the North had any effect on Hanoi's capacity to infiltrate and resupply the South. Heavier bombing prompted massive increases in Soviet aid to North Vietnam after 1965. US domestic opposition to the intervention in its early stages revolved mainly around the bombing, seen as both inefficient and immoral (Small 2005: 58–9).

The escalation of the intervention created strong domestic and international pressures for a negotiated settlement. The President repeatedly said the administration was ready to negotiate but there is little evidence that Johnson was prepared to compromise on the core objectives of the intervention. Consistent with US international order requirements, no concessions to Hanoi could threaten the status of South Vietnam as an independent non-communist state. In the absence of a strong military or political position in South Vietnam, Johnson could not enter into negotiations under favourable conditions. This stalemate led to a divisive domestic debate between Republican 'hawks' wanting maximum US power employed and the heterogeneous anti-war movement. The 'doves' included many influential and well-known Americans, but was only ever a small, although highly visible segment of the population. The war was questioned on the moral grounds that Washington was supporting a corrupt and decrepit authoritarian regime in South Vietnam and in the absence of a genuine material threat to national security, the devastation being wreaked on North Vietnam was repugnant. The wisdom of continuing the intervention was also called into question on pragmatic, realist grounds. The domino theory in Southeast Asia now lacked plausibility with Suharto's effective suppression of the communists in Indonesia and with China's internal problems in the wake of the Cultural Revolution.

Public support for the Vietnam intervention began to drop in 1967, with a majority of Gallup poll respondents indicating in July (52 per cent) that the war was a mistake. This figure never recovered, increasing steadily to 63 per cent toward the end of Johnson's term in October 1968 (Lunch and Sperlich 1979: 25). Civilians in the Defense Department led ironically by McNamara, one of the most forceful advocates for US intervention, began to change course (*FRUS* 1967, vol. 5: doc. 169, 177, 194). McNamara argued for the first time in 1967 that the bombing should be halted. Increases in US troop numbers had not brought security and an end to the external 'aggression'. There could be no confidence that further increases would improve the situation (*FRUS* 1967, vol. 5: doc. 375). Previously anathema to decision-makers, McNamara felt that the Saigon government must negotiate directly with the NLF to achieve a political solution (*FRUS* 1967, vol. 5: doc. 228, 330). In November 1967, McNamara followed Ball in resigning from the administration. Clark Clifford took up the position of Secretary of Defense on 1 March 1968.

Other advisors in the President's inner circle opposed a halt or any further 'pauses' to the bombing, despite its ineffectiveness. Johnson again opted for a middle-ground position. Consistent with his political experience, Johnson was more concerned to placate the JCS and Republican hawks than the anti-war left (*FRUS* 1967, vol. 5: doc. 330), and he expanded the bombing campaign to include targets in the Hanoi-Haiphong area. Further major troop requests were rejected, however. The President's instinct for the middle ground was at the expense of a logical policy. Johnson tried to placate the right, although still denying what his military commanders thought they needed, while also failing to ameliorate the much stronger and growing domestic opposition from the left. Given the contradictions identified at the beginning of this section, this course of action could only prolong the stalemate. Maximum air power could not be used against Hanoi because of the possible Soviet and Chinese reaction and further outrage on the left of domestic public opinion. But neither was Johnson prepared for a humiliating defeat on American objectives for the intervention.

The Tet Offensive launched on 30 January 1968 was a massive coordinated assault on the RVN's urban centres, including a highly symbolic attack on the US embassy in Saigon. Tet was a tactical defeat for the NLF. It suffered debilitating losses, and indeed, was never to recover as a fighting force. However, it was a profound psychological and political victory for the Vietnamese communists. After the attacks, Clifford recommended a modest additional deployment of a further 22,000 troops, a reserve call up, and serious pressure on Generals Thieu and Ky to take over more of the war effort. Johnson accepted the recommendations without debate. In early March 1968, it was agreed that a ceiling on force levels had been reached and that continued materiel assistance would be conditional on Saigon assuming greater control (*FRUS* 1968, vol. 6: doc. 105). This was the beginning of the policy of 'Vietnamization' that would be pursued under Nixon. It was effectively a return to the failed pre-1965 policies that had precipitated the intervention.

The President made a televised address on 31 March 1968. He announced that the bombing of North Vietnam would be substantially scaled-back. Then in a shock announcement, Johnson said he would not stand for re-election and focus on achieving a negotiated settlement. Johnson's decision marked the end of US escalation but Washington still would not compromise on its international order requirements. The United States refused to accept any settlement that did not guarantee the RVN as an independent non-communist state (Johnson 1968a: 470–76). Johnson's speech did not mark a change in overall Vietnam policy. It was another change of means, not ends. It was an attempt to appear conciliatory, but to stand firm and salvage his policy until the end of the term. Formal peace talks opened in Paris on 13 May but the President refused to compromise on core US objectives (Johnson 1968b). Johnson left office without securing a resolution to the conflict.

## Conclusion

The purpose of this chapter was to evaluate a case of armed intervention to prevent state failure in the contested postcolonial international order of the Cold War. The findings of the research in this chapter further support the main claims of the book. The US combat intervention in Vietnam in 1965 can be understood as a response to a normative threat to Washington's requirements for international order in Southeast Asia. The collapse of South Vietnam was a fundamental breach of US expectations for a stable, non-communist 'free world' order in the postcolonial periphery. Between 1961 and early 1965, the flow of information into Washington's decision-making processes clearly places the deteriorating effectiveness of the RVN as an acute risk to US objectives of maintaining an independent, non-communist South Vietnam. In the zero-sum ideological and strategic bipolarity of the Cold War, international order and the distribution of capabilities were tightly interlocked. Even though events in South Vietnam presented no direct material threat to the United States, with a few notable exceptions most members of the US policy community considered its 'loss' as threatening the 'free world' position in Southeast Asia and by extension, East Asia, the Pacific and the world.

The American identity narrative during the Cold War held that the United States carried a special burden of responsibility, as it had in World War II, to defend freedom in the world. This was a motif repeatedly emphasized in President Johnson's public statements about Vietnam, which were invariably placed within the narrative of Cold War containment policy across three previous administrations and expressed in a moral discourse of fulfilling responsibilities and keeping promises. The impending collapse of South Vietnam to communism was a serious challenge to US ontological security requirements because of the gap between events on the ground and how Washington needed to see itself according to its identity narrative.

In this case, domestic politics was also critical to the interpretation of state failure in South Vietnam. Johnson decided in March 1964 that despite worsening reports about the viability of the RVN, he was not prepared to take decisive action in an election year. South Vietnam was judged by the President to be a state 'failure' requiring direct military intervention only after his election victory in late-1964. The Defense Department and military and intelligence establishments had all assessed that the state was unviable without direct US intervention by late-October 1964. Ambassador Taylor and the Country Team converged with this interpretation by the end of November 1964. Many observers commented during 1964 and early 1965 that South Vietnam appeared to have no operating civilian government infrastructure whatsoever.

The analysis in this chapter also supports the claim made in Chapter 2 that what counts as a state failure in any given period is relative to factors other than the empirical conditions within weak states. There was some consideration in this case, particularly by Taylor, of the unpropitious political culture and social dynamics within South Vietnam that would work against the consolidation of an effective state even in the absence of the NLF insurgency. The point was also explicitly made in Washington that South Vietnam in itself was not worth the massive resources or effort being expended, but that the prestige and maintenance of the US world position meant that the RVN could not be allowed to collapse.

The threshold for state failure and permissible intervention in the postcolonial pattern of international order was the most stringent of the three case studies considered in the book. The UN Charter explicitly provided for a pluralistic international society. Armed intervention was only permissible in international law in the event of overt external aggression. The evidence shows that in public statements, US policy-makers always emphasized the external aggression of Hanoi and sometimes Beijing in supporting the NLF insurgency, rather than the internal weaknesses of South Vietnam. In a prudential sense, the US response to South Vietnam's failure was heavily constrained in the bipolar system by strategic considerations. Decision-makers in Washington had to balance the imperatives of demonstrating the credibility of America's global commitments by preventing the collapse of South Vietnam, while also avoiding a wider war with China as in Korea, or a general war with the Soviet Union. This was consistent with the incentives and constraints of domestic politics and the US identity narrative. The American public required both strength and peace.

The evidence demonstrates that it was the challenge to US normative requirements for a stable, non-communist 'free world' order in the postcolonial periphery that first activated the prestige motive for Washington. For US policy-makers, communist gains in Southeast Asia eroded its reputation for resolve in maintaining a non-communist international order in the region. A serious challenge to the reputation of status quo powers affects the way they feel about themselves. The chapter shows that US policy elites were acutely sensitive to the humiliation of losing South Vietnam to communism. Throughout 1964, the steadily deteriorating situation was regularly compared by President Johnson to the humiliating 'loss' of China under the Truman administration. The evidence presented in the chapter clearly shows that in formulating Vietnam policy the President and other key advisors, such as Defense Secretary Robert McNamara, were motivated by the need to avoid humiliation, both in a national and personal sense. This is supported by the repeated statements that South Vietnam could not be abandoned for reasons of national honour. The United States, across three administrations, had made a promise to defend South Vietnam. It would be dishonourable not to keep that promise. Parallel with these emotional fears, the possible collapse of South Vietnam became indelibly linked with US credibility in broader Cold War context vis-à-vis the Soviet Union and China.

The primary motive for undertaking the intervention was to maintain US prestige in global Cold War context by protecting South Vietnam from communist aggression. This would also meet the Johnson administration's requirements for strength and national honour in the domestic political sphere. The objectives for the intervention were consistent with the pluralist international order: the protection of South Vietnam from external aggression, and the maintenance of a free, independent and stable RVN, consistent with the provisions of the UN Charter and 1954 Geneva Accords.

There were two major inconsistencies in US intervention policy that denied it success in achieving its objectives. The first was that the indefinite duration of the intervention was incompatible with domestic political sentiment: there could be no protracted ground war. The second problem for US policy was that it became more and more apparent that Hanoi would not curtail the insurgency in the South unless faced with severe aerial devastation. But Cold War strategic competition ruled out this option. Johnson's middle ground policy of graduated escalation by ground and air was never likely to achieve the intervention's objectives while also prolonging it indefinitely. Domestic dissatisfaction then increased in almost direct proportion to increases in the application of force until Johnson signalled de-escalation in March 1968. Under the contested international order norms that precipitated the intervention, the Johnson and subsequent Nixon administrations were unwilling to change their objectives to the point of complete and humiliating failure with the eventual collapse of South Vietnam in 1975.

# Chapter 6
# French Intervention in Ivory Coast, 2002

This chapter examines the book's third case study of state failure and intervention within the liberal international order of the first decade of the twenty-first century. The French military intervention in the Ivory Coast political crisis and civil war from September 2002 can be understood as a response to a normative threat to international order in a region of historic French influence and responsibility. The notion of a special French duty and responsibility for Africa has endured into the post-Cold War era. For example, former French Ambassador to South Africa, Tristan d'Albis (1998: 5) wrote that 'France's attitude towards Africa is rooted in the recognition of its responsibility in a situation inherited from the colonial past, and an inherent sense of duty'. While the reputational consequences of the French intervention may have been mixed, its motive under the neo-Gaullist governments of Presidents Jacques Chirac and Nicolas Sarkozy is relatively clear. The intervention in Ivory Coast was undertaken to reverse the shame and dishonour of French policies and actions that were implicated in the genocide in Rwanda. The intervention in Ivory Coast was a litmus test of a new French policy in sub-Saharan Africa – the pursuit of a meaningful sense of *grandeur* through the robust promotion of liberal order norms.

It could be argued that for France, the pursuit of prestige through interventions in the periphery is anachronistic, and unique to its particular history, political culture and Gaullist legacy. However it should be noted that other interventions in the 2000s were also taken for similar prestige-based reasons. The US intervention in Afghanistan from 2001 was motivated in large part to reverse the humiliation of the 9/11 attacks by publicly meting out retribution in order to restore national self-respect (Saurette 2006). Australia's 2003 intervention to restore order in Solomon Islands was ostensibly to prevent the transnational security threats of people and drug trafficking, money laundering and potentially, terrorism. In conjunction with this, however, Australia's Prime Minister in 2003, John Howard, stated repeatedly that an important motive for the intervention was to bolster Canberra's reputation in the war on terror vis-à-vis its 'coalition of the willing' allies by being seen to keep order in its South Pacific sphere of responsibility (Prime Minister of Australia 2003a, 2003b).

The violent political instability in Ivory Coast between 1999 and 2011 may be viewed partly in the context of regionalized state failure in West Africa (Englebert and Tull 2008: 109). The postcolonial political economy of Ivory Coast shared some patterns with neighbouring 'shadow states' in Liberia and Sierra Leone. According to the International Crisis Group (ICG 2004: 4), there were transnational linkages with the conflict in Liberia and Ivorian rebel forces sought to gain control of lucrative natural resources. However, the Ivory Coast conflict does not altogether fit within the typical models of 'new wars' or failed state political economy in sub-Saharan Africa. The conflict in Ivory Coast displays a more traditional political rationale of contested citizenship claims based around a complex mosaic of ethnic identities (Bah 2010: 597–8).

The French intervention on 25 September 2002 officially took the form of a classic peacekeeping operation, in creating an impartial buffer zone to keep apart the northern rebels and southern government forces. This 'impartial', stabilizing role was more ambiguous and complex than it appeared, particularly in the volatile west of the country bordering Liberia, and also in dealing with violent civil unrest in Ivory Coast's largest city and commercial capital, Abidjan. The 'impartial' French role and its justifications also changed a number of times in response to events on the ground. In this it differs from recent failed state interventions of a comparable scale, such as the British intervention in Sierra Leone in 2000 or Australia's 2003 Regional Assistance Mission Solomon Islands (RAMSI). In both of these, a robust military intervention came in on the side of the recognized government, swiftly quelled the violence and the focus moved quickly to governance reforms and capacity-building. It was only in the final days of the Ivory Coast crisis in early April 2011 that French forces acted in direct support of the newly elected President Alassane Ouattara. And even these operations were 'impartially' carried out under UN mandate to protect civilians from heavy weapons.

The immediate French response in the late-1990s to the policy debacles of Rwanda and the DRC was to disavow intervention in Africa altogether. According to Richburg (2003a), France was so roundly criticized for its Rwanda mission in 1994, that it 'vowed a hands-off approach to Africa's future civil wars'. France was concerned about the instability and divisive identity politics of '*ivoirité*' that developed in Ivory Coast in the late-1990s and culminated in the country's first coup d'état in 1999. But in response to the 1999 coup, France reiterated its new policy of non-intervention in Africa. So soon after its failures in Rwanda and the DRC a policy reversal to intervene in Ivory Coast would have further damaged rather than bolstered France's reputation. But rather than ameliorating Ivory Coast's political crisis with new, more representative elections, xenophobic identity politics continued under coup leader General Robert Gueï and intensified with the election in 2000 of Laurent Gbagbo as President.

Non-interventionist sentiment was particularly strong in the French Socialist Party. Lionel Jospin had successfully opposed French intervention in Ivory Coast in 1999 as Prime Minister in the *cohabitation* government with Chirac from 1997 to 2002 (Smith 2003, Médard 2005: 51). The changed dynamics in French domestic politics in 2002 with a unified centre-right government certainly played an important part in facilitating the 2002 Ivory Coast intervention. But, as shown below, the turn of events in Ivory Coast in 2002 was a much more serious threat to international order norms than in 1999, with a coordinated nation-wide coup attempt, the partition of the country, violent ethnic conflict and serious threats to the safety of French nationals. Perhaps most importantly, however, was the solidification in the south of the country of an illiberal, xenophobic and increasingly authoritarian regime under Gbagbo.

The exclusion of northern ethnic groups and Muslims from citizenship rights in Ivory Coast was viewed with growing outrage by French policy-makers in the period between 1999 and 2002. But it was the explosion into ethnic violence and civil war with the September 2002 coup that strongly engaged French prestige concerns. Compared with the bloodless 1999 coup, the events of 2002 marked a more profound challenge to France's reputation for maintaining order in what had formerly been one of its most successful colonies. The potential for ethnic conflict in Ivory Coast to descend into a Rwanda-style 'catastrophe' was a visceral threat to liberal norms and French expectations for order in the region. In 2002, the emerging situation in Ivory Coast resonated deeply with French ontological security needs.

The flow of events shows that the emotional dimension of prestige became explicit after the failure of the French-brokered Linas-Marcoussis peace accords of January 2003 along with escalating anti-French violence in the south of the country over the next year. This culminated in November 2004 with an air attack by Gbagbo forces on a French military base killing nine soldiers and wounding 31. France responded with overwhelming force by destroying Ivory Coast's small air force. It then unilaterally mounted large-scale military operations over several days in the commercial capital Abidjan, using deadly force against civilian protestors to protect French nationals and restore calm. The disproportionate use of force in exacting retribution from the Gbagbo government and quelling the violence against French nationals shows the authenticity of the emotional dimension of the prestige motive.

Instrumental concerns for credibility also became implicated in the French handling of the Ivory Coast crisis as the situation worsened in 2003 and 2004. French military doctrine in Africa holds that pre-positioned troops and rapid reaction forces are for the purpose of deterring coups, political instability and civil unrest. It was feared that failing to gain control of the situation and allowing French troops and citizens to be attacked with impunity could give rise to similar risks in other African trouble spots. In this sense, the concerns for regional instability stated by French policy-makers throughout the episode reflected humanitarian concerns, but also prudential ones of costs and risks.

The normative threat of ethnic violence descending into genocide dissipated from early 2005 until violence flared again after the long-awaited October 2010 elections. French policy did not support Gbagbo personally, but Paris remained committed to the liberal principle that political change in Ivory Coast must come through constitutional processes and not by force. After Ouattara's election in 2010, France was instrumental in preparing the ground for Gbagbo's final removal by pushing for a UN Security Resolution that banned the use of heavy weapons in Abidjan. This cleared the way for decisive French military action in taking out Gbagbo's last defences and allowing his capture by pro-Ouattara forces.

## Historical Background and Case Overview

Ivory Coast was considered to be one of Africa's most wealthy and successful countries from decolonization in 1960 until the shift to multiparty democracy in 1990. Ivory Coast did not suffer from the postcolonial and then post-Cold War international neglect experienced by many African states because it was the anchor of francophone West Africa. Operating independently of the superpower blocs during the Cold War, France continued to provide significant military and economic assistance to former colonies in its West African sphere of influence. France also remained the most comprehensively engaged external power in Africa in the immediate post-Cold War era.

A critical view suggests that French involvement in postcolonial Africa had little to do with building strong states and prosperous societies, and was more about sustaining and reproducing systems of mutual benefit for Franco-African elites (Charbonneau 2008: 18). Jean François Médard (2005: 44) argues that French policy was only ever responsive to African developmental challenges when they affected French aims or interests. At the end of the Cold War in 1989, many African states seemed just as fragile as they had been during the turbulent post-independence years of 1963–66 when thirteen coups had taken place (Chipman 1989: 169–70). According to Médard (2005: 46–7), French aid to Africa during the Cold War was not development-oriented, but dedicated to maintaining stable bilateral relationships. Political instability in francophone Africa was kept in check by periodic French intervention, but the root causes of the problems were not ameliorated.

The state failure and civil war in the Ivory Coast during the first decade of the twenty-first century was a consequence of the inability of Ivorian political elites to adapt from the postcolonial system of governance established by President Felix Houphouët-Boigny after 1960. This system was destabilized by external pressures for democratization that came with the change to a solidarist liberal order in the early 1990s. The postcolonial Ivorian model was that of a plantation economy based mainly on cocoa and coffee. The agricultural sector grew rapidly after independence with high levels of French investment, privileged access to European markets and favourable pricing agreements. To support the industry, Houphouët-Boigny encouraged large-scale labour immigration to the southern cocoa and coffee belt, whether internal from other regions, or from neighbouring states Burkina Faso and Mali (ICG 2003).

Ivory Coast is home to more than 60 ethnic groups located within five broader cultural and language clusters. The Akan are dominant in the southeastern and central regions comprising 42.1 per cent of Ivory Coast's population. The Baoulé are the largest ethnic group within the Akan cluster. The Krou are dominant in the southwestern region at 11 per cent of the population, with the Bété the largest tribal grouping. The north of Ivory Coast is divided between three main ethnic clusters. The Northern Mandé in the northwest comprises 16.5 per cent of the population, with the Malinké the dominant group. In the centre-west, the Southern

Mandé account for 10 per cent of the population. The Yacouba are the main tribal grouping within the Southern Mandé cluster. The Gur or Voltaic peoples inhabit the northeast, making up 17.6 per cent of the Ivory Coast population, with the Sénoufos as the main ethnic group within this cluster (Chirot 2006: 65–6, CIA World Factbook 2012).

Many people belonging to these 'northern' ethnic groups live and work in southern Ivory Coast. These ethnic divisions are interwoven with a regional, communal divide between the predominantly Muslim north of the country and the Christian-dominated south. The Akan and Krou are predominantly Christian. The Northern Mandé is almost exclusively Muslim. The other ethnic groups are more mixed including animist elements. Islam is the country's largest religion if resident foreigners are included. This divide is also reflected in an economic disparity between the impoverished north and wealthier south. There are also large immigrant populations resident across Ivory Coast, mainly from Burkina Faso and Mali. These populations, estimated at 26 per cent of the country's total population before the 2002 crisis, have been living in Ivory Coast for a number of generations and share a similar culture with northern Ivorians (Langer 2005: 29, Bah 2010: 601). In 2002, there were also 130,000 Lebanese people in the country and up to 20,000 French nationals (CIA World Factbook 2012).

On the surface Ivory Coast appeared successful as a postcolonial state, unlike most of its neighbours. This was despite its lack of a centred and cohesive ethnic basis for political community. Arnim Langer (2005: 30–31) identifies four factors that help to explain how Ivory Coast maintained political stability under Houphouët-Boigny for the 30 years after independence in 1960. The first was that in the absence of genuine democratic institutions, the President played the role of mediator in the political process. The Houphouët-Boigny government 'was characterized by a culture of dialogue, compromise, rewards, punishments, forgiveness and integration' (Langer 2005: 30). Second was the use of economic incentives to co-opt opposition leaders and the military. Regime opponents were accommodated with lucrative places in Ivorian government or business and rarely imprisoned or forced into exile. Third was a system of ethnic quotas that, while Akan-dominated, also ensured that other major ethnic groups were represented (Langer 2005: 30–31). Elite politics at the national level was characterized by regional, ethnic factions jockeying for advantage but kept tied to the centre by presidential patronage (Boone 2007: 71). Finally, France provided a stabilizing element by maintaining mutually-cooperative relations with Ivorian elites in a relationship known as *la Françafrique* (Langer 2005: 30).

France maintained close ties during the Cold War period with corrupt and repressive regimes in francophone West and Central Africa in a relationship that has been likened to 'international clientilism'. This was marked by informal personal relationships, business and economic linkages, military aid and assistance, and direct armed intervention under bilateral defence accords. These networks, officially labelled as *coopération*, attracted increasing criticism after the Cold War as corrupt and neo-colonial. The state-based nature of this elite network began to break down in the 1990s into more fragmented and privatized arrangements in the wake of greater public scrutiny and a number of corruption scandals (Chafer 2005: 7–14, 2008: 39–41, Majumdar and Chafer 2010: 212–4).

At the diplomatic level, the French relationship with Africa began to be recast, or 'normalized' in the 1990s in line with the post-Cold War liberal international order and the evolution in French thinking outlined in Chapter 3. In 1990, President Mitterrand announced that French aid and technical assistance to Africa would be premised on democracy and progress on human rights. In 1993, the 'Balladur Doctrine' mandated that bilateral aid from France would be conditional on recipients having agreements in place with the World Bank and International Monetary Fund (IMF). Jospin announced in 1998 that French aid to Africa would in future be allocated to all countries according to need, not only to traditional French partners. These developments in the French view of international order in Africa, despite periodically being sacrificed for stability, marked a serious shift away from Cold War thinking (Quinn and Simon 2006: 301–2). This reorientation toward liberal order norms was supported by changes in personnel, particularly the death of Jacques Foccart in 1997, who had headed variously over 35 years the autonomous Africa cell that operated from the President's Elysée palace, and was instrumental in maintaining the *Françafrique* network (Charbonneau 2008: 76–7, Chafer 2002: 351–2). And although the neo-Gaullist President Chirac elected in May 1995 promised that France would maintain a privileged relationship with francophone Africa, it seemed clear that this pattern would be increasingly re-ordered according to liberal norms (Charbonneau 2008: 83, 91).

Another important development from the mid-1990s has been the restructuring of French military forces away from territorial defence to a focus on overseas operations (see Gregory 2000a). Chirac abolished national service in 1996 and the French military was fully professionalized. Land-based nuclear forces were dismantled in favour of mobile sea and air platforms. Conventional forces were geared toward long-range, high-tech force projection (Keiger 2005: 143). Longstanding deployments in Africa were retained, but streamlined and backed by new rapid reaction forces based in France. Pre-positioned troops in Africa under the doctrine of *prévention* were seen by Paris to be a crucial stabilizer and deterrent against political unrest (Charbonneau 2008: 97). The most recent 2008 Defence White Paper stated that the 'key determinant' of French force structures was now 'intervention abroad' (*Présidence de la République* 2008: 11). These military reforms reflect the post-Cold War change in international order that emphasizes human security, peace building and democratization, and after 9/11, preventing state failure and transnational threats. They also reflect the need to reduce costs but maintain in Africa an arena where France can still act like a great power, but now in the service of the reputational norms of liberal international order.

The postcolonial political settlement in Ivory Coast began to unravel in the 1980s with economic recession and international trade liberalization. Houphouët-Boigny opened the political system to its first multiparty election on 28 October 1990 under external pressures for democratization and internal dissent within his ruling party. The long-time President won the election but introduced the new post of Prime Minister to bolster the country's democratic credentials. This position was filled by Alassane Ouattara, a northern Muslim and technocrat who had previously worked for the IMF. Ouattara was responsible for overseeing unpopular IMF and World Bank austerity packages that prompted violent demonstrations in Abidjan in 1991. The leader of this protest movement was a leftist history professor, Laurent Gbagbo, of the Bété ethnic group, part of the southwestern Krou family. Gbagbo had lost the 1990 presidential election to Houphouët-Boigny and headed the increasingly nationalistic *Front Populaire Ivoirien* (*FPI*) (ICG 2003).

When Houphouët-Boigny died in office in 1993, the speaker of parliament Henri Konan Bédié assumed the presidency as per constitutional arrangements. Ouattara left the country and took up a post with the IMF in September 1994. Bédié then launched the divisive policy of '*ivoirité*'. A new electoral code distinguished between 'pure' Ivorians and those of foreign or mixed heritage. Muslim northerners lost seats in parliament and positions in the state bureaucracy. Many immigrants were forced to leave the country. *Ivoirité* also affected populations in the west of the country with ethnic connections to Liberia. This move by Bédié effectively disqualified Ouattara from politics as his father was reportedly a 'Burkinabe' from Burkina Faso. *Ivoirité* was also a response to the establishment of a new political party, *Rassemblement des Républicains* (*RDR*), which had split from Bédié's ruling *Parti Démocratique de Côte d'Ivoire* (*PDCI*) (ICG 2003). Both Gbagbo and Ouattara refused to contest the 1995 presidential election.

While Bédié's mobilization of *ivoirité* may have been for expedient political purposes, it resonated with southern intellectuals who sought a more authentic postcolonial Ivorian identity. They felt that under the 33-year one-party regime of Houphouët-Boigny, decolonization from France had never meaningfully occurred and the bases for Ivorian independence never properly established (Banégas 2006). But the assertion of *ivoirité* and the policies flowing from this were deeply disturbing to northerners and those of immigrant origins as it undermined their claims to citizenship and civil rights.

A successful military coup took place against the Bédié government on 24 December 1999 without French intervention. The junta was led by General Robert Gueï who maintained the ideology of *ivoirité*. The respective political parties of Ouattara and Bédié then boycotted the October 2000 presidential elections leaving Gueï and Gbagbo as the main candidates. Gueï declared himself winner but official results released later by the electoral commission indicated that Gbagbo had won. With French pressure, Gueï went into exile and Gbagbo was declared President.

Disaffected soldiers mounted a second coup d'état on 19 September 2002 aimed simultaneously at the major cities of Abidjan in the south of the country, Bouaké in the centre and Korhogo in the north. The attempt on Abidjan, Ivory Coast's major commercial centre failed, but Bouaké was held. The rebels, now named the *Mouvement Patriotique de la Côte D'Ivoire* (*MPCI*), rapidly seized the Muslim north of the country. French military forces intervened at Bouaké on

25 September to evacuate foreign nationals from the war zone. This also blocked any southward advance by the rebels toward Abidjan. A truce was brokered on 17 October with a ceasefire line dividing the country into northern and southern halves separated by a 'confidence zone'. The 700-strong French military deployment, named *Operation Licorne* (Unicorn), was reinforced and mandated to remain until relieved by a peacekeeping force from the Economic Community of West African States (ECOWAS). South of the ceasefire line, two anti-Gbagbo insurgent groups emerged in the west of the country. Not parties to the ceasefire, they advanced south toward the important port city of San Pedro, but were again halted by French forces. The anti-Gbagbo insurgent groups coalesced at the end of 2002 into the *Forces Nouvelles* (New Forces) (*FN*).

A 2000-strong ECOWAS Mission to Ivory Coast (ECOMICI) was scheduled to deploy on 31 December 2002, but was delayed with only 500 troops on the ground in February 2003. By this time France had deployed 3000 of a total 4000 troops. France provided the key military, logistical and financial backing for the ECOWAS peacekeeping effort which took over the policing of the ceasefire line in late-April 2003. Peace talks were held in France at Linas-Marcoussis from 15 to 24 January 2003. These talks provided for a transitional government to lead the country to new, more inclusive elections in 2005. On 4 February, the UN Security Council retrospectively authorized the Linas-Marcoussis Accords, the French Licorne operation and ECOMICI.

The peace agreement triggered sustained and violent anti-French demonstrations in Abidjan by pro-Gbagbo supporters. After this, thousands of French nationals fled the country. Gbagbo subsequently backtracked on important provisions of the peace accords. In May 2003, the UN Security Council established a small political mission to monitor and facilitate the Linas-Marcoussis Accords. This was followed in February 2004 with the establishment of the 7000-strong UN Operation in Ivory Coast (UNOCI) to commence on 4 April 2004. ECOWAS forces were absorbed into the new UN mission with French forces in cooperation but independent.

The continued north–south division of the country solidified the ethnic and political divide that predated the crisis. In the south, communal violence raged between pro-*FPI* 'Young Patriots' and opposition supporters. In the northern zone, the *MPCI* set up a parallel government. Inter-ethnic violence in the west of the country remained ongoing while the *FPI* continued to mount xenophobic campaigns in the south towards northerners and foreigners. The question of citizenship, of who was an Ivorian and who was not, remained at the centre of the crisis at the end of 2003. By this time, approximately 700,000 refugees had been displaced and large but unknown numbers killed.

On 4 November 2004, Gbagbo forces bombed both rebel positions and a French military base in Bouaké killing nine French soldiers and wounding 31. In response, the French military destroyed the Ivorian air force. This fuelled further violent anti-French protests among the southern population between 6 and 9 November 2004. Thousands of French and other foreign nationals fled the country after systematic intimidation and harassment by pro-Gbagbo militias. French forces mounted a number of military operations in Abidjan to secure military bases and the airport so that foreigners could be evacuated.

In November 2006, Gbagbo opened direct contact with the rebels leading to the Ouagadougou Accord of 4 March 2007. This provided for opposition politicians to enter a new power-sharing government, a more reasonable identification and residency system for all Ivorians, the disbanding and reintegration of militia groups, and the gradual removal of the confidence zone. But new elections continued to be postponed until 31 October 2010 and the north maintained its parallel government.

In the first round of the long-awaited 2010 election, Gbagbo secured 38 per cent of the vote compared with 32 per cent for Ouattara and 25 per cent for Bédié. After this, Bédié withdrew and endorsed Ouattara for the second round held on 28 November 2010. On 2 December, the electoral commission declared Ouattara winner with 54.1 per cent of the vote to Gbagbo's 45.9 per cent. The following day the President of the Constitutional Council intervened. The electoral commission had failed to confirm the results within the required statutory period. Sixteen per cent of votes cast were cancelled. The result was reversed and Gbagbo was declared winner. The UN recognized Ouattara as the legitimate President of Ivory Coast on 23 December. The northern rebels, now openly backing Ouattara, launched a nationwide offensive against the Gbagbo regime on 28 March 2011. On 30 March a UN Security Council Resolution authorized foreign forces in the country to take all necessary measures to protect civilians. On 4 April, French and UN troops secured the airport in Abidjan as rebel fighters gathered around the city. The following day, after French troops had destroyed heavy weapons deployed to protect the presidential palace, Ouattara's supporters surrounded Gbagbo's home in the government compound. After a weeks' stand-off, Gbagbo surrendered and was arrested on 11 April.

## The 1999 Military Coup, *Cohabitation* and Non-Intervention

This section examines French policy during the period from the first military coup in Ivory Coast in December 1999 until the election of the second Chirac government in France in mid-2002. This period saw the continuation and deepening in Ivory Coast of a divisive ethnic politics based on the exclusion of northern, Muslim groups from political office and a denial of their citizenship rights. In response to the coup d'état, France reiterated its late-1990s commitment to non-intervention in Africa that emerged after the failure of its policies in Rwanda and the DRC. Juxtaposed to this however, were expressions of growing concern by French policy-makers at the increasingly illiberal and xenophobic turn Ivorian politics was taking first under General Gueï and then Laurent Gbagbo. France's *cohabitation* government was divided on what to do about Ivory Coast. There was a strong commitment to non-intervention in the Socialist Party. But as the evidence below shows, French policy-makers were increasingly outraged by developments in Ivory Coast. Despite this, France's reputational requirements during this period were seen to be better served by non-intervention than intervention. The results of the October 2000 election in Ivory Coast returned Gbagbo on a platform of xenophobic identity politics. This set the conditions for state failure, French intervention and a decade of violence and instability in the country.

On 24 December 1999, details began to emerge that a bloodless military coup had taken place in Ivory Coast. This was reportedly over the non-payment of bonuses to soldiers for UN peacekeeping operations, deterioration of the armed forces and rampant government corruption. The military junta was led by retired General Robert Gueï, a Yacouba from the Southern Mandé ethnic group in the west of the country (Chirot 2006: 70). The French Foreign Ministry condemned the '"resort to force currently under way in Cote d'Ivoire"' and called 'for the "immediate restoration of order and security"' (*Agence France-Presse* [*AFP*] 1999a). The US State Department, Britain's Africa Minister and UN Secretary-General Kofi Anan all followed suit with condemnations of the coup action. The Organization of African Unity (OAU) declared it would not recognize the post-coup regime. Paris expressed vigilance about the safety of its 20,000 citizens resident in Ivory Coast. The security situation on the streets of Abidjan remained tense in the days after the coup with looting and sporadic gunfire. In Paris, the Foreign Ministry announced that France's existing military contingent of 550 personnel, based adjacent to the Abidjan international airport, would be increased as a precautionary measure for the protection of French nationals. Extra troops were immediately deployed from Libreville, Gabon, while 300 were to be flown to Dakar, Senegal, to wait on standby (*AFP* 1999b). This seems to have been a genuine precautionary measure and not a precursor to intervention.

The position of General Gueï's military junta was initially conciliatory. Opposition leaders Gbagbo and Ouattara, both out of the country and remaining silent were invited to consultations for a 'consensus government'. France also remained quiet on the political dimensions of the coup. A number of sources argue that Chirac favoured a traditional interventionist French response to prop up Bédié but initiatives in this direction were blocked in the *cohabitation* government by Jospin (see Chafer 2005: 16, Rouach 1999b). Foreign and security policy in Fifth Republic France is considered to be the '*domaine réserve*' of the President and advisors at the Elysée Palace. The President takes major policy decisions which are implemented by the Prime Minister's government. If the President's party has a majority in the National Assembly, his authority in foreign and defence policy is virtually absolute. This pattern has also been maintained in periods of *cohabitation* when left-right agreement has been possible on the objectives and direction of foreign policy (Keiger 2001, Wood 2005: 73). Where agreement cannot be reached, as at times during the 1997–2002 *cohabitation*, responsibility for foreign and security policy must be shared because the Prime Minister can block the implementation of any presidential policy initiatives (Wood 2005: 74).

Two days after the coup, Bédié was flown out of the country by France. French policy remained muted. Consistent with liberal order norms, Foreign Ministry spokesperson Anne Gazeau-Secret said simply that '"France would like to see the restoration of democracy and the rule of law in the shortest possible time"' (*AFP* 1999c). The first clear statements of French policy on the new situation in Ivory Coast were made on 27 December 1999, three days after the coup. The Cooperation Minister for francophone Africa, Charles Josselin (in Rouach 1999b), first said that France's approach to the coup 'reflected a "new policy" of non-intervention in Africa'. Paris would no longer intervene on the old model of its political relationships with Africa. It was out of the question that France would maintain '"a leader against the people's will"'. This did not, however, imply indifference or abandonment. France would work with its African partners to ensure that democracy could return to Ivory Coast as soon as possible. On 28 December, France withdrew its emergency military deployments. It is a reasonable judgement that in late-1999 under the *cohabitation* government, French reputational concerns were better served through non-intervention and African mediation in the crisis. The situation in Abidjan was calming and Paris had expounded a very recent and public policy of non-intervention in Africa. A policy reversal would have generated severe criticism in the international community and renewed accusations that France had not moved on from old-style neo-colonialism.

In early January 2000, Gueï refused to rule out standing as a candidate in post-coup presidential elections scheduled for later in the year, although he did pledge to abolish the controversial citizenship law that discriminated against Ouattara (*AFP* 2000a). Despite this initial impression that Gueï was a political ally of Ouattara, the exclusionary focus on ethnicity resurfaced in drafts for a new constitution and presidential eligibility requirements. The result was that a candidate must be born in Ivory Coast to a mother *or* father of Ivorian origin and never to have claimed a foreign nationality. Gueï unilaterally altered the draft constitution before it was put to referendum by changing it to both a mother *and* father of Ivoirian origin. This again disqualified Ouattara from politics in a move that was supported by Gbagbo (ICG 2003).

The retention of the exclusionary ethnic qualification was defended by the *FPI* as reflecting the aspirations of the people who had taken part in the sub-commissions that informed the Constitution's drafting (*BBC Monitoring Africa* 2000). The constitutional referendum passed resoundingly with 86.5 per cent of the vote but with only a 56 per cent turnout. The regional distribution of voter turnout was unclear. The continuation of an exclusionary identity politics in the wake of the coup began to cause concern for French policy-makers at the illiberal direction the regime in Ivory Coast was taking. France sent a clear message in the days after the referendum that Paris supported Ouattara's eligibility to be a candidate in the upcoming presidential election. Josselin (in Rouach 2000) said '"[t]here should be no artificial exclusion of any candidate"' and alluding to Rwanda, warned '"I would not like events before us to give rise to tension or violence between communities who live in Ivory Coast"'. He added that France did not support the nomination of coup leader, General Gueï, as a presidential candidate.

France again increased its forces in Ivory Coast and West Africa in preparation for unrest associated with the post-coup presidential election scheduled for 22 October 2000. This was not opposed by Gueï, who did warn, however, that foreign powers were not welcome to interfere in the national debate over election eligibility (*AFP* 2000d). France responded by repeating that it hoped Ivorians would have a full choice of candidates (*AFP* 2000c). The Ivory Coast Supreme Court confirmed on 7 October that the new Constitution would exclude 14 of the 19 nominated presidential candidates, including Ouattara. This left Gueï and Gbagbo as the main contenders for office. A French Foreign Ministry spokesperson denounced the poll as anti-democratic (Leighton 2000). Foreign Minister in Jospin's Socialist government, Hubert Védrine (in *AFP* 2000e) later clarified that the poll was 'legal' because it was consistent with Ivory Coast's constitution, but reiterated that '"France and Europe have condemned the fact that the (voters') free choice has been restricted"'.

Védrine's comments reflected the difficult situation posed by Ivory Coast for a status quo Western power in promoting liberal order norms. A democratic constitutional process in Ivory Coast had produced a fundamentally illiberal political outcome. People from northern, Muslim origins were treated as second-class citizens and denied civil and political rights. This confounds technocratic and rationalist approaches to state effectiveness and supports my critique of the orthodox view of governance advanced in Chapter 2. Putting in place the appropriate liberal institutions and procedures cannot overcome problems with a country's political culture. As argued in Chapter 2, to the contrary, political cultures will reverberate through institutional structures producing outcomes other than those intended by liberal governance models.

Gueï declared himself winner of the election on early results announced by the Minister of the Interior and suspended the official electoral commission count. This was condemned by French President Chirac as an attempted coup (*AFP* 2000b). Gbagbo claimed the presidency on 25 October 2000 and called on his *FPI* supporters to take to the streets in protest against Gueï's attempt to 'confiscate' the election. Official results released later by the electoral commission indicated that Gbagbo had indeed won. This led immediately to mass demonstrations with a number of deaths reported in clashes between Gbagbo and Gueï loyalists. Under French pressure, Gueï went into exile in neighbouring Benin and Gbagbo was declared President. After Gbagbo refused Ouattara's request that new elections be held, government security forces targeted supporters of the *RDR*, mainly immigrants and Ivorians from northern, Muslim areas. On 29 October, some 60 supporters of the *RDR* were allegedly murdered (Langer 2005: 34). France accepted the new result as legitimate. External pressure from France for new elections would damage its reputation by causing further unrest and accusations of neo-colonial interference in Ivory Coast's internal affairs (*AFP* 2000f).

Former President Bédié returned from exile on 15 October 2001 at the invitation of Gbagbo to participate in a National Reconciliation Forum. Ouattara originally refused to attend unless the government restored his citizenship but returned from France anyway on 30 November without the demand being met. Ouattara denounced the Gbagbo regime as illegitimate and dismissed proposals that his party participate in government while the exclusionary ethnic laws remained in force (Lhuillery 2001). Gbagbo's commitment to the Reconciliation Forum does not appear to have been genuine. In November 2001, an onerous national identification measure was initiated aimed at establishing a person's village of origin. In January 2002, the army was reformed in line with the ethnic divisions in politics. Supporters of Gueï and Ouattara were removed, while recruitment and promotion favoured Gbagbo's clients (ICG 2003). This sharpened the fault lines within the country and set the stage for the escalation of the crisis later in 2002.

The end of *cohabitation* in France also paved the way for a change in French policy back to intervention in Africa. The first Chirac presidency from 1995 was marked by unpopularity and the gross political miscalculation in 1997 of prematurely dissolving the National Assembly, which wiped out the President's centre-right majority. This brought the Socialists and left-wing allies to power in the *cohabitation* government that lasted until 2002. Chirac was politically rehabilitated in 2002 when the National Front's Jean-Marie Le Pen outpolled Jospin in the first round of the presidential election. The French republican establishment rallied behind Chirac delivering him a resounding second-round victory. In National Assembly elections shortly thereafter, Chirac's newly created *Union pour la Majorité Présidetielle* (*UMP*) also enjoyed a solid victory. Chirac entered his second term as president with a unified government under Prime Minister Jean-Pierre Raffarin and with heightened presidential authority (Atkin 2005: 181–95, Gaffney 2010: 168–78).

## The 2002 Coup, Civil War and French Intervention

This section examines the aftermath of the September 2002 coup in Ivory Coast, the French intervention, and north-south partition of the country along ethnic and communal lines. It shows that this adverse turn of events was viewed by France as a much more serious threat to its expectations for order in the region than the previous 1999 coup d'état. This normative threat to France in its area of historic responsibility, and so soon after the shame of Rwanda, made the Ivory Coast an acute reputational concern for Paris. The flow of events shows that there was indecision in its early stages as to whether the purpose of the French intervention would be limited to evacuating foreign nationals or if it was intended to prevent the situation from deteriorating into a humanitarian disaster that would also destabilize Ivory Coast's fragile neighbours. Some evidence suggests that this ambiguity reflected policy indecision within the French government during the early days after the coup. Given its commitment to non-intervention and sensitivity to accusations of neo-colonialism in Africa, limiting its military action to the evacuation of French nationals was a plausible alternative policy to the deepening of the intervention that followed. Indeed, similar to the Egypt case considered in Chapter 4, external pressures from France to force a solution contributed to the escalation of violence in the pro-government south of Ivory Coast.

It is also possible that the ambiguity in French intervention policy was deliberate. This may have been partly for reputational reasons in deflecting accusations of neo-colonialism and a return to discredited past practices in Africa. Ambiguity over the French role also sowed uncertainty on the ground and appeared to contribute to restraint at least on the part of the main rebel force. As the gravity of the situation became clearer in the weeks after the coup, French policy moved more firmly to a robust but politically neutral posture of preventing large-scale violence and stabilizing the situation pending a multilateral African peacekeeping force and a comprehensive political settlement. In December 2002, just prior to a French-sponsored peace initiative scheduled for January, intervention policy moved explicitly to peace enforcement. These actions in response to the evolving local situation were consistent with liberal order norms and French reputational concerns.

Rebel Ivorian soldiers mounted a coordinated nationwide coup attempt on 19 September 2002 aimed simultaneously at the major cities of Abidjan, Bouaké and Korhogo. The initial reaction from new French Foreign Minister Dominique de Villepin appeared to misjudge the situation. He attributed the unrest to another mutiny from disgruntled soldiers about the conditions of their demobilization (*BBC Monitoring European* 2002). Defence Minister Michèle Alliot-Marie (in *AFP* 2002) maintained the non-interventionist stance of the previous Socialist government. She said the attempted coup 'was a "purely internal affair"' and that France would not get involved.

The attempt by the northern forces to take Abidjan, Ivory Coast's largest city and major commercial centre failed, but Bouaké was held by the rebels, sparking fighting between loyalist troops and the breakaway army faction. It was estimated that 270 people were killed in the unrest in Abidjan alone. Bolstered by former Ivorian soldiers over the border in Burkina Faso, the *MPCI* quickly and successfully seized towns in the country's largely Muslim northern and central regions (ICG 2003). The ease of the takeover of the north of the country suggests a strong social base of support for the rebels. Details emerged later that the 2002 coup was planned and executed from Ouagadougou with the support of Blaise Compaoré, President of Burkina Faso (ICG 2003). The main grievances of the Ivorian rebels, initially numbering some 700–800 troops, related to land tenure, criteria for election candidature, citizenship and identity, and more generally, the political domination of the south over the north (Langer 2005: 35).

Atrocities were carried out by each side. Leader of the 1999 coup, General Gueï, his bodyguards and family were allegedly murdered during the events of 19 September 2002 although it was unclear which side was responsible. Opposition leader Ouattara took refuge at the French embassy when his house in Abidjan was attacked, looted and later set on fire by Gbagbo's security forces. Ouattara and the opposition *RDR*, with their main support base among Ivorians of northern Muslim and immigrant origins, were quick to disassociate themselves from the attempted coup (*BBC Monitoring Africa* 2002a). This did not stop reprisals in Abidjan against Muslims and northerners, with immigrant 'shantytowns' reportedly torched by government security forces with some 4,000 people displaced (*AFP* 2002g).

French Defence Minister Alliot-Marie announced that French forces in Ivory Coast would be reinforced from garrisons in Gabon, Senegal and Chad as the seriousness of the situation became clearer. Most of the estimated 20,000 French expatriates were in the Abidjan area, but around 600 were in rebel-held Bouaké and 80 in Korhogo. On 22 September 2002, a contingent of French troops was deployed to Ivory Coast's administrative capital of Yamoussoukro, 350 kilometres north-west of Abidjan and approximately 100 kilometres south of Bouaké (*AFP* 2002g). French military sources were reported on 24 September as saying that government reinforcements had left Yamoussoukro for Bouaké and that a loyalist attack against the rebels was imminent (*All Africa News* [*AFNWS*] 2002a). Later in the day, a French contingent also moved north to a position closer to Bouaké, while Washington said it would also deploy forces to evacuate US nationals, mostly Christian missionaries running a school in the city (Chanda 2002b). On 25 September, French troops mounted an operation to evacuate 191 Americans and other foreigners from the school and escort them to Yamoussoukro to a US military transport aircraft. In Abidjan on the same day, protestors attacked the French embassy demanding that Ouattara be turned over to the government (Chonghaile 2002).

After the evacuation was completed, French forces took up a position 20 kilometres east of Bouaké at Brobo. A military spokesperson said that troops would '"stay in proximity to the city, capable of intervening very rapidly if there are any problems"' (in *AFP* 2002l). Despite French insistence that the deployment was strictly to evacuate foreign nationals from the war zone, this marked a decisive French intervention in the crisis, and was seen as such by both the government and rebel side (e.g., Zavis 2002a, 2002b, *AFNWS* 2002b). This assessment is also supported by statements from Senegalese President Abdoulaye Wade (in *BBC Monitoring Africa* 2002b), ECOWAS mediator in the crisis, who said that the French mission in Ivory Coast was more than just the protection of French citizens 'but also to possibly prevent certain excesses'. A second and crucial motivation was to prevent large-scale ethnic violence and atrocities.

By 28 September 2002, the rebels were in control of large swathes of the north of the country, including most major towns. On the same day, the Gbagbo government unilaterally activated its defence agreement with France seeking logistical support to help defeat the rebels and restore government control over the country (*AFP* 2002j). A French Foreign Ministry statement agreed to provide undisclosed 'logistical support' to the Ivory Coast authorities (in *AFP* 2002c). This was later clarified as assistance in the form of vehicles, communications and food, but not weapons (*AFP* 2002h). It is unclear if this was a residue of earlier postcolonial French policies or if it was intended to contribute to stabilizing the volatile situation. Momentum was with the rebel forces and France sought to stall any further southward advance into government-held areas.

A clearer statement of French policy intentions in the aftermath of the coup was made on 30 September 2002. Counter to Gbagbo's expectations in activating the bilateral defence agreement, France was not entering the conflict on the government side, nor would it help the rebels. Its objective was to prevent violence and the break-up of the country until a political settlement could be reached and an African peacekeeping force deployed. French troops on the ground were 'strictly neutral' (Lhuillery 2002b). The objectives of stability, preventing ethnic violence and supporting regional multilateral initiatives were all indicative of the broader changes in France's Africa policy that had developed throughout the 1990s and reflected the norms of liberal international order. This was stability for reasons of humanitarianism and preventing regional contagion from affecting fragile neighbouring states. During the Cold war, stability had meant that of African client elites and their ties with France.

In line with this policy direction, France became more deeply involved in the Ivorian crisis from 1 October 2002. An unspecified number of Foreign Legion troops arrived in Bouaké. French troops also established positions between rebel-held Bouaké and Ivory Coast's administrative capital Yamoussoukro, on the main road to Abidjan. A further deployment was made to Duekoue in the west of the country closer to the border with Guinea. Duekoue was on the road south from rebel-held Odienne toward San Pedro, Ivory Coast's main port (Chanda 2002a). Any southward rebel advance would have to contend with French forces determined to keep the sides apart. These French military deployments, which marked a further decisive intervention in the conflict, coincided with an ECOWAS delegation in Abidjan for talks with Gbagbo (Chanda 2002a). These developments suggest a firm policy decision had been made in Paris.

A Defence Ministry spokesperson said the aim of the French military presence was to foster mediation and help to facilitate an African peacekeeping force. He said the troops were not acting directly as a buffer between the two sides, 'but did note that some French positions had "complicated the rebels' march towards the capital Yamoussoukro"' (in Serot 2002). A French military spokesperson referred to an 'evacuation zone' around Yamoussoukro, the main staging point for the evacuation of foreigners from the north. This zone had a radius of 15 to 20 kilometres, extensive enough to protect the staging points from heavy weapons fire. Rebel forces would not be allowed into this zone. It was an effective barrier to any rebel move south and consistent with the objective of maintaining stability in the situation (Goujon 2002). Rebel officers said French troops were indeed the only obstacle to an offensive on Yamoussoukro. A French commander on the ground acknowledged '"that indirectly we have contributed to freezing the situation"', but that this affected both sides (in Zavis 2002a). France remained impartial.

Reports in the French press began to canvass the reasons for the more assertive action after the current coup, compared with the hands-off approach in 1999. The main factor was considered to be the end of the *cohabitation* government. Chirac now had a cohesive government after his re-election in May and a broad majority in parliamentary polls held in June. The French government was united but knew that this 'was a litmus test – could it intervene militarily, if only to safeguard its nationals, without reviving old demons?' (Lhuillery 2002a). The evacuation of foreigners had been effective and impressive, but the crisis was becoming more complicated by the day. Whatever the public statements about protecting foreigners, French troops were acting as a buffer preventing a rebel advance. Paris appeared to be sending mixed messages. An unnamed French soldier on the ground more or less confirmed this by saying '"Our mission is clear but ambiguous"' (in Lhuillery 2002a).

Sources from inside Raffarin's *UMP* government suggested a level of indecision over France's role in the crisis. It was case 'of being "damned if we do and damned if we don't"' (Graham 2002). Any French intervention in Africa beyond rescuing nationals would be labelled in some quarters as a return to neo-colonialism and the failed policies of the past. But on the other hand, the conflict in Ivory Coast was fuelled by ethnic grievances. Another Rwanda in France's historic sphere of influence while its troops were on the ground would be a near fatal blow to French prestige in the world. De Villepin told the National Assembly, that other than the evacuation of French and foreign nationals, there were two main policy aims in Ivory Coast. These were relatively vague and unspecified allowing some room for manoeuvre. The first was to ensure the sovereignty and territorial integrity of Ivory Coast and the stability of the region. The second was to 'provide the framework for African mediation in the conflict' and deployment of an ECOWAS peacekeeping force for which France would provide logistical support (Graham 2002).

A ceasefire was brokered by President Wade of Senegal on 17 October 2002 after a number of further serious clashes between the two sides and much wrangling over the details (ICG 2003). Political leader of the *MPCI*, Guillaume Soro, said the ceasefire would be respected but the rebels would not disarm until Gbagbo stood down as President. By 21 October 2002, French troops had fanned out in a thin line across the middle of the country. The buffer zone operation involved about half of the 1,200 French troops deployed in Ivory Coast at the time (*AFP* 2002e). The posture of French troops would be to carry out patrols, deploy observation posts and checkpoints and establish contact points with both sides. French troops would retaliate decisively in response to any hostile activity against them (Merrill 2002).

In the first of many such incidents, pro-Gbagbo demonstrators attacked the main French military base in Abidjan on 23 October. They demanded opposition leader Ouattara be handed over and denounced France for imposing the ceasefire that allowed the rebels to consolidate their hold over the north (*AFNWS* 2002c). Reports also began to emerge that uniformed government security forces were engaged in reprisal killings of northerners in the western cocoa producing town of Daloa (Shea 2002, *AFP* 2002n). In December 2002, French troops discovered a mass grave with more than one hundred bodies northwest of the town. The government and rebels blamed each other for the atrocities (Carroll 2002).

Paris toughened its stance on the Gbagbo government the day after the protests in Abidjan. De Villepin (in Campagne 2002) called on the Ivory Coast President '"to do everything possible to avert possible attacks by uncontrolled elements against French and foreign nationals, as well as French troops"'. Gbagbo was told to rein in the hardliners in his entourage who were promoting xenophobic sentiments. And while President Chirac had been publicly reserved about the Ivory Coast crisis, both he and de Villepin had 'firmly warned' Gbagbo not to let the situation get out of control and spread to neighbouring states (Campagne 2002). The view in Paris that Ivory Coast was a failed state requiring a more robust intervention seems to have firmed by the end of 2002 with an intractable ethnic conflict, the discovery of mass graves and xenophobic violence and propaganda. The French military posture became less ambiguous from the end of 2002, moving to an explicit policy of peace enforcement to prevent the conflict from escalating and provide the conditions for a political settlement.

The French assessment in the post-Cold War period of what constitutes state failure, which differs somewhat from the Anglo-American view, is coloured by its deeper and more enduring involvement in postcolonial Africa and the experiences of Yugoslavia and Rwanda in the 1990s. For France, state failure is primarily a humanitarian and 'civilizing' concern. It is a result of politico-ethnic grievances that carry the risk of spiralling out of control into 'irrational' genocidal violence. The French role in this situation is to '"prevent, contain, and strictly control the escalation of violence"' (Bloch in Charbonneau 2006: 221). The phrase 'uncontrolled elements' used above by de Villepin was regularly used by French military commanders throughout the Ivory Coast intervention to justify the use of deadly force in quelling violence. In failed state contexts with the potential for genocidal ethnic conflict, violence itself becomes the enemy, with French military doctrine dedicated to the 'mastery of violence' (Dyson 2008: 758, Charbonneau 2008: 93–112). The objective of intervention in failed state contexts 'is not the destruction of the belligerent, but to establish stability and order by controlling, dominating, and eliminating the sources of violence' (Charbonneau 2006: 221). The logic of state failure on this view is that its ultimate cause is illiberal government that 'cannot accommodate multiple existing identities within its borders or when it instrumentalizes these differences to consolidate its power' (Charbonneau 2006: 223). This was certainly the case in Ivory Coast under Gbagbo's contested rule from 2000 to 2011. The *FPI*'s ideology and power base rested on ethnic grievance, xenophobia and the exclusion of foreigners. The solution to this form of state failure is not technocratic 'governance' on the dominant Anglo-American model, which was the basis of the critique presented in Chapter 2, but a genuine representative democracy than can accommodate and consolidate cultural diversity.

South of the ceasefire line to the west of Ivory Coast near the Liberian border, two new anti-Gbagbo insurgent groups emerged with connections to murdered 1999 coup leader, General Gueï: the *Mouvement Populaire du Grand Ouest* (Popular Movement of the Far West) (*MPIGO*) and *Mouvement pour la Justice et la Paix* (Movement for Justice and Peace) (*MJP*). Not parties to the ceasefire, they advanced south toward the port city of San Pedro, vital to Ivory Coast's commodity exports, but were halted by French forces that moved into the area ostensibly to evacuate foreign nationals from the new fighting (ICG 2003). A number of serious clashes occurred between French forces and rebel groups in the west that included ill-disciplined Liberian fighters. Around the end of 2002, the three anti-government forces (*MPCI*, *MPIGO* and *MJP*) coalesced into the *Forces Nouvelles*, or 'New Forces' (*FN*), under *MPCI* leader Soro (Bah 2010: 604).

In December 2002, the posture of French forces, particularly in the restive west of the country appeared to change. For example, French army spokesperson, Colonel Christian Baptiste (in *AFP* 2002i), 'said that French operations ... were entering a "third phase" aimed "at ending the progressive destabilisation of Ivory Coast"'. Referring to the 'second phase' of cease-fire monitoring (the first phase having been the evacuation of foreign nationals), Baptiste said '"[t]his time, we are going one step further"'. French forces now had 'orders to "open fire"' on anyone threatening their stabilizing function. This was backed up by de Villepin the following day. He said that French troops now being reinforced 'will have a mandate to shoot at anyone blocking their mission'. This 'was a "mark of its will"' to pursue a policy of '"backing democratic authorities who were legitimately elected; the preservation of the territorial integrity and sovereignty of Ivory Coast"' and support for regional efforts to end the crisis (in *AFP* 2002a). French efforts at this point still seemed to be predominantly targeted at the rebels as the main party destabilizing the country, rather than the government. De Villepin's statement appeared to lend support to Gbagbo or at least to the democratically elected office of president. French statements supporting democratic legitimacy can also be interpreted through the more instrumental lens of credibility. If the rebels were allowed to take over in Ivory Coast, this could lead to similar instability in neighbouring countries for which France also carried a level of responsibility.

Commanders on the ground in Ivory Coast were more explicit. French military spokesperson, Frederic Thomaso said that troops would no longer simply monitor the ceasefire, but would now enforce it. He said that '"[b]efore we did not react when they violated the ceasefire, but from now on we will make it understood to all that they have to respect the ceasefire and not endanger the stability of the Ivory Coast"' (in *AFP* 2002f). In response to bitter rebel complaints and violent demonstrations in Bouaké about the more assertive French approach, de Villepin (in *AFP* 2002m) commented that '"[i]f France was not there, a catastrophe would have already taken place"'. This again reflected the French view that resolving state 'failure' was not about restoring government capacity or one side in the conflict prevailing, but about preventing large-scale violence.

French prestige was now directly on the line in Ivory Coast. The intensification of the intervention, and scale of the French military presence, made it 'the country's riskiest venture in Africa since Rwanda'. The change in the nature of the rules of engagement to peace enforcement marked 'a major shift from the hands-off policy in Africa pursued since France's disgrace in Rwanda in 1994' (Schofield 2002). President Chirac was also investing his personal standing in bringing a political settlement to Ivory Coast. Reports late in December suggested that 'President Jacques Chirac is determined that France play the lead in restoring order' (Sciolino 2002). Raffarin (in *AFP* 2002d) said 'that France was "at the stage of moving from a security mission to the search for a political solution"'. Military actions were for the purpose of '"preventing the disintegration of the country"'. On 21 December 2002, French forces directly engaged an advancing *MPIGO* rebel convoy near Duekoue in the west with heavy weapons in the first of a number of serious engagements. A number of vehicles were destroyed by tank fire and up to seven rebels killed. This was the first time that French forces had directly stopped any of the rebel factions from capturing new territory (*AFP* 2002k). This was consistent with the new mandate of maintaining stability until a political settlement could be reached.

French sponsored peace talks were scheduled for 15 January 2003 in Paris. There would first be a week long summit meeting between French leaders, West African mediators and representatives of all Ivory Coast parties to the conflict. This would be followed on 26 January by a meeting of West African heads of state and UN Secretary General Kofi Annan. Commentary in the lead up to the talks began to focus on the apparent shifts in French policy during the crisis thus far. A number of motives for the French intervention were canvassed in the lead up to the Paris talks. The first was interest-based. France was wary that the battle would shift to the main cities of Abidjan and the port of San Pedro, where most French nationals and foreign citizens lived. This would require a massive evacuation of expatriates to France similar to the resettlement from Algeria some decades earlier. Many of these people had been born and lived all their lives in Ivory Coast and had few ties with France proper. This explains the French deployments that blocked rebel approaches to these major cities (Richburg 2003a).

Other reasons were less tangible and directly engaged with the reputation of France. The intervention was a test for the new post-Rwanda French policy in Africa. Reports suggested that France views 'its job as keeping Ivory Coast out of the ranks of "failed states"'. It could stand aside and do nothing and let Ivory Coast fall apart, but this would profoundly damage the promotion of international order norms in the region (Vaisse in Richburg 2003a). Credibility was also at stake. A related consideration was the signal it would send to the turbulent region if France and the international community let a legally elected government be overthrown. This would encourage further regional instability and the potential for other costly and risky French interventions. France had no enthusiasm for the increasingly illiberal Gbagbo regime, but at this time, there was little alternative but to back the elected government (Richburg 2003a).

### The Linas-Marcoussis Accords, Anti-French Violence and Retribution

This section examines the turbulent period from the Linas-Marcoussis peace agreement in January 2003 until the end of 2004, after which a tense relative calm prevailed until 2010. I first show that the prestige of France and personal standing of President Chirac were heavily invested in the French sponsored peace agreement, which was endorsed by West African heads of state, the UN and international community. While a sense of alarm among French policy elites had already been growing about the potential for Ivory Coast to descend into a Rwanda-style 'catastrophe', it was during the 2003–04 period that the emotional dimension of prestige was most powerfully engaged for France.

Rather than resolving the conflict, the peace agreement turned out to be a humiliating failure. This aroused negative emotions of anger and frustration among French policy-makers toward the Gbagbo government. The peace accord failed because of bitter anti-French sentiment in the pro-government south of Ivory Coast and Gbagbo's intransigence in implementing it. The situation escalated to intimidation and violence against French nationals and culminated with the air attack on a French military base killing nine soldiers. This was an insult to French national honour from a low status actor. France unilaterally deployed overwhelming military force in response to this in destroying Ivory Coast's entire air force and using deadly force to suppress civilian protests in Abidjan. The disproportionate use of force to exact retribution against the Gbagbo regime and quell the civilian violence demonstrates the authenticity of the emotional dimension of the prestige motive. Instrumental concerns for French credibility in the region were also implicated in these events. The failure of France to control the situation and allow its soldiers to be killed and citizens attacked with impunity could give rise to similar risks elsewhere in the world.

In the days leading up to the Paris talks, the *MPCI* leaders reiterated their demands. They wanted Gbagbo to step down as president and new elections to be held (Schofield 2003). Gbagbo's response was that he expected the peace talks would end the civil war, but was unyielding to rebel demands. Gbagbo wanted rebel belligerence to cease and government control again established over the whole of the country (*AFP* 2003c). Gbagbo declined to attend the peace talks, sending his Prime Minister instead. He would, however, attend the West African head of state talks to follow.

The stakes were high for Paris. Commentators argued that by taking responsibility for brokering a settlement, '"France is risking its credibility in Africa"' (Domergue in Smith 2003). This is indicated, for example, in Foreign Ministry statements that the government feared that a breakdown in Ivory Coast could lead to similar problems in neighbouring Mali, Burkina Faso and Guinea, all countries in which France had historical responsibilities similar to Ivory Coast (Schofield 2003). But more was at stake than French credibility in Africa. A report in *The New York Times* argued that French interests in Ivory Coast, such as the safety of its citizens and economic investments, were not the main motive for French involvement. France had long positioned itself as a supporter of developing countries '"to distinguish itself in world affairs"'. Because it was no longer strong enough to be a true world power, France's reputation and heightened international status was based on being seen to keep order in areas not of prime strategic importance in a global sense, predominantly in sub-Saharan Africa (Marchal in Smith 2003). This was a role that French politicians were eager to protect and one that would suffer if the country failed to stop the civil war in Ivory Coast (Smith 2003).

The peace talks were held at Linas-Marcoussis, outside Paris, from 15-24 January 2003. The talks appeared initially successful with both sides compromising. The Linas-Marcoussis Accord provided for a transitional government, including most players in the crisis, to lead the country to new elections scheduled for 2005. In meetings between Soro and Gbagbo presided over by Chirac and Kofi Annan, it was agreed that *MPCI* would control the defence and interior ministries in an interim government of national unity, while Gbagbo would remain president and nominate a consensus prime minister approved by France (ICG 2003). The other main political parties, the *PDCI* and Ouattara's *RDR* would also share ministerial responsibilities. The accords included measures to disarm belligerents, including government security forces and end the division of the country. Politically, the agreement provided for free and fair elections, an end to impunity for security forces, and most importantly, an end to hate campaigns and the policy of ethnic exclusion (ICG 2003, *AFP* 2003g).

Information that later emerged suggested that Chirac had taken a tough line during this meeting, 'with the underlying message that Gbagbo had no choice but to accept the treaty' (Lhuillery 2003b). By forcefully brokering the peace deal, Chirac invested his personal reputation and political standing in its success along with the risk of humiliation if the deal fell apart. The UN Security Council (2003) retrospectively authorized the Linas-Marcoussis Accords, the French Licorne operation and the ECOWAS mission with Resolution 1464 on 4 February 2003.

The deal struck at the talks prompted three days of violent anti-French protests in Abidjan by pro-Gbagbo supporters, which also spilled over into looting and killing in parts of the city inhabited by northerners. Gbagbo allegedly instructed his *FPI* supporters, the 13,000-strong 'Young Patriots', to carry out demonstrations against the accords while the peace talks in Paris were still going on (ICG 2003). Tens of thousands of people besieged the French embassy brandishing machetes, lighting bonfires and hurling burning tyres into the embassy compound. French shops were looted (Chanda 2003). In a later meeting in Paris, Chirac told Gbagbo that 'he must do what is necessary to restore calm'. Observers said the 'meeting was short and the message clear' (*AFP* 2003a). The tone of this report suggests that French frustration with Gbagbo and anger about the situation was rising.

On his return to Abidjan, Gbagbo backtracked on provisions of the accords, labelling them as only a 'set of proposals'. Government security forces, who claimed to have not been represented at the peace talks, refused to allow the rebels into a unity government (*AFP* 2003d). A peaceful demonstration of an estimated one hundred thousand protestors marched through Abidjan on 1 February denouncing the French-brokered deal. The tone was fiercely anti-French, with tricolour flags burned and crowds chanting death to Chirac (Koffi 2003, Aboa 2003). These events in Abidjan prompted a major exodus of French nationals. The

French Foreign Ministry advised its then approximately 16,000 citizens to leave the country unless their presence was essential. The airport had been besieged for two days by people trying to get out. They were attacked by protestors and French soldiers were deployed to secure the airport (*AFP* 2003f).

The upsurge of popular opinion against France and the peace deal was recognized internationally as damaging to French prestige. In Britain, for example, *The Daily Telegraph* (2003) wrote that the 'failure of the peace deal' was 'particularly wounding' for Chirac and de Villepin. They now found themselves mired in a worsening African civil war. For decades the Ivory Coast had been 'the success story of former French West Africa'. Its collapse represented 'a failure for France's post-colonial policies'. In *The Washington Post*, Keith Richburg (2003b) wrote that the peace accord was 'in tatters'. It was rejected by Ivory Coast's army. Gbagbo had refused to endorse it after personally agreeing to it with Chirac. Even more humiliating was that French citizens and interests were being openly attacked by Gbagbo's supporters. French influence in the country had collapsed, with its harassed citizens fleeing in droves.

Gbgabo (in *AFP* 2003e) made a televised address pledging to respect '"the spirit of the text of Marcoussis"'. He qualified the agreement, however, by stating that where it clashed with the Ivory Coast Constitution, the latter would be applied. This would disqualify those parts of the peace plan that abolished discrimination against northerners and foreigners. Gbagbo also ruled out any disarmament of government security forces or police. Gbagbo's continued intransigence must have further provoked French ire. Defence Minister Alliot-Marie (in *BBC Monitoring Africa* 2003c) said on the same day that Licorne had been reinforced to 3,200 troops with a mandate to protect foreigners 'whatever the circumstances'. This indicated a tougher posture in response to the attacks on French nationals. It appears to have been taken unilaterally, without the consent of the Gbagbo government. The additional troops would be located mainly in Abidjan where recent attacks and harassment had taken place. Helicopter over flights of the city were now constant in monitoring potential flashpoints. It is a reasonable assumption that the ubiquitous presence of French military helicopters over the city was intended to intimidate 'uncontrolled elements' with an overbearing reminder of the force that could be applied (*BBC Monitoring Africa* 2003c).

In an address to the Council of French Nationals Living Abroad on 3 September 2003, Alliot-Marie (in *BBC Monitoring Africa* 2003b) made some candid comments about French motivations in Ivory Coast. These were based on French responsibilities in Africa, preventing another Rwanda and maintaining regional stability. She first recognized France's historic responsibility for order in the region. France was 'playing a big brother role … in a certain number of cases because of our attachment to these countries'. She then alluded to the 1990s experience of Rwanda in saying that we 'know quite well that if we allow some situations to blow up or if we allow ethnic rivalries to thrive, we know very well how it is going to end'. No one wanted a military intervention, but without French stabilization, 'the country might break up'. This had implications for regional stability and French prestige. If France failed in Ivory Coast, the situation would 'spread to all the other countries in the region'. France would be judged accordingly.

A Radio France journalist was murdered by police in Abidjan on 23 October 2003. This provoked the anger of President Chirac on the eve of a state visit to Africa. Chirac said he expected 'exemplary justice' on this case from Ivorian authorities. He demanded that Gbagbo's government 'ensure the security of foreign nationals in general and French nationals in particular' (*BBC Monitoring Africa* 2003a). Details came out later that the journalist was waiting outside the national police headquarters attempting to gain access to arrested opposition militants when shot point blank in the head. Amnesty International and Paris-based lobby group, Reporters without Borders, said there had been an atmosphere of impunity for security forces and pro-government militias in the south since the September 2002 rebellion. Chirac (in Lhuillery 2003a) angrily condemned 'what he called "the irrational, irresponsible behaviour of certain Ivorian leaders"'.

While the confidence zone remained relatively quiescent, Abidjan became the focus of further violence. On 26 March 2004, 12 people were killed during a demonstration by opposition supporters over Gbagbo's failure to implement the peace accords (Peel 2004). Human rights groups claimed that up to 200 people were killed and 600 injured during and in the days after the demonstration by pro-government militias (*AFP* 2004c). The UN described these events as '"a huge setback"' to reconciliation efforts. A rebel spokesperson said disarmament was now completely off the agenda while Gbagbo remained in power (in Sengupta 2004a).

The UN Mission in Ivory Coast (UNOCI) was initially ineffective as it lacked logistical support and was slow to deploy. Because of its limited mandate, it also failed to prevent Gbagbo's troops from breaking the cease-fire and again attacking the rebels. In a new development perhaps designed to break the military deadlock, the government mounted a series of air attacks on rebel positions in and around Bouaké and Korhogo from 4 to 6 November 2004. Paris expressed 'worry' at the deteriorating situation and called for all parties to fully respect the cease-fire. Government sources said the bombing would continue, the rebel-held territory reconquered and Ivory Coast reunified (*AFP* 2004a, Sengupta 2004b). These attacks culminated on 6 November when Gbagbo forces bombed a French military base near Bouaké killing nine French soldiers and wounding 31. This was apparently in retaliation for UN and French troops turning back a government attack on Bouaké (*BBC Monitoring Africa* 2004a), although this was later denied by Gbagbo (*AFP* 2004f). The French military command in Ivory Coast said later that this air attack could not have been a mistake. The French base was well-marked and known to all parties (*AFP* 2004d).

In response to the air strike, and at the direct command of President Chirac, French military forces soon after destroyed the entire Ivorian air force, including its fighter-bombers and helicopters, on the ground at its base in Yamoussoukro (Bovcon 2009a: 11, Chirot 2006: 73). Later reports alleged that French troops made a point of killing the Belarusian mercenaries that had piloted the aircraft used in the attacks (see Hoagland 2004). The motive of retribution against the Gbagbo regime is prominent here, both for the direct attack on French soldiers and humiliation over the failed peace deal. On a personal level, Chirac was known to be impulsive and emotional (Thody 1998). Revenge can be considered emotionally as an end it itself that restores self-respect after a past humiliation. An article in *The Guardian*, for example, likened the French destruction of Ivory Coast's aircraft to 'a revenge rampage' (Adams 2004). Prime Minister Raffarin (in *AFP* 2004f) said 'no one could expect to kill French soldiers and get away with it. "One cannot kill French soldiers with impunity – end of discussion"'. Retribution in this sense can also be considered instrumentally, with the goal of maintaining French credibility. If French forces could be attacked with impunity in Ivory Coast, it might encourage attacks on French troops engaged in other controversial deployments.

Shortly after these events, a French school in Abidjan was attacked and set on fire by demonstrators while Gbagbo security forces skirmished with French troops at the airport. A demonstration numbering in the tens of thousands marched on the airport but was dispersed by French helicopters and cannon fire. Three demonstrators were reported killed (*AFP* 2004b). Concerned about the potential for massacres and hostage-taking, French forces in armoured vehicles and helicopter gunships mounted a series of intense military operations in Abidjan between 6 and 10 November 2004 to secure military bases, the airport and to airlift foreigners out of trouble spots. A further 8000 expatriates from 63 countries left Ivory Coast between 10 and 18 November. Evidence suggests that the anti-French protests were not spontaneous. Preparations had been made that identified the houses and businesses of French nationals along with a disinformation campaign claiming that French aircraft had bombed the Presidential palace (Bovcon 2009b: 285–6, Amnesty International 2006).

The French military actions seem to have been a unilateral decision without Ivory Coast government authorization. Leading figures in Gbagbo's ruling *FPI* seemed shocked. Government spokespeople called on France to order its troops back to their bases and stop shooting civilians. It was estimated that between 20 and 57 Ivory Coast civilians were killed in French military actions in Abidjan (Amnesty International 2006: 4). Media reports suggested that France had now abandoned 'its policy of strict neutrality in the country's civil war and take decisive military action to curb Gbagbo's forces' (*AFP* 2004b). This assessment was supported by French government statements. For example, Foreign Minister Barnier (in Kouassi 2004) said '"Gbagbo is personally responsible for what has happened"'. The violence against France was '"unexplainable, unjustifiable"'.

Details emerged later that an estimated 100 French businesses and 300 French-owned houses were looted and destroyed in the violence. French nationals and other white people were beaten, and 50 to 60 women, mainly Ivorians married to French husbands, allegedly raped (Bovcon 2009b: 285–6). French Chief of Defence Staff, General Henri Bentegeat (in *AFP* 2004e) described the pro-government mobs with disgust as '"a pack of looters and rapists, uncontrolled or manipulated people"'. Alliot-Marie (in *BBC Monitoring Africa* 2004b) later said that people close to Gbagbo had called 'for an anti-white witch-hunt'. They had 'carried out acts of violence, destruction and attacks against people, and – in some cases – rape'. The attacks on French troops and civilians in Abidjan were seen as an intolerable insult to French national honour by an actor of much lower status. Fears for the safety of large numbers of French nationals and the restoration of the respect due to France explain the heavy handed use of force against protesters in Abidjan. In the wake of this tougher French military action, the situation quietened by mid-December 2004.

## Stalemate and Endgame

This section first briefly covers developments during the period of political stalemate between 2005 and 2010 before moving to its main focus on the October 2010 elections and their aftermath in which the Gbagbo regime was removed and the crisis ended. France withdrew some of the extra troops deployed in November 2004 as calm was restored in the country. Over the next five years the French deployment was progressively drawn down to around 900 troops by early 2011. The UN mission took the leading role for maintaining security, and after the failed 2003 French-brokered peace agreement, further initiatives toward a political settlement were left to African mediators (Youngs 2006: 349). This suggests that the French objective in failed state contexts of the mastery of violence was judged to have been achieved to a satisfactory extent. The threat of ethnic violence descending into the Rwanda-style 'catastrophe' feared by French policy-makers dissipated from 2005 until violence flared again after the long-awaited October 2010 elections. This went some way to satisfying French reputational requirements and ontological security concerns. The events of November 2004 turned France against the Gbagbo regime, but consistent with liberal norms, Paris continued to insist that change must come through legitimate constitutional processes.

In November 2006, Gbagbo made the surprise initiative of opening direct contact with New Forces leader, Guillaume Soro. This was based on the premise 'of finding an "Ivorian solution to the Ivorian problems"' and overcoming the diplomatic and military stalemate (Bovcon 2009a: 12). With the facilitation of President Compaoré of Burkina Faso, then acting president of ECOWAS, the Ouagadougou Accord was concluded on 4 March 2007. A month later Soro took the office of Prime Minister in a new power-sharing government. This new accord provided for a more reasonable identification and residency system for all Ivorians based on place of birth and not on proving village ancestry, the disarmament and reintegration of rebel forces and other militias and the gradual removal of the confidence zone by replacing Licorne and UNOCI forces with mixed forces made up of both rebel and government soldiers. This latter process began on 16 April 2007 and was finished on 15 September, with international forces repositioned instead at seventeen observation points (Bovcon 2009a: 12, Bah 2010: 610–13).

Nicolas Sarkozy was elected President of France on 6 May 2007. Sarkozy continued the French policy of not supporting Gbagbo personally, but maintaining support for the peace accords already in place and legitimate constitutional processes. Sarkozy (in Agyeman 2007) said he would meet with Gbagbo, but indicated French displeasure by saying he 'would much prefer to meet with a president who had been democratically elected as opposed to one who has "overstayed his welcome"'. In June 2007, Sarkozy's Foreign Minister Bernard Kouchner met with New Forces leader Guillaume Soro, now Ivory Coast's Prime Minister, in Mali. Soro was assured of France's continued and unwavering support for the Ouagadougou Accord (*AFP* 2007). The new accord was meant to signal the end of the civil war, the start of a new national reconciliation process and another rescheduling of a presidential election for 2009. But with mounting frustration on all sides, the elections were postponed a total of six times until 31 October 2010, and the north maintained its parallel government and armed forces (Förster 2010).

The first round of the long awaited presidential election was held on 31 October 2010, contested by longstanding rivals Gbagbo (Presidential Majority, LMP), Ouattara (*RDR*) and former President Bédié (*PDCI*). Turnout was high at around 80 per cent of 5.7 million registered voters. Gbagbo secured 38 per cent of the vote compared with 32 per cent for Ouattara and 25 per cent for Bédié (ICG 2011a). Although Gbagbo gained the highest proportion of votes, the result fell far short of the 50 per cent necessary to win in the first round. The Gbagbo camp immediately began to voice doubts about the credibility of the result (*AFNWS* 2010). On 8 November, Bédié withdrew from the race and endorsed Ouattara for the second round of elections to be held on 28 November (*BBC Monitoring Africa* 2010). The backdrop to this was vitriolic and unrestrained verbal attacks by campaign organizers on both sides and violent clashes and several deaths across the country. Despite a veneer of professionalism, text messages and films of atrocities committed by both sides deliberately incited ethnic hatreds. The Gbagbo campaign focused on Ouattara's alleged complicity with the 2002 rebellion in trying to make the election a referendum on the civil war (ICG 2011c).

On 2 December 2010, under UN protection and certification, the electoral commission declared Ouattara the winner of the election with 54.1 per cent of the vote to Gbagbo's 45.9 per cent. This was after days of wrangling behind the scenes in which electoral commission officials were physically prevented from declaring the result. The Gbagbo camp claimed that there had been massive fraud, violence and vote-rigging in the rebel-held north (ICG 2011c). The following day the President of the Constitutional Council personally intervened, stating that the electoral commission had failed to confirm the results within the required statutory period and that there had been irregularities, intimidation and violence in Ouattara strongholds in the centre and north of the country. Some 660,000 ballots, representing 16 per cent of votes cast, were subsequently cancelled. With these new results, Gbagbo was declared winner in what detractors labelled a 'constitutional coup', sparking angry demonstrations and the resumption of the political crisis. Gbagbo was sworn in as President on 4 December 2010 (ICG 2011c).

Throughout the month of December 2010, Gbagbo's security forces mounted a campaign of repression in the south to shut down demonstrations and terrorize opposition supporters into submission. This allegedly involved extrajudicial executions, indiscriminate murder, torture, rape and forced disappearances. Firstly this was against opposition party officials, then moving on to anyone with family names indicating connections with the Muslim north. In response, militias associated with the opposition sporadically attacked and killed members of the security forces (ICG 2011c). Spurred on by xenophobic propaganda against so-called foreign occupiers, Young Patriot militias loyal to Gbagbo resumed attacks on UNOCI peacekeepers (ICG 2011c, see Strauss 2011 for a detailed analysis of the dynamics of post-election violence from both sides). As the situation spiralled downwards, observers concluded that these events were emblematic of a concerted strategy by Gbagbo to remain in power whatever the result of the 2010 election (ICG 2011c).

Sarkozy issued a public ultimatum to Gbagbo on 17 December 2010 to step down, but afterwards remained publicly silent, leaving it to ECOWAS, the African Union (AU) and EU to lead the push for Gbagbo's departure. Sarkozy's hands-off approach in public was reportedly to avoid giving Gbagbo the opportunity to rally anti-French sentiment to his cause (Hall 2010). By making an ultimatum, however, Sarkozy had invested his own political standing and French prestige in Gbagbo's removal. By December 2010, French troops numbered only 950 and their mission had officially returned to protecting French and foreign nationals leaving the major responsibility for peace enforcement to the larger UN force of 7,500 (Hall 2010). Winner of the election, Ouattara, remained blockaded by pro-Gbagbo forces in his temporary headquarters in Abidjan under UN protection. Ouattara first pursued a diplomatic and political strategy of isolating Gbagbo internationally, trying to cut off his finances and attempting to wrest control of parts of the state administration (Banégas 2011: 461). The UN recognized Ouattara as the legitimate President on 23 December following similar declarations from the AU and ECOWAS.

In early February 2011, Ouattara was calling for a targeted military operation to remove Gbagbo from office. By 26 March, Gbagbo's Young Patriot supporters were again setting up checkpoints and patrolling the streets of Abidjan with clubs and machetes. Reports also surfaced that Gbagbo loyalists were readying heavy weaponry for use in the city. The UN Security Council was under international pressure for a new resolution banning the use of heavy weapons. Sarkozy announced that behind the scenes France had indeed prepared such a draft resolution, which was now being considered. This would open the way for the use of force by UN and French forces to remove Gbagbo's defences (Nebehay 2011).

The New Forces, now renamed the Republican Forces of Côte d'Ivoire (RFCI) launched a nationwide offensive against Gbagbo's government on 28 March 2011. On 30 March, UN Security Council Resolution 1975 recognized Ouattara as legitimate President and authorized UN-mandated forces to take all necessary measures to protect civilians, especially from the use of heavy weaponry in Abidjan (UN Security Council 2011). On the same day the RFCI captured

San Pedro on the southern coast of the country. On 2 and 3 April mass violence with up to 1000 deaths was reported as northern rebel forces now openly backing Ouattara captured the city of Duekoue in the country's volatile southwest (Bellamy and Williams 2011: 834). The following day French and UN troops secured the airport in Abidjan as fighters gathered around the city. On 4 April, Ouattara's supporters advanced after heavy fighting and surrounded Gbagbo's home in the Presidential palace the following day. Most of the government's regular security forces and police had melted away by this time. Only the hardcore loyalist elements of the Presidential guard and Young Patriots remained to defend Gbagbo (Wallis 2011).

UN Secretary-General Ban Ki-Moon instructed UN-mandated forces to take all necessary measures to protect civilians from Gbagbo's heavy weapons on 5 April 2011. Ban (in *News Press* 2011) said that the security situation was deteriorating rapidly, which was '"a direct consequence of Mr. Gbagbo's refusal to relinquish power and allow a peaceful transition to President Ouattara"'. The country had again been plunged into violence as a result with a heavy toll on the civilian population. Gbagbo supporters had opened fire on UN peacekeepers with mortars, rocket-propelled grenades and heavy machine-guns. It remained unclear how many civilians had been killed by heavy weapons fire, although it was estimated that 500 had died in Abidjan since the election. Any actions by UN mandated forces would be for the purposes of self-defence and protection of the population in line with the Security Council Resolution (*News Press* 2011). Removing Gbagbo's heavy weapons would, however, also remove his last defences from the RFCI. Bellamy and Williams (2011: 835) note that this 'use of force by UN peacekeepers and French troops blurred the lines between human protection and regime change'. This drew protests from Russia, India and Brazil that UN actions exceeded the mandate under Resolution 1975.

The final rebel advance on the presidential palace was shortly preceded by a joint French and UN operation with French helicopter gunships taking out Gbagbo's heavy weapons and ammunition stockpiles with rocket fire (Roberts 2011). Just prior to Gbagbo's surrender, French helicopters destroyed a number of remaining armoured vehicles within the palace grounds and UN forces attacked residual pro-Gbagbo positions around the city. Gbagbo surrendered to the RFCI and was arrested on 11 April 2011, marking a decisive dénouement in Ivory Coast's twenty years of political turmoil (*BBC Monitoring Africa* 2011).

International media reports tended to be positive about the French role in bringing the Ivory Coast conflict to a conclusion. France had risked its reputation for humanitarian reasons under circumstances where success was far from certain. Under Sarkozy, France had undeniably 'taken back the initiative … and radically changed its image' with its leading role and decisive actions in Libya and Ivory Coast. Sarkozy had pledged during his election campaign to increase France's influence on the world stage. This was consistent with the French identity narrative of pursuing *grandeur* through meaningful action in the world. According to some commentators, France indeed appeared to have '"scored some points"' with regards to its '"position in the world"' (Heisbourg in Rater 2011).

Other reports praised France by pointing out that 'the Ivorian despot would still be defying election results and waging civil war were it not for French military intervention' (*The Christian Science Monitor* 2011). An editorial in *The Times* (2011) said that Sarkozy may have 'many domestic critics. But his role in international affairs is big, beneficial and much to France's credit'. The French intervention in Ivory Coast was 'far from an exercise in imperial power'. It was in the service of the norms of liberal international order. Its intent was a defence of the civilian population of Ivory Coast from an illegitimate ruler that likely prevented a humanitarian catastrophe. While French intervention policy since 2002 had changed in reaction to events on the ground, each phase was clearly predicated on liberal order norms. Despite criticisms that French policy intentions in Ivory Coast were at times indecisive and ambiguous, its main motive remained consistent with the evolution of French Africa policy outlined in Chapter 3: the pursuit of a meaningful sense of *grandeur* through the promotion of liberal norms in France's historic sphere of responsibility.

Other French preoccupations were also reflected in the positive media commentary. *The Times* (2011) also noted that Sarkozy's handling of the crisis 'combined decisiveness and determination to make an effective diplomatic force of the UN'. The French view that multilateral institutions are a power multiplier for France is evident in Sarkozy's working within the UN Security Council to secure a Resolution that would protect civilians while allowing Gbagbo to be forced from power. This action had served Africa well and provided a wider lesson to the international community that such crises were 'better confronted than ignored' (*The Times* 2011). It was lethargy by major powers that had compounded the humanitarian catastrophes in Bosnia and Rwanda. This was a particular lesson for France, from which it had clearly learned. With Rwanda, not only had France 'failed to protect a threatened population from genocide: it aided the wrong side' (*The Times* 2011). Sarkozy had shown a resolve and determination to correct past mistakes and inglorious past episodes. This demonstrates the importance of the emotional dimension of the prestige motive in the French intervention. It was primarily past-oriented in transforming feelings of disgrace and humiliation back to self-respect.

On 30 November 2011, Gbagbo was turned over to the International Criminal Court (ICC) to face four counts of crimes against humanity, including murder, rape and persecution. This hardened the position of Gbagbo's associates who announced their suspension of all participation in reconciliation processes and boycotted the legislative elections of 11 December. Members of the extreme wing of Gbagbo's *FPI* went into exile in neighbouring Ghana where they remain isolated but still capable of disrupting the post-war reconciliation process (ICG 2011b). At the time of writing in early 2012, the situation remains fragile in Ivory Coast with a population awash with weapons and ammunition, and a fragmented security vacuum as defeated pro-Gbagbo forces abandoned their posts with the

RFCI yet to be integrated into a cohesive command and organizational structure. Ouattara has also forged strong ties with France and the international community, which played a decisive role in his victory (ICG 2011a).

## Conclusion

My purpose in this chapter was to consider a contemporary case study of state failure and intervention in the present liberal international order of the early twenty-first century using the interpretive framework developed in Chapter 3. The idea that Ivory Coast was a failed state is less controversial compared with previous chapters as the type of disorder fits within the generally-accepted pattern of post-Cold War state failure. The evidence presented and conclusions drawn from this chapter do however support the book's argument that even in the present period, interventions to restore order in the periphery are undertaken primarily for prestige-based motivations. The intervention in Ivory Coast can be understood as a normative threat to French expectations for liberal order in its historic West African sphere of responsibility. Against a backdrop of xenophobic and divisive identity politics, the 2002 coup, civil war, threat to the safety of foreign nationals and partition of the country, were a gross breach of the norms of liberal international order.

The post-Cold War pattern of international order is homogenising and solidarist. Leading Western actors and international institutions view convergence toward liberal-democratic statehood and 'good' governance practices as normative for all states. The thresholds for state failure and permissible intervention are therefore low relative to the previous pluralistic international orders considered in the book. This was even lower in the case of France in Ivory Coast where a defence agreement provided for a troop deployment of around 500 personnel at a permanent French military base. The unipolar international system of the early twenty-first century does not feature intense strategic competition at the system-level. Unlike the book's previous case studies, there were no strategic constraints on a French intervention in Ivory Coast. Indeed, French actions were welcomed by Washington, many African states and the international community more broadly as contributing to regional stability. This is despite earlier strategic tensions in the region with Nigeria, and more recent attention on West Africa by the United States and China in the 2000s.

Unlike the other status quo powers considered in the book, prestige is an explicit part of the French identity narrative. The purpose of French foreign and security policy in the Fifth Republic has been the evocation of national *grandeur* and an elevated sense of global standing. Prestige, as an end in itself, is a major motive for French action in the world. The mid-1990s policy failures in Rwanda and Zaire that implicated France in the genocide and humanitarian catastrophes that followed were profoundly damaging to France's reputation in the world, and therefore to its self-respect and sense of national honour. When similar dynamics of ethnic conflict appeared in Ivory Coast in 2002, the threat to French ontological security was acute. But the tactics adopted in the service of prestige had changed with the end of the Cold War and shift to a solidarist liberal international order. French tactics in the early 2000s, exemplified in the Ivory Coast intervention, moved to the pursuit of *grandeur* through the promotion of liberal order norms. The insistence that the crisis must be resolved according to liberal norms was clear and consistent in French policy throughout the episode.

The chapter has demonstrated that each theoretical dimension of the prestige motive was evident in this case to varying but convincing degrees. After the shame of Rwanda, the normative threat to France in its area of historic responsibility made the disorder in Ivory Coast an acute reputational concern for Paris. Allusions to events in Rwanda were made by French policy-makers throughout the Ivory Coast crisis. There was some ambiguity in its early stages as to whether French intervention policy was limited to evacuating foreign nationals or if it was intended to prevent the situation from deteriorating into a humanitarian disaster that would also destabilize Ivory Coast's fragile neighbours. As the gravity of the situation quickly became clear, French policy moved more firmly to a robust but politically neutral posture of preventing large-scale violence and stabilizing the situation pending a multilateral African peacekeeping force and a political settlement. These actions were consistent with liberal order norms, French reputational concerns and ontological security requirements.

While a sense of unease among French policy elites had been growing about the potential for Ivory Coast to descend into a Rwanda-style 'catastrophe', it was during the 2003–4 period that the emotional dimension of prestige was most powerfully engaged. The evidence suggests that the failure of the 2003 Linas-Marcoussis agreement and subsequent intimidation and harassment of French nationals in Ivory Coast was felt as an insult to national honour. Rather than resolving the conflict, the peace agreement had turned out to be a humiliating failure, which aroused negative emotions of anger and frustration toward the Gbagbo government. Linked to national honour, the motive of retribution is also clear in the disproportionate French response to the air attack on its military base at Bouaké and the heavy handed use of force against civilians to quell the anti-French violence in Abidjan. These events also raised instrumental concerns for French credibility in Africa and other turbulent regions of the world where its forces were engaged. Being shown to be unable to control the situation and allowing its soldiers to be killed and citizens attacked with impunity could give rise to similar risks elsewhere in the world.

French actions in the final stages of the Ivory Coast conflict in 2011 remained consistent with liberal international order norms and French identity and ontological security requirements. The ontological security of France relies on its capacity and willingness to take action and wield influence in the world. In its final stages in 2011, France acted through the UN Security Council in maximizing its impact on the outcome of the Ivory Coast crisis, while retaining international legitimacy with the justification of protecting civilians.

# Chapter 7
# Conclusions

This study has used the contemporary problem frame of state 'failure' to shed light on an enduring question in international politics: why do great powers intervene in disordered states on the periphery? This is a perennial puzzle because such disorder is rarely a direct security threat to the great powers of the international society, and in most cases rational interest-based alternatives to military intervention are available to policy-makers. These types of interventions in the periphery are also clearly distinguishable from conquest or colonization because their purpose is not to absorb the territory or extinguish the sovereignty of the targeted state. Rather, interventions in the periphery seek to build or restore viable sovereign states in conformity with norms of appropriate statehood in the international society. Why status quo great powers choose to undertake this task through the use of military force has been the subject of this book.

The book has two main conclusions. First, what great powers perceive as disorder from the periphery, or state failure in the current period, cannot be adequately understood through a narrow materialist lens. State failure is not a condition unique to the post-Cold War era that can be defined by empirical indicators. It is a normative threat to international order that is interpreted in historical context. This was established in Chapter 2 initially through a critique of current empirical methods of defining state failure and associated concepts of fragility and collapse. Chapter 2 demonstrated that an amorphous, context-specific set of shifting empirical indicators could not plausibly define the concept of state failure. This finding suggested that the more deeply held assumptions inherent in the orthodox view of state failure were also flawed. Two important points were drawn from the theoretical and philosophical critique that followed in Chapter 2.

The first was that state failure cannot primarily be the result of a breakdown in formal institutions of governance within a state because institutions are epiphenomenal. They can only transit the effects of the conditions that gave rise to them and that sustain them. State failure must then be relative to these conditions within the international society. The second point drawn from this critique was that state failure cannot be the result of a breakdown in the domestic social contract between state and citizen. This is because state cohesion and legitimacy do not derive from the instrumental provision of public goods. Effective statehood relies on a shared bond of value consensus or cultural identity that precedes any imagined or contrived social contract. The case studies in the book illustrate that in each historical period, disordered states on the periphery lacked the basis for centred political community necessary to meet the norms of legitimate statehood laid down by the leading actors of international society. Indeed, an important pattern evident throughout the book is that external pressures for state transformation resulted in the types of empirical disorder that engage the attention of great powers as a normative threat.

In drawing these lines of critique together, I concluded in Chapter 2 that normative beliefs about appropriate statehood are driven by ideational and material changes that are largely independent of the empirical conditions within peripheral states. For instance, the contemporary failed state phenomenon is a product of the change to international ordering principles in the post-Cold War era that views a convergence towards good governance on the liberal-democratic model as normative for all states. Shifts in international order norms are relative to changes in the structural conditions of the international system. The current solidarist liberal international order has only been possible due to US strategic unipolarity after the collapse of the competing Soviet model. The book has traced this historical pattern back over more than a century through three international orders and system structures. The book has shown that the meaning of state failure in any historical period is judged by policy-makers against the pattern of international order promoted and legitimized by the great powers of the day.

A crucial observation from the ontological security literature canvassed in Chapters 1 and 3 is that being recognized as a source and exemplar of international order is an integral and meaningful part of the identity narrative of status quo great powers. Rather than their physical security or material interests, disordered states on the periphery threaten the ontological security of great powers by challenging their role identity as the source and guarantor of international order in areas for which they carry responsibility. The normative threat to international order posed by failed states directly impinges on the ontological security and identity needs of status quo great powers.

International order, the distribution of capabilities and ontological security were expounded systematically in Chapter 3 as providing the conceptual foundations for understanding state failure and intervention in the periphery. The chapter defined these concepts and the dynamics between them before locating them in case-specific and historical context to provide an interpretive framework to evaluate the book's case studies. I concluded Chapter 3 by arguing that the prestige motive is the 'three-pronged' linkage that connects these large and diffuse influences into a concrete policy of intervention to restore order. Prestige has been considered in the book across three dimensions: the normative (reputation), instrumental (credibility) and emotional (national honour).

This leads into the book's second main conclusion. Armed interventions to restore order in the periphery are undertaken by great powers primarily for prestige-based motives. The prestige motive, as conceptualized in Chapter 3, is central to understanding intervention in the periphery across different historical settings and patterns of international order. There is an intrinsic association for status quo great powers between prestige and upholding international order norms in geographical areas they consider to be their responsibility. From a relational perspective, disorder in these areas challenges the reputation of such powers for maintaining order and also engages their more instrumental concerns for credibility in other parts of the world. More importantly, though, a state's perception of its reputation among its peers deeply affects the way it feels about itself – its sense of self-respect and national honour. The evidence presented in the book has shown that normative threats from the periphery are experienced emotionally by political leaders in the form of anger or frustration. These emotions are typically expressed as an affront or insult to the national honour of a great power at the hands of a lower status actor. The book has demonstrated that these emotions quickly extend to humiliation and the desire for retribution if normative threats result in tangible consequences.

There were some variations in its emphasis throughout the case studies and the dimensions of prestige engaged at any given time were relative to events on the ground in the failed state in question. But prestige remained a constant across all three cases including in the current period. This finding is a major challenge to the orthodoxy in the failed state literature in which transnational security threats or humanitarian imperatives are viewed as the main reasons for these types of interventions. As I have shown in this book, these may be part of the objectives or justifications for failed state interventions, but as motives they are indirect. Harmful transnational activity that strikes at the core, or the potential for a humanitarian catastrophe, ultimately motivates great powers to intervene because it threatens their ontological security. It creates a gap between real-world events and how a great power needs to see itself consistent with its identity narrative. This gap needs to be closed to restore a meaningful sense of national honour.

The findings of the study also make a useful contribution to the emerging literature that seeks to develop prestige-related themes from a constructivist perspective. Where it is considered at all in IR theorizing, prestige has generally been used only in an instrumental sense as credibility. Credibility remained an important motive in each of the case studies examined here, but by considering the normative and emotional dimensions of prestige, I have been able to show that prestige is a much more complex and multifaceted concept. The emotional dimension of prestige was particularly important in each case study and illustrates the importance in political science of taking 'non-rational' motivations seriously. In each case, the negative emotional aspects of national honour, such as insult, humiliation and retribution were past-oriented. The military actions that were taken, especially in the British and French cases, were in part intended to reverse a past shame or humiliation by restoring self-respect. In the United States' case, military action was taken to avoid a possible future humiliation.

Glory, as the positive emotional dimension of prestige was weakest and most difficult to demonstrate throughout the case studies in the book. It was evident in the British case in the nineteenth century, particularly in the disposition of the press. Needless to say, there was no glory to be celebrated by Washington in South Vietnam. Because of the lack of archival sources, expressions of glory were also difficult to discern in the French case. It is a reasonable assumption from this that in an emotional sense, restoring order on the periphery is more about reversing negative emotions rather than something to be glorified in a positive sense. This supports the proposition made in the introduction and evident throughout the empirical material in the book that political leaders only undertake these interventions reluctantly and belatedly in areas where they perceive a burden of responsibility.

## Patterns across the Cases

From the British perspective considered in Chapter 4, Egypt's state failure in 1882 can be understood as a normative threat to stable expectations for international order in the Near East. Britain saw itself as the primary arbiter of international order in this area because of the importance of the Ottoman Empire and Egypt to its position in India. Urabi's revolt first breached the pattern of international order represented by the 'standard of civilization' by removing the legitimate government in Egypt recognized by the international society. As increasing external pressure was applied, the deterioration from political unrest to violent civil disorder threatening the lives and property of British subjects was a further and irrevocable breach of the standard. The disorder in Egypt presented no direct threat to the British Empire and a rational alternative to military action was available. Britain could have come to terms with the Urabi regime as the Continental Powers and Chairman of the Suez Canal Company had already done. The evidence shows that Prime Minister Gladstone did not believe that the Suez Canal was under any genuine threat unless a foreign intervention was mounted. Urabi also pledged to respect Egypt's international financial obligations, and indeed, only defaulted on these when Britain and France increased the external pressure with gunboat diplomacy.

The state failure of South Vietnam considered in Chapter 5 can be understood as a normative threat to Washington's requirements for international order in the contested Southeast Asian region. The RVN regimes failed to maintain even minimal levels of administrative competence and territorial control. Nor were they able to effectively carry out rural pacification against the NLF. The steady deterioration in the political stability and military effectiveness of the Saigon regime was an acute risk to US Cold War objectives of maintaining an independent, non-communist state in South Vietnam. More broadly, the collapse of the RVN was a fundamental challenge to US expectations for a stable, non-communist 'free world' order in the postcolonial periphery. The insurgency in South Vietnam presented no direct security threat to the United States, but under the ideological and strategic bipolarity of the Cold War, much of the US policy community considered that the 'loss' of South Vietnam to communism would imperil the 'free world' strategic position. There were a number of prominent critics of Johnson administration policy such as Vice President Humphrey, Senator Mike Mansfield and Undersecretary of State, George Ball. Each predicted the problems that would befall the United States in Vietnam. They offered a rational alternative to the intervention by arguing that both America's position in the world, and the administration's domestic standing, would be better served by negotiating its way out of South Vietnam without a ground intervention. Any short term losses to US credibility would be trivial compared with the costs to prestige that would be incurred if the greatest military power in the world was unable to defeat a guerrilla insurgency.

The 2002 state failure in Ivory Coast can be understood as a normative threat to French expectations for liberal international order in its historic African sphere of responsibility. Ivory Coast presented no direct security threat to France in a traditional sense. The state failure in Ivory Coast, characterized by xenophobic identity politics, civil war, ethnic violence and human rights atrocities, was however, a gross breach of the norms of liberal international order. The room for a rational interest-based policy alternative to a French intervention in Ivory Coast is smallest of the three cases considered in the book. A plausible alternative would have been to maintain the Socialist Party stance of non-intervention in Africa with the caveat of small, targeted operations to evacuate French nationals and others that wished to leave. But the looming spectre of Rwanda ensured that a hands-off policy would have been difficult to maintain for any French government as the situation in Ivory Coast descended into ethnic violence and atrocities.

The thresholds for permissible intervention were high in the pluralist international orders considered in Chapters 4 and 5. In Chapter 4, the rebel military in Egypt circumvented the legitimate government under international law in a revolutionary capture of the state. This met the accepted threshold for military intervention to restore order in the European international society of the nineteenth century. The postcolonial international order considered in Chapter 5 held the most stringent requirements for permissible intervention. According to the UN Charter, armed intervention was only permissible in the case of overt external aggression. Despite the ambiguity of the conflict in South Vietnam, US policy-makers were always very careful throughout the entire episode to emphasize that the insurgency was driven by external aggression from Hanoi and Beijing rather than by internal South Vietnamese disaffection with the inept and corrupt Saigon government.

By contrast to these historical examples, the threshold for failed state interventions in the current liberal international order is very low. The current solidarist international order is densely packed with rules and thick normative claims which mean that it is easily breached by peripheral states. The UN and major powers are also under increasing pressure to enforce the emerging norm in the international community of a responsibility to protect civilians from violence. The threshold for intervention was even lower in the case of Ivory Coast because France maintained a permanent military presence under a bilateral defence agreement. Different to the two historical cases, however, French military actions were not taken on behalf of the existing government, but in the service of the appropriate principles and procedures of liberal statehood. This demonstrates the difference between pluralist and solidarist international orders. Pluralist patterns of order are concerned primarily with state behaviour and its effect in the international society.

They hold only minimal requirements for state identity. Solidarist international orders, on the other hand, are primarily concerned with appropriate state identity, which, it is believed, will then inform responsible behaviour.

Each case study also lends support to the proposition made in Chapter 2 that not all political communities can be socialized to the prevailing norms of international order at any given time. The book has shown that external pressures for state transformation in conformity with international order norms weakens existing political structures and can result in the types of disorder perceived by status quo great powers as a normative threat. In the Egypt case, the modernizing pressures of industrialization and nationalism contributed to the breakdown of the hereditary Khedival autocracy. Pressures for modern industry and infrastructure led to a debt crisis, foreign interference and local resentment. The growing pressures of nationalism led to an Arab revolt spearheaded by the military against imperial Turkish rule and European interference. Arab proto-nationalism as the basis for effective political community in Egypt could not be realized under the institutions of Ottoman suzerainty.

South Vietnam was an 'artificial' state created by Cold War strategic and ideological bipolarity. Its existence was supported by the US belief drawn from modernization theory that the bases of nation-statehood in the postcolonial Third World were performance-based rather than primordial or constitutional. This proved to be a dismal failure. There was no coherent basis for statehood in South Vietnam separate from the remainder of the country. It was noted, particularly by Ambassador Taylor, that the unfavourable political culture and social dynamics in South Vietnam would work against the consolidation of an effective state even in the absence of the NLF insurgency.

In the book's third case study, the intense normative pressures of a solidarist liberal international order directly contributed to the political instability and violent unrest in Ivory Coast. Pressures for democratization in the early 1990s profoundly destabilized the postcolonial Ivorian settlement maintained under founding President Houphouët-Boigny. The breakdown of Houphouët-Boigny's politics of patronage unleashed a virulent debate claiming that French paternalism and Ivory Coast's postcolonial political economy had never allowed Ivorians to establish an authentic and independent national identity. Constitutional and democratic processes in Ivory Coast then produced a series of increasingly xenophobic and illiberal outcomes that denied civil rights to large parts of the population and resident foreigners. This illustrates the point argued in Chapter 2 that institutions of liberal-democratic governance will not deliver the outcomes anticipated if they are incompatible with underlying political cultures.

The Egypt and Vietnam cases were mounted against a backdrop of intense strategic competition and both were subject to heavy prudential constraints on decision-making. In the multipolar system of the late-nineteenth century, the Egypt crisis was part of the broader Eastern Question of Ottoman decline and subject to the scrutiny and interference of all the great powers. To assuage prudential concerns, Britain first sought the intervention of Turkey as legitimate suzerain, and then aimed for a European-mandated intervention before finally exploring the possibility of joint intervention with France and Italy. It was only after all other options had failed that a unilateral British intervention was undertaken. In the bipolar Cold War system, Washington's prudential concerns were focused on the parameters of armed intervention. Any proposed military action needed to be kept limited to the extent that it would avoid a wider war with China or escalation to a general war with the Soviet Union while achieving US objectives in South Vietnam. Both of these approaches were consistent with the pressures of domestic politics and each state's identity narrative. The British and American publics required both peace and strength. By contrast, in the unipolar international system of the early twenty-first century, there was no evidence of any strategic constraints on French military action in West Africa. French actions were generally welcomed by other interested states as contributing to regional stability. This is despite earlier tensions with Nigeria and the greater recent attention paid to West Africa in the 2000s by China and the United States. Residual historic tensions were perhaps reflected in Nigeria's refusal to participate in the ECOWAS peacekeeping mission to Ivory Coast.

The case study chapters have demonstrated that the three dimensions of the prestige motive – normative, emotional and instrumental – were evident to varying but convincing degrees across the different historical periods and international orders considered. For Britain, the military revolt in Egypt challenged its reputation as the primary arbiter of order in the Near East. For US policy-makers, the threat of the collapse of South Vietnam to communist insurgency eroded its reputation for resolve in maintaining a non-communist international order in Southeast Asia. Again differing from the two historical cases, France entered the Ivory Coast crisis nursing a profoundly damaged reputation because of the recent failure of its policies in Rwanda and the DRC. When the situation in Ivory Coast began to display similar dynamics after September 2002, it became an acute reputational concern for Paris. Being a source of international order in geographical areas for which they carry responsibility is a meaningful part of the identity narrative of status quo great powers. Normative threats to international order in these areas will threaten their ontological security.

Because of this, disorder from the periphery evokes negative emotional responses from the political leaders of great powers because it disrupts stable expectations for the future. In Egypt, the disorder fostered by Urabi's rebellion against the Khedivate was experienced as an insult to Britain's reputation as the leading status quo actor with primary responsibility for stability in the area. It was a lack of due respect from an actor without international status. The emotional dimension of prestige became more acute with the Alexandria massacre in June 1882. Along with the failed ultimatum to Urabi's regime in May, this was profoundly damaging to British national honour. The subsequent naval bombardment of Alexandria was disproportionate to the scale of the preceding 'massacre', which was likely exaggerated by British representatives on the ground. The bombardment was openly justified as retribution. These factors point to the authenticity of revenge taken as a non-rational, past-oriented motive dedicated to transforming feelings of humiliation back to self-respect.

The emotional dimension of prestige played out differently in the case of the United States and South Vietnam. US policy elites were acutely sensitive to the personal and political humiliation of 'losing' Vietnam to communism. This was particularly evident for President Johnson and Defense Secretary McNamara. Ironically, an important aspect of the prestige-based motive for the South Vietnam intervention was to avoid the potential humiliation of seeing the state collapse and be taken over by the communists. This was supported by repeated statements, made both publicly and in private, that South Vietnam could not be abandoned for reasons of national honour. Across three administrations, Washington had made a commitment to defend South Vietnam from communism. It would be dishonourable to break that commitment and shameful to leave the people of the country to the terror and repression that communist rule would surely bring.

For France in Ivory Coast, the emotional dimension of prestige was displayed in a similar pattern to the Britain-Egypt case. Resentment increased in the pro-Gbagbo south of Ivory Coast as greater French military pressure was applied in stabilizing the north-south partition of the country pending a political settlement. This erupted during 2003 into violent anti-French sentiment that began to strongly engage the emotional dimension of prestige for France. It culminated with the air attack and killing of French troops in November 2004, the destruction of Ivory Coast's air force, and the subsequent French military actions taken against civilian protestors in Abidjan. The failure of the Linas-Marcoussis Accord of January 2003 and the violence against France aroused negative emotions of anger and frustration among French political leaders. Similar to the Egypt case, the disproportionate French response to the killing of its soldiers and its heavy-handed use of deadly force in suppressing civilian protestors in Abidjan demonstrated the authenticity of the revenge motive.

In each case in the book, the imperative to be seen to be able to control the situation and restore order also raised instrumental concerns for credibility in other parts of the world. In the British case, policy elites in London came to the belief that armed intervention to restore order in Egypt was also required to maintain credibility abroad, particularly to head off any further challenges to British rule in India in the immediate decades after the Mutiny. For the United States, preventing the collapse of South Vietnam was indelibly linked with the domino theory and US global credibility in Cold War context. In the French case, credibility was implicated in two ways. First, allowing an armed rebellion to overthrow the legitimately elected government of Ivory Coast might encourage similar political instability elsewhere in francophone Africa. Second, allowing its soldiers to be killed and French citizens to be attacked with impunity could give rise to similar risks in other turbulent regions of the world where France was engaged.

While the primary motives behind each military intervention in the book were prestige-based, the objectives of each were consistent with the pattern of order in the international society. In Egypt, Britain sought to restore the legitimate authority of the Khedive, reinstate sound financial governance to ensure Egypt's international obligations would be met, and more vaguely, to assist in the prudent development of self-governing institutions. The United States sought to maintain a free, independent and stable South Vietnam consistent with the provisions of the 1954 Geneva Accords and the UN Charter. France sought to stabilize Ivory Coast by maintaining its territorial integrity and preventing ethnic violence to provide the conditions for a comprehensive peace settlement and free and fair democratic elections. Of the three cases considered in the book, the French intervention appears to be the most successful in achieving its objectives at the time of writing in 2012, although its duration was longer than anticipated. The French actions in Ivory Coast may provide some useful lessons for future responses to state failure especially when compared with Anglo-American approaches that focus on governance and capacity-building.

## Implications for the Future

A number of current and longer-term implications may be drawn from the study. The first is that interventions in the periphery in states deemed to be failed are unlikely to be more than partly successful in achieving their objectives. The book has shown that interventions in the periphery are driven by international order considerations and the domestic political circumstances of great powers. Intervening powers do not genuinely attempt to address the structural conditions of state weakness in targeted states. A fundamental incongruence therefore exists between externally-generated intervention objectives and local conditions in failed states. The evidence from the book's historical case studies suggests that this incongruence leads to either the failure and humiliating withdrawal of the intervention when it becomes clear its objectives cannot be achieved, or an indefinite presence and administrative guidance until the structure of the international system and pattern of international order is altered. Even with the current case, ostensibly the most successful considered in the book, the situation in Ivory Coast remains fragile in early 2012 and France retains an indefinite troop presence. Policy-makers should expect mixed results from interventions in the periphery and have few illusions about the likelihood that successful or timely exits can be made. Prudence strongly suggests that great powers should not become directly involved in the internal problems of weak states given the unpropitious chances of success. Rather, they should seek under most circumstances to quarantine or address the risks of state failure externally. This will likely be the trend in the longer-term if the international system moves towards a multipolar structure and pluralist pattern of order in the twenty-first century.

In the short to medium-term, however, the relatively successful French approach to state failure examined in Chapter 6 may provide some useful and transferrable lessons for the future. Rather than regime change or building formal institutions of governance, the French intervention sought to quell the violence and stabilize the situation pending an indigenous political process mediated by regional leaders and organizations. French actions in Ivory Coast, however self-serving, were able to reasonably satisfy humanitarian imperatives, while also allowing for a representative political process to eventually take place. And as I established in Chapter 2, it is political structures appropriate to the society in question that is most important for viable statehood. Formal institutions of governance are secondary and derivative. Local political cultures and processes must be worked through despite their inadequacies, rather than being sidelined as corrupt and ineffective. This may not always lead to liberal-democracy as the most appropriate form of state (see Englebert and Tull 2008, Kaplan 2008 on this approach more generally). But the imperative for democracy will naturally diminish in importance in a future pluralist order where stable international behaviour will be valued over state identity.

To reiterate, the study suggests that pluralist orders hold stringent requirements for state behaviour in the international society but minimal requirements for identity. Pluralist international orders are the preserve of multipolar or bipolar system structures and feature formidable strategic constraints on state decision-making and action. The normative criteria giving substance to the pattern of international order will be contested and open to interpretation. Thresholds for both state failure and permissible intervention will therefore be high relative to a solidarist international order. Solidarist international orders hold stringent requirements for both state identities and behaviours. These will reflect the deontological claims of the hegemon and its close allies. In a solidarist international order underwritten by strategic unipolarity, there is less room for norm contestation and low thresholds for state failure and permissible intervention to restore order.

The longer-term patterns identified in the study suggest that reputational pressures on Western status quo powers to promote liberal norms are likely to increase as international order becomes more contested with the likely evolution toward multipolarity in the twenty-first century. This is because the rise of authoritarian and postcolonial great powers will challenge the deeply-held assumption that a global liberal-democratic order on the Western model is normative for all states (Gat 2007). This will be an acute and visceral threat to the ontological security of status quo Western powers that will impinge directly on their prestige requirements across the three dimensions considered in the study. There will be intense pressure to respond to the pluralist challenge by promoting liberal international order norms in the periphery. Running counter to these pressures, however, the book demonstrates that the objectives of interventions in the periphery are less likely to be achieved successfully where international order norms are contested. The evolution from a solidarist to pluralist order is therefore likely to produce greater pressures for armed interventions by Western states in circumstances where success is highly uncertain, along with greater multipolar competition and attendant strategic risks and constraints.

Entering the second decade of the twenty-first century, the global distribution of capabilities appears to be shifting irrevocably away from the West (Bell 2007,

National Intelligence Council 2008). China's continued economic rise and military modernization is seemingly inexorable. Russia and India are increasingly assertive in pressing their claims on the world and regional stages. The United States is mired in a series of interlocking problems that suggests a status-quo power in long-term relative decline (Haas 2008: 46–7, Buzan 2011: 6). The country is deep in economic recession and with an unsustainable fiscal position that both sides of politics seem incapable of solving. The Obama administration has withdrawn US combat forces from George W. Bush's Iraq misadventure as civil unrest, political instability and terrorist violence continue to plague the country. Washington has also pledged to withdraw its troops from Afghanistan in 2014 while a bloody counterinsurgency war against the Taliban continues to rage with no end in sight. The desirability and sustainability of the liberal model embodied by the United States has come under increasing contestation (Buzan 2011: 10–12). Washington is now less able to translate its military preponderance into diplomatic influence on many important international issues (Haas 2008: 47). Added to these concerns is a complex and evolving global security context of intense competition over energy and other strategic natural resources that are often located in chronically unstable regions, and dangerous climate change and the potential for mass movements of displaced peoples.

If, as present trajectories suggest, the structure of the international system moves toward multipolarity, there will be greater acceptance of heterogeneity in state identities. The numbers of 'failed' states in such an international system will therefore be fewer. In a multipolar system, international order norms will be oriented toward regulating state behaviour rather than constituting state forms. A pluralist international order will be predicated on the stable and predictable behaviour of states with less concern for their regime type. Thresholds for permissible intervention will again become much higher than in the present solidarist order. New descriptors for state failure may be found. State weakness will likely be of greatest concern to major powers if close to home or located in regions subject to strategic competition. Elsewhere, disorderly weak states will attract less great power attention and resources. As described in Chapter 3, the nature of international order in a future multipolar system will be that of a 'civil' association rather than an 'enterprise' association. Recent research confirms, for example, that 'Chinese elites reject the sort of solidarism that would result in most of the world's leading states becoming democratic' (Lynch 2007: 703). This pluralism will be buttressed by authoritarian and postcolonial great powers that do not share a civilizational worldview comparable to that prevailing in the nineteenth century European international society considered in Chapter 4.

The collapse of Soviet communism is generally regarded as an epochal event portending a new era of human security in a global liberal-democratic order. A longer perspective suggests that the Cold War clash of ideologies was itself the historical anomaly. An emerging twenty-first century multipolar system will likely mark the return of a more typical pluralistic pattern of international politics (Gray 2003: 44, 59–61). The geographical zones of chronic state weakness lie mainly in resource rich areas of the world such as the Caucuses, Middle East, West Africa and Central Asia. These regions are likely to become the subject of energy security competition among a heterogeneous group of great powers that may be authoritarian such as China, illiberal democracies such as Russia, or post-colonial democracies as in India, in addition to the United States and other liberal-democratic actors. Stability in these regions will be of paramount concern for great power relations. The patterns identified in the study suggest that the current good governance concerns elicited by state failure, and the liberal state-building agenda, will diminish in importance as the international system returns to multipolarity and pluralism. For Western policy-makers, a closed mindset that assumes conflict over the nature of governance has ended will be ill-prepared to manage the shifting nature of state failure in an evolving multipolar international system, the ordering principles of which will be increasingly contested in the coming decades.

# References


Aboa, A. 2003. Loyalists march through Ivory Coast. *Associated Press*, 1 February [Online]. Available at: Factiva [accessed: 26 February 2012].

Adams, R. 2004. France's little Iraq: after the violence meted out by its former colonial masters, Ivory Coast is looking to the African Union. *The Guardian*, 21 December [Online]. Available at: Factiva [accessed: 26 February 2012].

Adebajo, A. 2008. Hegemony on a shoestring: Nigeria's post-Cold War foreign policy, in *Gulliver's Troubles: Nigeria's Foreign Policy after the Cold War*, edited by A. Adebajo and A.R. Mustapha. Scottsville, South Africa: University of KwaZulu-Natal Press, 1–37.

*Agence France-Presse* (*AFP*). 1999a. France condemns the use of force in Cote d'Ivoire, 24 December [Online]. Available at: Factiva [accessed: 26 February 2012].

*Agence France-Presse* (*AFP*). 1999b. Ivorian strongman urges departure of President, calls for unity, 25 December [Online]. Available at: Factiva [accessed: 26 February 2012].

*Agence France-Presse* (*AFP*). 1999c. Ousted Bedie flees Cote d'Ivoire on French plane, 26 December [Online]. Available at: Factiva [accessed: 26 February 2012].

*Agence France-Presse* (*AFP*). 2000a. Cote d'Ivoire's new strongman Guei could run for President, 2 January [Online]. Available at: Factiva [accessed: 26 February 2012].

*Agence France-Presse* (*AFP*). 2000b. 'Grave consequences' if legality not restored after I Coast vote – France, 25 October [Online]. Available at: Factiva [accessed: 26 February 2012].

*Agence France-Presse* (*AFP*). 2000c. France calls for 'full and calm' elections in Ivory Coast, 26 September [Online]. Available at: Factiva [accessed: 26 February 2012].

*Agence France-Presse* (*AFP*). 2000d. I Coast ruler warns foreigners not to intervene in Ouattara debate, 21 September [Online]. Available at: Factiva [accessed: 26 February 2012].

*Agence France-Presse* (*AFP*). 2000e. Paris says upcoming Ivory Coast election will be legal, 8 October [Online]. Available at: Factiva [accessed: 26 February 2012].

*Agence France-Presse* (*AFP*). 2000f. Up to Ivorians to decide on new presidential poll: French PM, 27 October [Online]. Available at: Factiva [accessed: 26 February 2012].

*Agence France-Presse* (*AFP*). 2002a. France makes all-out effort to end Ivory Coast's conflict, 13 December [Online]. Available at: Factiva [accessed: 26 February 2012].

*Agence France-Presse* (*AFP*). 2002b. France says will not interfere in Ivory Coast, 20 September [Online]. Available at: Factiva [accessed: 26 February 2012].

*Agence France-Presse* (*AFP*). 2002c. France to give Ivory Coast logistical support, 28 September [Online]. Available at: Factiva [accessed: 26 February 2012].

*Agence France-Presse* (*AFP*). 2002d. France wants to help ensure political solution to Ivorian Crisis: PM, 27 December [Online]. Available at: Factiva [accessed: 26 February 2012].

*Agence France-Presse* (*AFP*). 2002e. French deploy in Ivory Coast buffer zone to monitor ceasefire, 21 October [Online]. Available at: Factiva [accessed: 26 February 2012].

*Agence France-Presse* (*AFP*). 2002f. French military to step up activity in Ivory Coast, 13 December [Online]. Available at: Factiva [accessed: 26 February 2012].

*Agence France-Presse* (*AFP*). 2002g. French troop reinforcements arrive in Ivory Coast, 22 September [Online]. Available at: Factiva [accessed: 26 February 2012].

*Agence France-Presse* (*AFP*). 2002h. Fresh fighting in I. Coast as France pledges logistical support, 28 September [Online]. Available at: Factiva [accessed: 26 February 2012].

*Agence France-Presse* (*AFP*). 2002i. Ivorians enlist to fight, France to send more troops to Ivory Coast, 12 December [Online]. Available at: Factiva [accessed: 26 February 2012].

*Agence France-Presse* (*AFP*). 2002j. Ivory Coast activating Defense Accords with France amid conflict: PM, 28 September [Online]. Available at: Factiva [accessed: 26 February 2012].

*Agence France-Presse* (*AFP*). 2002k. Ivory Coast rebels warn French troops of all-out war, 22 December [Online]. Available at: Factiva [accessed: 26 February 2012].

*Agence France-Presse* (*AFP*). 2002l. Last French vehicle quits Bouake, 27 September [Online]. Available at: Factiva [accessed: 26 February 2012].

*Agence France-Presse* (*AFP*). 2002m. More French troops deploy in Ivory Coast to end three-month conflict, 15 December [Online]. Available at: Factiva [accessed: 26 February 2012].

*Agence France-Presse* (*AFP*). 2002n. Protestors storm France's main military base in Ivory Coast, 23 October [Online]. Available at: Factiva [accessed: 26 February 2012].

*Agence France-Presse* (*AFP*). 2003a. Chirac asks I. Coast's Gbagbo to restore calm, 26 January [Online]. Available at: Factiva [accessed: 26 February 2012].

*Agence France-Presse* (*AFP*). 2003b. France hands over charge of eastern Ivorian post to African peacekeepers, 15 March [Online]. Available at: Factiva [accessed: 26 February 2012].

*Agence France-Presse* (*AFP*). 2003c. I Coast president says peace talks must restore 'legal order', 15 January [Online]. Available at: Factiva [accessed: 26 February 2012].

*Agence France-Presse* (*AFP*). 2003d. Ivory Coast military rejects peace deal, ministries for rebels, 28 January [Online]. Available at: Factiva [accessed: 26 February 2012].

*Agence France-Presse* (*AFP*). 2003e. Ivory Coast President accepts French peace deal but with conditions, 7 February [Online]. Available at: Factiva [accessed: 26 February 2012].

*Agence France-Presse* (*AFP*). 2003f. Ivory Coast rebels rule out sacrifice to save peace deal, 4 February [Online]. Available at: Factiva [accessed: 26 February 2012].

*Agence France-Presse* (*AFP*). 2003g. Main points of the Marcoussis Agreement on Ivory Coast, 24 January [Online]. Available at: Factiva [accessed: 26 February 2012].

*Agence France-Presse* (*AFP*). 2004a. Ivorian military renews attacks on rebels: French government, 6 November [Online]. Available at: Factiva [accessed: 26 February 2012].

Agence France-Presse (*AFP*). 2004b. Ivory Coast engulfed in violence, French reinforcements expected, 7 November [Online]. Available at: Factiva [accessed: 26 February 2012].

*Agence France-Presse* (*AFP*). 2004c. Ivory Coast opposition supporters ignore calls for new demos, 29 March [Online]. Available at: Factiva [accessed: 26 February 2012].

*Agence France-Presse* (*AFP*). 2004d. 'There is no way he did not see us,' French Captain says of I. Coast attack, 11 November [Online]. Available at: Factiva [accessed: 26 February 2012].

*Agence France-Presse* (*AFP*). 2004e. Thousands of Europeans flee mob violence in Ivory Coast, 13 November [Online]. Available at: Factiva [accessed: 26 February 2012].

*Agence France-Presse* (*AFP*). 2004f. 'We are not at war with France,' says I Coast President as thousands flee, 11 November [Online]. Available at: Factiva [accessed: 26 February 2012].

*Agence France-Presse* (*AFP*). 2007. French Foreign Minister assures I Coast of full backing: Soro, 9 June [Online]. Available at: Factiva [accessed: 26 February 2012].

Agyeman, K. 2007. The effect of France's presidential win on West Africa. *Global Insight Daily Analysis*, 8 May [Online]. Available at: Factiva [accessed: 26 February 2012].

Alkopher, T.D. 2007. The role of rights in the social construction of wars: from the Crusades to humanitarian interventions. *Millennium: Journal of International Studies*, 36(1), 1–27.

*All Africa News* (*AFNWS*). 2002a. France sends troops to Cote d'Ivoire, 24 September [Online]. Available at: Factiva [accessed: 26 February 2012].

*All Africa News* (*AFNWS*). 2002b. Ivorien civil war – French troops halt rebels' advance, 3 October [Online]. Available at: Factiva [accessed: 26 February 2012].

*All Africa News* (*AFNWS*). 2002c. Ivory Coast demonstrators attack French military base, demanding Ouattara be handed over, 23 October [Online]. Available at: Factiva [accessed: 26 February 2012].

*All Africa News* (*AFNWS*). 2010. Gbagbo and Ouattara set for run-off vote, 5 November [Online]. Available at: Factiva [accessed: 26 February 2012].

Amnesty International. 2006. Côte D'Ivoire clashes between peacekeeping forces and civilians: lessons for the future. AI Index: AFR 31/005/2006 [Online]. Available at: http://www.amnesty.org/en/library/asset/AFR31/005/2006/en/f3e364cc-d3ff-11dd-8743-d305bea2b2c7/afr310052006en.pdf [accessed: 20 May 2012].

Anderson, D.L. 1993. Presidential leadership and U.S. intervention in Southeast Asia: the buck stops – and starts – here, in *Shadow on the White House: Presidents and the Vietnam War, 1945–1975*, edited by D.L. Anderson. Lawrence, KS: University Press of Kansas, 1–18.

Anderson, L. 2004. Antiquated before they can ossify: states that fail before they form. *Journal of International Affairs*, 58(1), 1–16.

Anderson, M.S. 1966. *The Eastern Question 1774–1923*. London: MacMillan.

Aquinas, St Thomas. 1970. *Selected Political Writings*, translated by J.G. Dawson. Oxford: Blackwell.

Aristotle. 1962. *The Politics*, translated by T.A. Sinclair. Harmondsworth: Penguin.

Aron, R. 2003. *Peace & War: A Theory of International Relations*. New Brunswick, NJ and London: Transaction Publishers.

Atkin, N. 2005. *The French Fifth Republic*. Basingstoke and New York: Palgrave MacMillan.

Atzili, B. 2006/07. When good fences make bad neighbours: fixed borders, state weakness, and internal conflict. *International Security*, 31(3), 139–73.

Augustine, St. 1972. *Concerning the City of God against the Pagans*, translated by H. Bettenson. Harmondsworth: Penguin.

Ayoob, M. 1995. *The Third World Security Predicament: State Making, Regional Conflict, and the International System*. Boulder and London: Lynne Rienner.

Bach, D. 2008. The European Union and China in Africa, in *Crouching Tiger, Hidden Dragon? Africa and China*, edited by K. Ampiah and S. Naidu. Scottsville, South Africa: University of KwaZulu-Natal Press, 278–93.

Bah, A.B. 2010. Democracy and civil war: citizenship and peacemaking in Côte D'Ivoire. *African Affairs*, 109(437), 597–615.

Baker, P.H. and Stremlau, J.J. 1999. Nigeria: U.S.–European stakes in Africa's largest state, in *Transatlantic Tensions: The United States, Europe, and Problem Countries*, edited by R.N. Haas. Washington, DC: Brookings Institution Press, 179–204.

Banégas, R. 2006. Côte D'Ivoire: patriotism, ethnonationalism and other African modes of self-writing. *African Affairs*, 105(421), 535–52.

Banégas, R. 2011. Post-election crisis in Côte D'Ivoire: the *Gbonhi* War. *African Affairs*, 110(440), 457–68.

Barrett, D.M. 1993. *Uncertain Warriors: Lyndon Johnson and His Vietnam Advisors*. Lawrence, KS: University Press of Kansas.

Bator, F.M. 2008. No good choices: LBJ and the Vietnam/Great Society connection. *Diplomatic History*, 32(3), 309–40.

*BBC Monitoring Africa*. 2000. Cote d'Ivoire – war of words on Constitution resumes, 16 May [Online]. Available at: Factiva [accessed: 26 February 2012].

*BBC Monitoring Africa*. 2002a. Cote d'Ivoire – opposition leader 'deeply saddened, shocked' by coup attempt, 21 September [Online]. Available at: Factiva [accessed: 26 February 2012].

*BBC Monitoring Africa*. 2002b. Cote d'Ivoire – Ouattara said given refuge at French Embassy with state consent, 26 September [Online]. Available at: Factiva [accessed: 26 February 2012].

*BBC Monitoring Africa*. 2003a. France's Chirac demands 'exemplary justice' from Cote d'Ivoire, 23 October [Online]. Available at: Factiva [accessed: 26 February 2012].

*BBC Monitoring Africa*. 2003b. French Defence Minister says country playing 'big brother' role in Africa, 3 September [Online]. Available at: Factiva [accessed: 26 February 2012].

*BBC Monitoring Africa*. 2003c. French Defence Minister says evacuation plan for Cote d'Ivoire is ready, 7 February [Online]. Available at: Factiva [accessed: 26 February 2012].

*BBC Monitoring Africa*. 2004a. French minister condemns Ivorian shelling, urges stronger UN force mandate, 6 November [Online]. Available at: Factiva [accessed: 26 February 2012].

*BBC Monitoring Africa*. 2004b. France tells Ivorian leader to end 'anti-white witch-hunt', 16 November [Online]. Available at: Factiva [accessed: 26 February 2012].

*BBC Monitoring Africa*. 2010. Cote d'Ivoire: losing candidate urges supporters to back opposition, 8 November [Online]. Available at: Factiva [accessed: 26 February 2012].

*BBC Monitoring Africa*. 2011. Minister Longuet says French army not involved in Ivorian leader's arrest, 12 April [Online]. Available at: Factiva [accessed: 26 February 2012].

*BBC Monitoring European*. 2002. French Foreign Minister says mutinous soldiers shooting in Ivory Coast, 19 September [Online]. Available at: Factiva [accessed: 26 February 2012].

Bell, C. 2007. *The End of the Vasco da Gama Era: The Next Landscape of World Politics*. Sydney: Lowy Institute for International policy.

Bellamy, A. and Williams, P.D. 2011. The new politics of protection? Côte D'Ivoire, Libya and the responsibility to protect. *International Affairs*, 87(4), 825–50.

Bentham, J. 1996. *An Introduction to the Principles of Morals and Legislation.* Oxford: Oxford University Press.

Berger, M.T. 2007. States of nature and the nature of states: the fate of nations, the collapse of states and the future of the world. *Third World Quarterly*, 28(6), 1203–14.

Berger, M.T. and Weber, H. 2006. Beyond state-building: global governance and the crisis of the nation-state system in the 21st century. *Third World Quarterly*, 27(1), 201–08.

Bergerud, E.M. 1991. *The Dynamics of Defeat: The Vietnam War in Hau Nghia Province*. Boulder: Westview Press.

Beschloss, M.R. 1997. *Taking Charge: The Johnson White House Tapes, 1963–1964*. New York: Simon & Schuster.

Blaufarb, D.S. 1977. *The Counterinsurgency Era: US Doctrine and Performance.* New York: Free Press.

Blunden, M. 2000. France, in *The Foreign Policies of the European Union Member States*, edited by I. Manners and R.G. Whitman. Manchester, UK: Manchester University Press, 19–43.

Bodin, J. 1955. *Six Books of the Commonwealth*, translated by M.J. Tooley. Oxford: Blackwell.

Boone, C. 2007. Africa's new territorial politics: regionalism and the open economy in Côte D'Ivoire. *African Studies Review*, 50(1), 59–81.

Bovcon, M. 2009a. France's conflict resolution strategy in Côte D'Ivoire and its ethical implications. *African Studies Quarterly*, 11(1), 1–24.

Bovcon, M. 2009b. French repatriates from Côte D'Ivoire and the resilience of *Françafrique*. *Modern & Contemporary France*, 17(3), 283–99.

Bowen, N. 2005. Multilateralism, multipolarity, and regionalism: the French foreign policy discourse. *Mediterranean Quarterly*, 16(1), 94–116.

Bozo, F. 1995. France and security in the new Europe: between the Gaullist legacy and the search for a new model, in *Remaking the Hexagon: The New France in the New Europe*, edited by G. Flynn. Boulder and Oxford: Westview Press, 213–32.

Brown, W. 2006. The Commission for Africa: results and prospects for the West's Africa policy. *Journal of Modern African Studies*, 44(3), 349–74.

Bull, H. 1966. The Grotian conception of international society, in *Diplomatic Investigations: Essays in the Theory of International Politics*, edited by H. Butterfield and M. Wight. Cambridge, MA: Harvard University Press, 51–73.

Bull, H. 1984. Introduction, in *Intervention in World Politics*, edited by H. Bull, Oxford: Clarendon Press, 1–6.

Bull, H. 2002. *The Anarchical Society: A Study of Order in World Politics*. 3rd edition. Basingstoke and New York: Palgrave.

Burke, E. 1910. *Reflections on the Revolution in France*. London: J.M. Dent & Sons Ltd.

Buzan, B. 2004. *From International Society to World Society?* Cambridge: Cambridge University Press.

Buzan, B. 2011. A world order without superpowers: decentred globalism. *International Relations*, 25(1), 3–25.

Buzan, B. and Little, R. 2000. *International Systems in World History: Remaking the Study of International Relations*. Oxford: Oxford University Press.

Cabinet Office Records (CAB). 1 January 1880 – 31 December 1916, series 37. The National Archives, Kew, UK.

Cain, P.J. and Hopkins, A.G. 2002. *British Imperialism, 1688–2000*. 2nd edition. London: Pearson.

Call, C.T. 2008. The fallacy of the 'failed state'. *Third World Quarterly*, 29(8), 1491–507.

Campagne, J-P. 2002. Paris takes hard line with I Coast, demands end to attacks on foreigners. *Agence France-Presse* (*AFP*), 23 October [Online]. Available at: Factiva [accessed: 26 February 2012].

Caplan, R. 2007. From collapsing states to neo-trusteeship: the limits to solving the problem of 'precarious statehood' in the 21st century. *Third World Quarterly*, 28(2), 231–44.

Carr, E.H. 1964. *What is History?* Harmondsworth: Penguin.

Carroll, R. 2002. French troops find mass grave in Ivory Coast – carnage on streets as three-sided civil war rages. *The Guardian*, 7 December [Online]. Available at: Factiva [accessed: 26 February 2012].

Cecil, G. 1932. *Life of Robert Marquis of Salisbury*, vol. 4. London: Hodder and Stoughton.

Chafer, T. 2002. Franco-African relations: no longer so exceptional. *African Affairs*, 101, 343–63.

Chafer, T. 2005. Chirac and '*la Françafrique*': no longer a family affair. *Modern & Contemporary France*, 13(1), 7–23.

Chafer, T, 2008. From confidence to confusion: Franco-African relations in the era of globalisation, in *France on the World Stage: Nation State Strategies in the Global Era*, edited by M. Maclean and J. Szarka. Basingstoke and New York: Palgrave MacMillan, 37–56.

Chafer, T. and Cumming, G. 2010. Beyond Fashoda: Anglo-French security cooperation in Africa since Saint-Malo. *International Affairs*, 86(5), 1129–1147.

Chamberlain, M.E. 1981. British public opinion and the invasion of Egypt, 1882. *Trivium*, 16, 5–28.

Chanda, A.K. 2002a. French troops deploy as mediation bid starts in Ivory Coast. *Agence France-Presse* (*AFP*), 1 October [Online]. Available at: Factiva [accessed: 26 February 2012].

Chanda, A.K. 2002b. French troops move closer to Bouake. *Agence France-Presse* (*AFP*), 24 September [Online]. Available at: Factiva [accessed: 26 February 2012].

Chanda, A.K. 2003. Tens of thousands protest French-brokered peace deal for I Coast. *Agence France-Presse* (*AFP*), 26 January [Online]. Available at: Factiva [accessed: 26 February 2012].

Chandler, D. 2006. *Empire in Denial: The Politics of State-Building*. London and Ann Arbor, MI: Pluto Press.

Charbonneau, B. 2006. Mastering 'irrational' violence: the relegitimization of French security policy in sub-Saharan Africa. *Alternatives*, 31, 215–41.

Charbonneau, B. 2008. *France and the New Imperialism: Security Policy in Sub-Saharan Africa*. Aldershot, UK and Burlington, VT: Ashgate.

Childers, S. 1901. *The Life and Correspondence of the Right Hon. Hugh C.E. Childers 1827–1896*, vol. 2. London: John Murray.

Chipman, J. 1989. *French Power in Africa*. Oxford and Cambridge, MA: Blackwell.

Chirot, D. 2006. The debacle in Côte D'Ivoire. *Journal of Democracy*, 17(2), 63–77.

Chonghaile, C.N. 2002. U.S., French mount W. Africa rescue. *Associated Press* (*AP*), 25 September [Online]. Available at: Factiva [accessed: 26 February 2012].

*The Christian Science Monitor*. 2011. A more assertive France in Africa, 12 April [Online]. Available at: Factiva [accessed: 26 February 2012].

CIA World Factbook. 2012. Cote D'Ivoire [Online]. Available at: https://www.cia.gov/library/publications/the-world-factbook/geos/iv.html [accessed: 19 May 2012].

Cicero. 1976. *On the Commonwealth*, translated by G.H. Sabine and S.B. Smith. Indianapolis, IN: Bobbs-Merrill, Inc.

Clayton, G.D. 1971. *Britain and the Eastern Question: Missolonghi to Gallipoli*. London: University of London Press.

Cole, J.R.I. 1989. Of crowds and empires: Afro-Asian riots and European expansion, 1857–1882. *Comparative Studies in Society and History*, 31(1), 106–33.

Colvin, A. 1906. *The Making of Modern Egypt*. London: Seeley & Co.

Commission on Weak States and US National Security. 2004. *On the Brink: Weak States and US National Security*. Washington, DC: Centre for Global Development.

Crawford, N.C. 2000. The Passion of world politics: propositions on emotion and emotional relationships. *International Security*, 24(4), 116–56.

Creppell, I. 2011. The concept of normative threat. *International Theory*, 3(3): 450–87.

Cromer, Earl of. 1908. *Modern Egypt*, vol 1. London: MacMillan.

Cumming, G.G. 2004. UK African policy in the post-Cold War era: from *realpolitik* to *moralpolitik*. *Commonwealth & Comparative Politics*, 42(1), 106–128.

*The Daily News*. 1882a. 28 January, 5.

*The Daily News*. 1882b. 26 April, 5.

*The Daily News*. 1882c. 30 May, 5.

*The Daily News*. 1882d. 14 June, 5.
*The Daily News*. 1882e. 12 July, 5.
*The Daily News*. 1882f. 13 July, 5.
*The Daily News*. 1882g. 14 July, 5.
*The Daily News*. 1882h. 17 July, 5.
*The Daily News*. 1882i. 28 July, 5.
*The Daily Telegraph*. 1882a. 2 June, 5.
*The Daily Telegraph*. 1882b. 14 July, 5.
*The Daily Telegraph*, 2003. French flee Ivory Coast as mobs attack soldiers, 1 February [Online]. Available at: Factiva [accessed: 26 February 2012].
D'Albis, T. 1998. France and Africa: continuity, change and paradoxes. *South African Journal of International Affairs*, 6(1), 1–6.
Dean, R.D. 1998. Masculinity as ideology: John F. Kennedy and the domestic politics of foreign policy. *Diplomatic History*, 22(1), 29–62.
De Gaulle, C. 1955. *The Complete War Memoirs of Charles de Gaulle: Volume I The Call to Honour*. New York: Simon and Schuster.
Department for International Development (DFID) (UK). 2005. *Why we Need to Work More Effectively in Fragile States*. London: DFID.
Dorff, R.H. 2005. Failed states after 9/11: what did we know and what have we learned? *International Studies Perspectives*, 6, 20–34.
Drake, H. 2010. France, Europe and the limits of exceptionalism, in *The End of the French Exception? Decline and Revival of the 'French Model'*, edited by T. Chafer and E. Godin. Basingstoke: Palgrave MacMillan, 187–202.
Drake, H. 2011. *Contemporary France*. Basingstoke and New York: Palgrave MacMillan.
Duara, P. 2008. The global and regional constitution of nations: the view from East Asia. *Nations and Nationalism*, 14(2), 323–45.
Duffield, M. 2001. *Global Governance and the New Wars: The Merging of Development and Security*. London and New York: Zed Books.
Duffield, M. 2002a. Social reconstruction and the radicalization of development: aid as a relation of global liberal governance. *Development and Change*, 33(5), 1049–71.
Duffield, M. 2002b. War as a network enterprise: the new security terrain and its implications. *Cultural Values*, 6(1–2), 153–65.
Duffield, M. 2005. Social reconstruction: the reuniting of aid and politics. *Development*, 48 (3), 16–24.
Dumbrell, J., with Barrett, D.M. 1990. *The Making of US Foreign Policy*. Manchester and New York: Manchester University Press.
Durrans, P.J. 1982. A two-edged sword: the Liberal attack on Disraelian imperialism. *The Journal of Imperial and Commonwealth History*, 10(3), 262–84.
Dyson, T. 2008. Convergence and divergence in post-Cold War British, French, and German military reforms: between international structure and executive autonomy. *Security Studies*, 17, 725–74.

Eldridge, C.C. 1973. *England's Mission: The Imperial Idea in the Age of Gladstone and Disraeli 1868–1880*. London and Basingstoke: MacMillan.

Elman, C. and Elman, M.F. 1997. Diplomatic history and international relations theory: respecting difference and crossing boundaries. *International Security*, 22(1), 5–21.

Elster, J. 1990. Norms of revenge. *Ethics*, 100(4), 862–85.

Englebert, P. and Tull, D.M. 2008. Postconflict reconstruction in Africa: flawed ideas about failed states. *International Security*, 32(4), 106–39.

Eriksen, S.S. 2011. 'State failure' in theory and practice: the idea of the state and the contradictions of state formation. *Review of International Studies*, 37, 229–47.

European Union (EU). 2003. *European Security Strategy: A Secure Europe in a Better World.* Brussels: Council of the European Union.

Evans, R.J. 1968. *The Victorian Age 1815–1914*. 2nd edition. London: Edward Arnold.

*The Evening News*. 1882a. 3 June, 3.

*The Evening News*. 1882b. 13 July, 3.

*The Evening News*. 1882c. 14 July, 3.

Farnie, D.A. 1969. *East and West of Suez: The Suez Canal in History 1854–1956*. Oxford: Clarendon Press.

Fattah, K. and Fierke, K.M. 2009. A clash of emotions: the politics of humiliation and political violence in the Middle East. *European Journal of International Relations*, 15(1), 67–93.

Fearon, J.D. and Laitin, D.D. 2004. Neotrusteeship and the problem of weak states. *International Security*, 28(4), 5–43.

Ferguson, N. 2004. *Colossus: The Rise and Fall of the American Empire*. London: Allen Lane.

Fieldhouse, D.K. 1976. *Economics and Empire 1830–1914*. London: Weidenfeld and Nicolson.

Finnemore, M. 2003. *The Purpose of Intervention: Changing Beliefs about the Use of Force*. Ithaca and London: Cornell University Press.

Flynn, G. 1995. French identity and post-Cold War Europe, in *Remaking the Hexagon: The New France in the New Europe*, edited by G. Flynn. Boulder and Oxford: Westview Press, 233–49.

Fordham, B.O. and Asal, V. 2007. Billiard balls or snowflakes? Major power prestige and the international diffusion of institutions and practices. *International Studies Quarterly*, 51, 31–52.

Foreign Office Records (FO). Confidential Print: Egypt and the Sudan. 1 January 1839 – 31 December 1958, series 407. The National Archives, Kew, UK.

*Foreign Relations of the United States* (*FRUS*). 1950, vol. 1, National Security Affairs; Foreign Economic Policy. Washington, DC: Government Printing Office.

*Foreign Relations of the United States* (*FRUS*). 1958–1960, vol. 3, National Security Policy; Arms Control and Disarmament. Washington DC: Government Printing Office.

*Foreign Relations of the United States* (*FRUS*). Kennedy Administration. 1961–1963, vol. 1, *Vietnam*, 1961 [Online]. Available at: http://history.state.gov/historicaldocuments/frus1961-63v01 [accessed: 12 May 2012].

*Foreign Relations of the United States* (*FRUS*). Kennedy Administration. 1961–1963, vol. 2, *Vietnam*, 1962 [Online]. Available at: http://history.state.gov/historicaldocuments/frus1961-63v02 [accessed: 12 May 2012].

*Foreign Relations of the United States* (*FRUS*). Kennedy Administration. 1961–1963, vol. 3, *Vietnam*, January–August 1963 [Online]. Available at: http://history.state.gov/historicaldocuments/frus1961-63v03 [accessed: 12 May 2012].

*Foreign Relations of the United States* (*FRUS*). Kennedy Administration. 1961–1963, vol. 4, *Vietnam*, August–December 1963 [Online]. Available at: http://history.state.gov/historicaldocuments/frus1961-63v04 [accessed: 12 May 2012].

*Foreign Relations of the United States* (*FRUS*). Kennedy Administration. 1961–1963, vol. 8, *National Security Policy* [Online]. Available at: http://history.state.gov/historicaldocuments/frus1961-63v08 [accessed: 12 May 2012].

*Foreign Relations of the United States* (*FRUS*). Johnson Administration. 1964–1968, vol. 1, *Vietnam*, 1964 [Online]. Available at: http://history.state.gov/historicaldocuments/frus1964-68v01 [accessed: 12 May 2012].

*Foreign Relations of the United States* (*FRUS*). Johnson Administration. 1964–1968, vol. 2, *Vietnam*, January–June 1965 [Online]. Available at: http://history.state.gov/historicaldocuments/frus1964-68v02 [accessed: 12 May 2012].

*Foreign Relations of the United States* (*FRUS*). Johnson Administration. 1964–1968, vol. 3, *Vietnam*, June–December 1965 [Online]. Available at: http://history.state.gov/historicaldocuments/frus1964-68v03 [accessed: 12 May 2012].

*Foreign Relations of the United States* (*FRUS*). Johnson Administration. 1964–1968, vol. 4, *Vietnam*, 1966 [Online]. Available at: http://history.state.gov/historicaldocuments/frus1964-68v04 [accessed: 12 May 2012].

*Foreign Relations of the United States* (*FRUS*). Johnson Administration. 1964–1968, vol. 5, *Vietnam*, 1967 [Online]. Available at: http://history.state.gov/historicaldocuments/frus1964-68v05 [accessed: 12 May 2012].

*Foreign Relations of the United States* (*FRUS*). Johnson Administration. 1964–1968, vol. 6, *Vietnam*, January–August 1968 [Online]. Available at: http://history.state.gov/historicaldocuments/frus1964-68v06 [accessed: 12 May 2012].

Förster, T. 2010. *Maintenant, on sait qui est qui*: statehood and political reconfiguration in northern Côte D'Ivoire. *Development and Change*, 41(4), 699–722.

François, M. and Sud, I. 2006. Promoting stability and development in fragile and failed states. *Development Policy Review* 24(2), 141–60.

Freedgood, E. 2003. *Victorian Writing about Risk: Imagining a Safe England in a Dangerous World*. Cambridge: Cambridge University Press.

Freeman, E.A. 1880. The election and the eastern question. *The Contemporary Review*, 37, 956–6.

Fukuyama, F. 1989. The end of history? *The National Interest*, (Summer), 3–18.

Fukuyama, F. 2004. *State-Building: Governance and World Order in the 21st Century*. Ithaca: Cornell University Press.

Fund for Peace/*Foreign Policy*. 2010. The failed states index. *Foreign Policy* (July–August), 76–79.

Furubotn, E.G. and Richter, R. 2005. *Institutions and Economic Theory: The Contribution of the New Institutional Economics*. 2nd edition. Ann Arbor, MI: University of Michigan Press.

Gaddis, J.L. 1982. *Strategies of Containment: A Critical Appraisal of Postwar American National Security*. New York and Oxford: Oxford University Press.

Gaffney, J. 2010. *Political Leadership in France: From Charles de Gaulle to Nicolas Sarkozy*. Basingstoke: Palgrave MacMillan.

Galbraith, J.S. 1960. The 'turbulent frontier' as a factor in British expansion. *Comparative Studies in Society and History*, 2(2), 150–68.

Galbraith, J.S. and Al-Sayyid-Marsot, A.L. 1978. The British occupation of Egypt: another view. *International Journal of Middle Eastern Studies*, 9(4), 471–88.

Galluci, R.L. 1975. *Neither Peace Nor Honour: The Politics of American Military Policy in Viet-Nam*. Baltimore, MD and London: John Hopkins University Press.

Gat, A. 2007. The return of authoritarian great powers. *Foreign Affairs*, 86(4), 59–69.

Ghani, A. and Lockhart, C. 2008. *Fixing Failed States: a Framework for Rebuilding a Shattered World*. Oxford: Oxford University Press.

Gilby, T. 1958. *Principality and Polity: Aquinas and the Rise of State Theory in the West*. London: Longmans, Green & Co., Ltd.

Gill, S. *Power and Resistance in the New World Order*. Basingstoke and New York: Palgrave MacMillan.

Gilpin, R. 1981. *War and Change in World Politics*. Cambridge: Cambridge University Press.

Gladstone, W.E. 1876. *Bulgarian Horrors and the Question of the East*. London: John Murray.

Gladstone, W.E. 1877. *Aggression on Egypt and Freedom in the East*. London: The National Press Agency.

Gladstone, W.E. 1971. *Midlothian Speeches 1879*. Leicester, UK: Leicester University Press.

Gong, G.W. 1984. *The Standard of 'Civilization' in International Society*. Oxford: Clarendon Press.

Gordon, P.H. 1993. *A Certain Idea of France: French Security Policy and the Gaullist Legacy*. Princeton, NJ: Princeton University Press.

Goujon, E. 2002. I. Coast rebels gain ground, but French say no entry to evacuation zone. *Agence France-Presse* (*AFP*), 2 October [Online]. Available at: Factiva [accessed: 26 February 2012].
Graham, R. 2002. France redrawing its Africa policy amid Ivory Coast turmoil. *Financial Times*, 3 October [Online]. Available at: Factiva [accessed: 26 February 2012].
Gray, J. 2003. *Al Qaeda and What it Means to be Modern*. New York and London: The New Press.
Gregory, S. 2000a. *French Defence Policy into the Twenty-First Century*. Basingstoke: MacMillan.
Gregory, S. 2000b. The French military in Africa: past and present. *African Affairs*, 99, 435–48.
Griffin, C. 2007. *France, the United Kingdom, and European Union Capacities for Military Action in Africa*. Paper prepared for the Sixth Annual Pan-European Conference on International Relations, Turin, Italy, 12–15 September.
Gros, J-G. 1996. Towards a taxonomy of failed states in the new world order: decaying Somalia, Liberia, Rwanda and Haiti. *Third World Quarterly*, 17(3), 455–71.
Gwynn, S. and Tuckwell, G.M. 1917. *The Life of the Rt. Hon. Sir Charles W. Dilke*, vol. 1. London: John Murray.
Haas, R.N. 2008. The age of nonpolarity: what will follow U.S. dominance. *Foreign Affairs*, 87(3), 44–56.
Hadfield-Amkhan, A. 2010. *British Foreign Policy, National Identity, and Neoclassical Realism*. Lanham, MD: Rowman & Littlefield Publishers, Inc.
Hall, B. 2010. Sarkozy keeps distance from former colony. *Financial Times*, 27 December [Online]. Available at: Factiva [accessed: 26 February 2012].
Hall, P.A. and Taylor, R.C.R. 1996. Political science and the three new institutionalisms. *Political Studies*, 44(5), 936–57.
Halvorson, D. 2010a. 'Bringing international politics back in': reconceptualising state failure for the twenty-first century. *Australian Journal of International Affairs*, 64(5), 583–600.
Halvorson, D. 2010b. Prestige, prudence and public opinion in the 1882 British occupation of Egypt. *Australian Journal of Politics and History*, 56(3), 423–40.
Hameiri, S. 2007. Failed states or a failed paradigm? State capacity and the limits of institutionalism. *Journal of International Relations and Development*, 10, 123–34.
Hampton, J. 1999. Hobbesian reflections on glory as a cause of conflict, in *The Causes of Quarrel: Essays on Peace, War, and Thomas Hobbes*, edited by P. Caws. Boston: Beacon Press, 78–96.
*Hansard's Parliamentary Debates*. 1882a. 3rd Series, 1830–1891, vol. 269.
*Hansard's Parliamentary Debates*. 1882b. 3rd Series, 1830–1891, vol. 270.
*Hansard's Parliamentary Debates*. 1882c. 3rd Series, 1830–1891, vol. 271
*Hansard's Parliamentary Debates*. 1882d. 3rd Series, 1830–1891, vol. 272.

*Hansard's Parliamentary Debates*. 1882e. 3rd Series, 1830–1891, vol. 273.
Harrison, R.T. 1995. *Gladstone's Imperialism in Egypt: Techniques of Domination*. Westport CT: Greenwood Press.
Helman, G.B. and Ratner, S.S. 1992. Saving failed states. *Foreign Policy*, 89, 3–20.
Helmke, G. and Levitsky, S. 2004. Informal institutions and comparative politics: a research agenda. *Perspectives on Politics*, 2(4), 725–40.
Herring, G.C. 1979. *America's Longest War: The United States and Vietnam, 1950–1975*. New York: John Wiley & Sons, Inc.
Hey, J.A.K. 2003. Refining our understanding of small state foreign policy, in *Small States in World Politics: Explaining Foreign Policy Behavior*, edited by J.A.K. Hey. Boulder and London: Lynne Rienner, 185–95.
Hilsman, R. 1963. The challenge to freedom in Asia. 22 April. *Department of State Bulletin*, 49(1254), 43–50.
Hoagland, J. 2004. Giving France a hand: in its Ivory Coast diplomacy, the U.S. resists retribution. *The Washington Post*, 25 November [Online]. Available at: Factiva [accessed: 21 May 2012].
Hobbes, T. 1996. *Leviathan*. Cambridge: Cambridge University Press.
Hobson, J.M. 1998. The historical sociology of the state and the state of historical sociology in international relations. *Review of International Political Economy*, 5(2), 284–320.
Holm, H-H. 2001. A disaggregated world order in the making: policy towards failed states as an example. *International Politics*, 38, 357–74.
Holm, U. 2004. The old France, the new Europe and a multipolar world. *Perspectives on European Politics and Society*, 5(3), 469–91.
Hopkins, A.G. 1986. The Victorians and Africa: a reconsideration of the occupation of Egypt, 1882. *The Journal of African History*, 27(2), 364–70.
Howe, H.M. 2005. Nigeria, in *The Politics of Peacekeeping in the Post-Cold War Era*, edited by D.S. Sorenson and P.C. Wood. Abingdon, UK and New York: Frank Cass, 176–95.
Howorth, J. 1996. A testing time for the pursuit of *grandeur*, in *Chirac's Challenge: Liberalization, Europeanization, and Malaise in France*, edited by J.T.S. Keeler and M.A. Schain. New York: St. Martin's Press, 383–400.
Hughes, B.B. 1978. *The Domestic Context of American Foreign Policy*. San Francisco, CA: W.H. Freeman and Co.
Huntington, S.P. 1968. *Political Order in Changing Societies*. New Haven, CT: Yale University Press.
Hurrell, A. 2007. *On Global Order: Power, Values, and the Constitution of International Society*. Oxford: Oxford University Press.
Hymans, J.E.C. 2006. *The Psychology of Nuclear Proliferation: Identity, Emotions, and Foreign Policy*. Cambridge: Cambridge University Press.
Ignatieff, M. 2005. Human rights, power and the state, in *Making States Work: State Failure and the Crisis of Governance*, edited by S. Chesterman, M. Ignatieff and R. Thakur. Tokyo: United Nations University Press, 59–75.

Ikenberry, G.J. 2005. Power and liberal order: America's postwar world order in transition. *International Relations of the Asia-Pacific*, 5, 133–52.
International Crisis Group (ICG). 2003. *Côte D'Ivoire: 'The War is Not Yet Over'*. ICG Africa Report no. 72, Brussels: ICG.
International Crisis Group (ICG). 2004. *Côte D'Ivoire: No Peace in Sight*. ICG Africa Report no. 82, Brussels: ICG.
International Crisis Group (ICG). 2011a. *A Critical Period for Ensuring Stability in Côte D'Ivoire*. ICG Africa Report no. 176, Brussels: ICG.
International Crisis Group (ICG). 2011b. *Côte D'Ivoire: Continuing the Recovery*. ICG Africa Briefing no. 83, Dakar, Senegal and Brussels: ICG.
International Crisis Group (ICG). 2011c. *Côte D'Ivoire: Is War the Only Option?* Africa Report no. 171, Brussels: ICG.
Irondelle, B. 2008. European foreign policy: the end of French Europe? *European Integration*, 30(1), 153–168.
Jackson, R.H. 1987. Quasi-states, dual regimes, and neoclassical theory: international jurisprudence and the Third World. *International Organization*, 41(4), 519–49.
Jackson, R.H. 1990. *Quasi-States: Sovereignty, International Relations, and the Third World*. Cambridge: Cambridge University Press.
Jackson, R.H. 1993. The weight of ideas in decolonization: normative change in international relations, in *Ideas and Foreign Policy: Beliefs, Institutions, and Political Change*, edited by J. Goldstein and R.O. Keohane. Ithaca and London: Cornell University Press, 111–38.
Jackson, R.H. 2000. *The Global Covenant: Human Conduct in a World of States*. Oxford: Oxford University Press.
Jeffery, R. 2011. Reason, emotion, and the problem of world poverty: moral sentiment theory and international ethics. *International Theory*, 3(1): 143–78.
Jervis, R. 2002. An interim assessment of September 11: what has changed and what has not? *Political Science Quarterly*, 117(1), 37–54.
Johnson, L.B. 1964a. Remarks in Manchester to the members of the New Hampshire Weekly Newspaper Editors Association, 28 September. *Public Papers of the Presidents of the United States of America*. 1963–64. Washington, DC: Office of the Federal Register, 1160–69.
Johnson, L.B. 1964b. Remarks in Memorial Hall, Akron University. 21 October. *Public Papers of the Presidents of the United States of America*. 1963–64. Washington, DC: Office of the Federal Register, 1387–93.
Johnson, L.B. 1964c. Television address to the American people. 7 October. *Public Papers of the Presidents of the United States of America*. 1963–64. Washington, DC: Office of the Federal Register, 1241–43.
Johnson, L.B. 1965a. Pattern for peace in Southeast Asia, 7 April. *Department of State Bulletin*, 52(1348), 606–10.
Johnson, L.B. 1965b. Statement by the President: 'tragedy, disappointment, and progress' in Viet-Nam, 17 April. *Public Papers of the Presidents of the United States*, 1966. Washington DC: Office of the Federal Register, 428–30.

Johnson, L.B. 1965c. The President's news conference of July 28, 1965. *Public Papers of the Presidents of the United States*, 1966. Washington DC: Office of the Federal Register, 794–803.

Johnson, L.B. 1965d. We will stand in Vietnam, 28 July. *Department of State Bulletin*, 53(1364), 262–65.

Johnson, L.B. 1968a President's address to the nation announcing steps to limit the war in Vietnam and reporting his decision not to seek reelection, 31 March. *Public Papers of the Presidents of the United States*, 1968–1969, vol. 1. Washington DC: Office of the Federal Register, 469–76.

Johnson, L.B. 1968b. The Vietnam War: the objectives of the United States. 9 August. *Vital Speeches of the Day*, 34(23), 712–16.

Johnson, R.H. 1994. *Improbable Dangers: US Conceptions of Threat in the Cold War and After*. New York: St. Martin's Press.

Kahin, G.M. 1986. *Intervention: How America Became Involved in Vietnam*. New York: Alfred A. Knopf, Inc.

Kaldor, M. 1999. *New and Old Wars: Organized Violence in a Global Era*. Stanford CA: Stanford University Press.

Kaplan, R.D. 1994. The coming anarchy. *The Atlantic Monthly*, 273(2), 44–76.

Kaplan, S.D. 2008. *Fixing Fragile States: A New Paradigm for Development*. Westport, CT: Praeger Security International.

Kearns, D. 1976. *Lyndon Johnson and the American Dream*. New York: Harper & Row.

Keiger, J.F.V. 2001. *France and the World since 1870*. London: Arnold.

Kennedy, J.F. 1961a. Annual message to the Congress on the state of the union, 30 January. *Public Papers of the Presidents of the United States of America*. Washington, DC: Office of the Federal Register, 19–28.

Kennedy, J.F. 1961b. Inaugural address, 20 January. *Public Papers of the Presidents of the United States of America*. Washington, DC: Office of the Federal Register, 1–3.

Kennedy, J.F. 1961c. Radio and television report to the American people on returning from Europe, 6 June. *Public Papers of the Presidents of the United States of America*. Washington, DC: Office of the Federal Register, 441–46.

Kennedy, J.F. 1961d. Remarks at the Eighth National Conference on International Economic and Social Development, 16 June. *Public Papers of the Presidents of the United States of America*. Washington, DC: Office of the Federal Register, 460–64.

Kennedy, J.K. 1961e. Special message to the Congress on foreign aid, 22 March. *Public Papers of the Presidents of the United States of America*. Washington, DC: Office of the Federal Register, 203–12.

Kennedy, J.F. 1961f. Special message to the Congress on the defense budget, 28 March. *Public Papers of the Presidents of the United States of America*. Washington, DC: Office of the Federal Register, 229–40.

Kennedy, J.F. 1961g. Special message to the Congress on urgent national needs, 25 May. *Public Papers of the Presidents of the United States of America.* Washington, DC: Office of the Federal Register, 396–406.

Kennedy, J.F. 1963. Special message to the Congress on free world defense and assistance programs, 2 April. *Public Papers of the Presidents of the United States of America.* Washington, DC: Office of the Federal Register, 294–303.

Kennedy, P. 1981. *The Realities behind Diplomacy: Background Influences on British External Policy, 1865–1980.* London and Boston, MA: Allen & Unwin.

Keys, B. 2011. Henry Kissinger: the emotional statesman. *Diplomatic History*, 35(4), 587–609.

Kissinger, H.A. 1964. *A World Restored: Metternich, Castlereagh and the Problems of Peace 1812–22.* Boston: Houghton Mifflin.

Klare, M. and Volman, D. 2006. America, China & the scramble for Africa's oil. *Review of African Political Economy*, 108, 297–309.

Knorr, K.E. 1963. *British Colonial Theories 1570–1850.* London: Frank Cass.

Knutsen, T.L. 1999. *The Rise and Fall of World Orders.* Manchester, UK and New York: Manchester University Press.

Koffi, C. 2003. Ivory Coast sees giant peaceful demo against French peace deal. *Agence France-Presse* (*AFP*), 1 February [Online]. Available at: Factiva [accessed: 26 February 2012].

Kouassi, P. 2004. French seize Abidjan after peacekeepers slain. *The Globe and Mail*, 8 November [Online]. Available at: Factiva [accessed: 26 February 2012].

Krasner, S.D. 2004. Sharing sovereignty: new institutions for collapsed and failing states. *International Security*, 29(2), 85–120.

Krasner, S.D. and Pascual, C. 2005. Addressing state failure. *Foreign Affairs*, 84, 153–63.

Krause, S.R. 2002. *Liberalism with Honor.* Cambridge, MA and London: Harvard University Press.

Krotz, U. and Sperling, J. 2011. The European security order between American hegemony and French independence. *European Security*, 20(3), 305–35.

Langer, A. 2005. Horizontal inequalities and violent group mobilization in Côte D'Ivoire. *Oxford Development Studies*, 33(1), 25–45.

Lansford, T. 1996. The question of France: French security choices at century's end. *European Security*, 5(1), 944–64.

Latham, M.E. 2000. *Modernization as Ideology: American Social Science and 'Nation Building' in the Kennedy Era.* Chapel Hill and London: The University of North Carolina Press.

Latham, M.E. 2006. Redirecting the revolution? The USA and the failure of nation-building in South Vietnam. *Third World Quarterly*, 27(1), 27–41.

Lathbury, D.C. 1880. The European Concert. *The Fortnightly Review*, new series, 28, 200–209.

Layne, C. 2006. *The Peace of Illusions: American Grand Strategy from 1940 to the Present.* Ithaca and London: Cornell University Press.

Lebow, R.N. 2008. *A Cultural Theory of International Relations*. Cambridge: Cambridge University Press.

Leffler, M.P. 1992. *A Preponderance of Power: National Security, the Truman Administration, and the Cold War*. Stanford, CA: Stanford University Press.

Leftwich, A. 2000. *States of Development: On the Primacy of Politics in Development*. Cambridge: Polity Press.

Leighton, C. 2000. France denounces exclusion of I Coast presidential candidates. *Agence France-Presse* (*AFP*), 7 October [Online]. Available at: Factiva [accessed: 26 February 2012].

Le Pere, G. 2008. The geo-strategic dimension of the Sino-African relationship, in *Crouching Tiger, Hidden Dragon? Africa and China*, edited by K. Ampiah and S. Naidu. Scottsville, South Africa: University of KwaZulu-Natal Press, 20–38.

Levering, R.B. 1978. *The Public and American Foreign Policy, 1918–1978*. New York: William Morrow and Co., Inc.

Lhuillery, J. 2001. Ouattara eyes top job in Ivory Coast after return from exile. *Agence France-Presse* (*AFP*), 5 December [Online]. Available at: Factiva [accessed: 26 February 2012].

Lhuillery, J. 2002a. Former colonial ruler gets sucked into the Ivorian Crisis. *Agence France-Presse* (*AFP*), 2 October [Online]. Available at: Factiva [accessed: 26 February 2012].

Lhuillery, J. 2002b. Ivory Coast's ties with former ruler France at a low after mutiny. *Agence France-Presse* (*AFP*), 30 September [Online]. Available at: Factiva [accessed: 26 February 2012].

Lhuillery, J. 2003a. Chirac urges Ivory Coast to end 'climate of hatred' after reporter killed. *Agence France-Presse* (*AFP*), 23 October [Online]. Available at: Factiva [accessed: 26 February 2012].

Lhuillery, J. 2003b. France goes to bat for former star colony Ivory Coast. *Agence France-Presse* (*AFP*), 26 January [Online]. Available at: Factiva [accessed: 26 February 2012].

Lin, M. 2009. China and the escalation of the Vietnam War. *Journal of Cold War Studies*, 11(2), 35–69.

Linantud, J.L. 2008. Pressure and protection: Cold War geopolitics and nation-building in South Korea, South Vietnam, Philippines, and Thailand. *Geopolitics*, 13, 635–56.

Lindner, E. 2006. *Making Enemies: Humiliation and International Conflict*. Westport, CT and London: Praeger.

Lirong, L. 2011. *The EU and China's Engagement in Africa: The Dilemma of Socialisation*, European Union Institute for Security Studies, Occasional Paper 93, August.

Locke, J. 1980. *The Second Treatise of Government*. Indianapolis, IN: Bobbs-Merrill, Inc.

Lowe, C.J. 1969. *The Reluctant Imperialists: British Foreign Policy 1878–1902*. New York: MacMillan.

Löwenheim, O. 2003. 'Do ourselves credit and render a lasting service to mankind': British moral prestige, humanitarian intervention, and the Barbary pirates. *International Studies Quarterly*, 47(1), 23–48.

Löwenheim, O. 2007. *Predators and Parasites: Persistent Agents of Transnational Harm and Great Power Authority*. Ann Arbor, MI: The University of Michigan Press.

Löwenheim, O. and Heimann, G. 2008. Revenge in international politics. *Security Studies*, 17, 685–724.

Lunch, W.L. and Sperlich, P.W. 1979. American public opinion and the war in Vietnam. *The Western Political Quarterly*, 32(1), 21–44.

Lynch, D.C. 2007. Envisioning China's political future: elite responses to democracy as a global constitutive norm. *International Studies Quarterly*, 51, 701–22.

MacDonald, D.J. 1991. The Truman Administration and global responsibilities: the birth of the falling domino principle, in *Dominoes and Bandwagons: Strategic Beliefs and Great Power Competition in the Eurasian Rimland*, edited by R. Jervis and J. Snyder. New York and Oxford: Oxford University Press, 112–44.

McLean, D. 1976. Finance and 'informal empire' before the First World War. *The Economic History Review*, 29(2), 291–305.

Maclean M. and Szarka, J. 2008. Globalisation and the nation state: conceptual lenses on French ambitions in a changing world order, in *France on the World Stage: Nation State Strategies in the Global Era*, edited by M. Maclean and J. Szarka. Basingstoke and New York: Palgrave MacMillan, 1–19.

McNamara, R.S. 1964. The defense of the free world, 21 May. *Department of State Bulletin*, 50(1302), 893–99.

Mahoney, D.J. 1998. The politics of *grandeur*: De Gaulle and national identity, in *Honor among Nations: Intangible Interests and Foreign Policy*, edited by E. Abrams. Washington, DC: Ethics and Public Policy Center, 51–67.

Majumdar, M.A. and Chafer, T. 2010. Back to the future? Franco-African relations in the shadow of France's colonial past, in *The End of the French Exception? Decline and Revival of the 'French Model'*, edited by T. Chafer and E. Godin. Basingstoke, UK: Palgrave MacMillan, 203–20.

Markey, D.S. 1999. Prestige and the origins of war: returning to realism's roots. *Security Studies*, 8(4), 126–72.

Marsh, P. 1979. Conscience and the conduct of government in nineteenth-century Britain: an introduction, in *The Conscience of the Victorian State*, edited by P. Marsh. Syracuse, NY: Syracuse University Press, 215–42.

Marshall, P.J. 1987. Empire and authority in the later eighteenth century. *The Journal of Imperial and Commonwealth History*, 15(2), 105–122.

Marten, K. 2006/07. Warlordism in comparative perspective. *International Security*, 31(3), 41–73.

Médard, J.F. 2005. France and Sub-Saharan Africa: a privileged relationship, in *Africa and the North: Between Globalization and Marginalization*, edited by U. Engel and G.R. Olsen. London and New York: Routledge, 38–54.
Medlicott, W.N. 1969. *Bismarck, Gladstone, and the Concert of Europe*. New York: Greenwood Press.
Mehta, U.S. 1999. *Liberalism and Empire: A Study in Nineteenth-Century British Liberal Thought*. Chicago and London: University of Chicago Press.
Mercer, J. 2006. Human nature and the first image: emotion in international politics. *Journal of International Relations and Development*, 9, 288–303.
Mercer, J. 2010. Emotional beliefs. *International Organization*, 64, 1–31.
Merrill, A. 2002. French forces monitor Ivory Coast. *Associated Press*, 19 October [Online]. Available: Factiva [accessed: 26 February 2012].
Miller, D.T. 2001. Disrespect and the experience of injustice. *Annual Review of Psychology*, 52, 527–53.
Mills, G. 2004. Africa's new strategic significance. *The Washington Quarterly*, 27(4), 157–69.
Mitzen, J. 2006. Ontological security in world politics: state identity and the security dilemma. *European Journal of International Relations*. 12(3), 341–70.
Morgenthau, H.J. 1978. *Politics among Nations: the Struggle for Power and Peace*, 5th Revised edition. New York: Alfred A. Knopf, Inc.
*The Morning Post*. 1882. 14 July, 5.
Mozaffari, M. 2001. The transformationalist perspective and the rise of a global standard of civilization. *International Relations of the Asia-Pacific*, 1(2), 247–64.
Mueller, J.E. 1973. *War, Presidents and Public Opinion*. New York and Toronto: John Wiley & Sons, Inc.
Nathan, J.A. and Oliver, J.K. 1994. *Foreign Policy Making and the American Political System*. 3rd edition. Baltimore, MD and London: The Johns Hopkins University Press.
National Intelligence Council. 2008. *Global Trends 2025: A Transformed World*. Washington, DC: US Government Printing Office.
Nebehay, S. 2011. U.N.: hundreds of thousands displaced in Ivory Coast. *The Washington Post*, 26 March [Online]. Available at: Factiva [accessed: 26 February 2012].
Newman, E. 2009. Failed states and international order: constructing a post-Westphalian world. *Contemporary Security Policy*, 30(3), 421–43.
*The News of the World*. 1882a. 4 June, 2.
*The News of the World*. 1882b. 11 June, 4.
*The News of the World*. 1882c. 16 July, 2.
*News Press*. 2011. Côte d'Ivoire: Ban instructs UN troops to take all necessary steps to protect civilians, 5 April [Online]. Available at: Factiva [accessed: 26 February 2012].
Ninkovich, F. 1994. *Modernity and Power: A History of the Domino Theory in the Twentieth Century*. Chicago and London: University of Chicago Press.

North, D.C. 1990. *Institutions, Institutional Change and Economic Performance.* Cambridge: Cambridge University Press.

North, D.C. 1997. Fundamental puzzles in economic history/development, in *The Economy as an Evolving Complex System II*, edited by W.B. Arthur, S.N. Durlauf and D.A. Lane. Reading, MA: Perseus Books, 223–37.

Nye, Jr J.S. and Keohane, R.O. 1972. Transnational relations and world politics: an introduction, in *Transnational Relations and World Politics*, edited by R.O. Keohane and J.S. Nye Jr. Cambridge MA: Harvard University Press, ix–xxix.

Oakeshott, M. 1975. *On Human Conduct.* Oxford: Clarendon Press.

Obi, C.I. 2008. Nigeria's foreign policy and transnational security challenges in West Africa. *Journal of Contemporary African Studies*, 26(2), 183–96.

Obi, C.I. 2009. Economic Community of West African States on the ground: comparing peacekeeping in Liberia, Sierra Leone, Guinea Bissau, and Côte D'Ivoire. *African Security*, 2, 119–35.

Oliver, K. 2004. Towards a new moral history of the Vietnam War? *The Historical Journal*, 47(3), 757–74.

Organisation for Economic Co-operation and Development (OECD). 2008. *Concepts and Dilemmas of State Building in Fragile Situations*. Paris: OECD.

Olson, M. 2000. Big bills left on the sidewalk: why some nations are rich and others poor, in *A Not-So-Dismal Science: A Broader View of Economics and Societies*, edited by M. Olson and S. Kahkonen. Oxford: Oxford University Press, 37–60.

Orr, R.C. 2004. The United States as nation builder: facing the challenge of post-conflict reconstruction, in *Winning the Peace: An American Strategy for Post-Conflict Reconstruction*, edited by R.C. Orr. Washington DC: Center for Strategic and International Studies, 3–18.

Osborn, R.D. 1882. The value of Egypt to Great Britain. *The Contemporary Review*, 41, 27–39.

Owen IV, J.M. 2002. The foreign imposition of domestic institutions. *International Organization*. 56(2), 375–409.

Packenham, R.A. 1973. *Liberal America and the Third World: Political Development Ideas in Foreign Aid and Social Science*. Princeton, NJ: Princeton University Press.

*The Pall Mall Gazette*. 1882a, 2 February, 1.

*The Pall Mall Gazette*. 1882b. 24 February, 12.

*The Pall Mall Gazette*. 1882c. 25 February, 2.

*The Pall Mall Gazette*. 1882d. 13 March, 1.

*The Pall Mall Gazette*. 1882e. 15 April, 7.

*The Pall Mall Gazette*. 1882f. 1 June, 1.

*The Pall Mall Gazette*. 1882g. 19 June, 11.

*The Pall Mall Gazette*. 1882h. 24 June, 8.

*The Pall Mall Gazette*. 1882i. 27 June, 11.

*The Pall Mall Gazette*. 1882j. 3 July, 10.

*The Pall Mall Gazette*. 1882k. 3 July, 11.

*The Pall Mall Gazette*. 1882l. 4 July, 11.

*The Pall Mall Gazette*. 1882m. 13 July, 8.

*Parliamentary Papers*. 1882. Egypt, no. 10. Copy of a Despatch from Earl Granville to the Earl of Dufferin Respecting the Affairs of Egypt.

*Parliamentary Papers*. 1884. Egypt, no. 10. Correspondence Respecting the Assent of Foreign Powers to the Law of Liquidation.

Patrick, S. 2011. *Weak Links: Fragile States, Global Threats, and International Security*. Oxford: Oxford University Press.

Peel, M. 2004. Ivory Coast peace process collapses. *Financial Times*, 26 March [Online]. Available at: Factiva [accessed: 26 February 2012].

Peters, B.G. 1998. *Institutional Theory in Political Science: The 'New Institutionalism'*. London and New York: Pinter.

Pham, J.P. 2007. Next front? Evolving United States – African strategic relations in the 'war on terrorism' and beyond. *Comparative Strategy*, 26, 39–54.

Phillips, A. *War, Religion and Empire: The Transformation of International Orders*. Cambridge: Cambridge University Press.

Porteous, T. 2008. *Britain in Africa*. London and New York: Zed Books.

Power, M. and Mohan, G. 2010. Toward a critical geopolitics of China's engagement with African development. *Geopolitics*, 15, 462–95.

Présidence de la République. 2008. *The French White Paper on Defence and National Security*. Paris. (English language summary of the full French version)

Prime Minister of Australia. 2003a. *Transcript of the Prime Minister the Hon John Howard MP interview with Steve Liebmann, Today Show, 23 July* [Online]. Available at: http://pandora.nla.gov.au/pan/10052/20031121-0000/www.pm.gov.au/news/interviews/Interview383.html [accessed: 19 May 2012].

Prime Minister of Australia. 2003b. *Transcript of the Prime Minister the Hon John Howard MP interview with Kerry O'Brien, The 7.30 Report, ABC, 25 June* [Online]. Available at: http://pandora.nla.gov.au/pan/10052/20031121-0000/www.pm.gov.au/news/interviews/Interview194.html [accessed: 19 May 2012].

Przeworski, A. 2004a. Institutions matter? *Government and Opposition*, 39(4), 527–40.

Przeworski, A. 2004b. The last instance: are institutions the primary cause of economic development? *European Journal of Sociology*, 45(2), 165–88.

Public Records Office (PRO). *Granville Papers*, series 30. The National Archives, Kew, UK.

Puchala, D.J. 2003. *Theory and History in International Relations*. London and New York: Routledge.

Quinn, J.J. and Simon, D.J. 2006. *Plus ça change, …* : the allocation of French ODA to Africa during and after the Cold War. *International Interactions*, 32, 295–318.

Rater, P. 2011. France stakes reputation on conflicts in Libya, I. Coast. *Agence France-Presse (AFP)*, 5 April [Online]. Available at: Factiva [accessed: 26 February 2012].

Reagan, R. 1989. Farewell Address to the Nation [Online]. 11 January. Available at: http://www.reagan.utexas.edu/archives/speeches/1989/011189i.htm [accessed: 13 May 2012].

Reeves, J. 2004. *Culture and International Relations: Narratives, Natives and Tourists*. London and New York: Routledge.

Reid, R.T. 1884. Our obligations in Egypt. *The Fortnightly Review*, new series, 36, 199–210.

Reus-Smit, C. 1999. *The Moral Purpose of the State*. Princeton, NJ: Princeton University Press.

Reus-Smit, C. 2005. Liberal hierarchy and the licence to use force. *Review of International Studies* 31, 71–92.

Richburg, K.B. 2003a. France abandons hands-off policy on Africa conflicts; some fear Ivory Coast quagmire. *The Washington Post*, 4 January [Online]. Available: Factiva [accessed: 26 February 2012].

Richburg, K.B. 2003b. France's influence wanes in Ivory Coast. *The Washington Post*, 4 February [Online]. Available: Factiva [accessed: 26 February 2012].

Richmond, J.C.B. 1977. *Egypt 1798–1952: Her Advance Towards a Modern Identity*. London: Methuen & Co Ltd.

Roberts, M. 2011. Ivorian republican forces launch final assault as French and UN helicopters attack bases. *Global Insight Daily Analysis*, 5 April [Online]. Available: Factiva [accessed: 26 February 2012].

Robinson, R. and Gallagher, J. 1961. *Africa and the Victorians*. London: MacMillan.

Ross, A. 2006. Coming in from the cold: constructivism and emotions. *European Journal of International Relations*, 12(2), 197–222.

Rotberg, R.I. 2002. Failed states in a world of terror. *Foreign Affairs*, 81(4), 127–40.

Rotberg, R.I. 2003. Failed states, collapsed states, weak states: causes and indicators, in *State Failure and State Weakness in a Time of Terror*, edited by R.I. Rotberg. Washington, DC: World Peace Foundation, 1–28.

Rotberg, R.I. 2004. Strengthening governance: ranking countries would help. *The Washington Quarterly*, 28(1), 71–81.

Rouach, H. 1999a. Paris moves troops after Cote d'Ivoire coup, ambiguous on Bedie. *Agence France-Presse (AFP)*, 27 December [Online]. Available at: Factiva [accessed: 26 February 2012].

Rouach, H. 1999b. Paris says hands off over Cote d'Ivoire was new 'French policy'. *Agence France-Presse (AFP)*, 25 December [Online]. Available at: Factiva [accessed: 26 February 2012].

Rouach, H. 2000. France warns I Coast against political exclusion. *Agence France-Presse (AFP)*, 25 July [Online]. Available at: Factiva [accessed: 26 February 2012].

Rousseau, J-J. 1968. *The Social Contract*, translated by M. Cranston. London: Penguin.

Rubin, B.R. 2006. Peace building and state-building in Afghanistan: constructing sovereignty for whose security? *Third World Quarterly*, 27(1), 175–85.

Rusk, D. 1963. The stake in Viet-Nam, 22 April. *Department of State Bulletin*, 48(1246), 727–35.

Rusk, D. 1965. Secretary Rusk's news conference of February 25. *Department of State Bulletin*, 52(1342), 362–71.

Salehyan, I. 2007. Transnational rebels: neighboring states as sanctuary for rebel groups. *World Politics*, 59, 217–42.

Samaan, J-L. and Gompert, D.C. 2009. French nuclear weapons, Euro-deterrence, and NATO. *Contemporary Security Policy*, 30(3), 486–504.

San Akca, B. 2009. Supporting non-state armed groups: a resort to illegality? *Journal of Strategic Studies*, 32(4), 589–613.

Sanin, F.G. 2011. Evaluating state performance: a critical view of state failure and fragility indexes. *European Journal of Development Research*, 23(1), 20–42.

Sasley, B.E. 2011. Theorizing states' emotions. *International Studies Review*, 13, 452–76.

Saunders, E.N. 2009. Transformative choices: leaders and the origins of intervention strategy. *International Security*, 34(2), 119–61.

Saurette, P. 2006. You dissin me? Humiliation and post 9/11 global politics. *Review of International Studies*, 32, 495–522.

Schofield, H. 2003. Paris brokers week of talks from Wednesday to end Ivory Coast war. *Agence France-Presse* (*AFP*), 13 January [Online]. Available at: Factiva [accessed: 26 February 2012].

Schölch, A. 1976. The 'men on the spot' and the English occupation of Egypt in 1882. *The Historical Journal*, 19(3), 773–85.

Schumpeter, J.A. 1951. *Imperialism and Social Classes*, translated by H. Norden. Oxford: Blackwell.

Schweller, R. 1999. Realism and the present great power system: growth and positional conflict over scarce resources, in *Unipolar Politics*, edited by E.B. Kapstein and M. Mastanduno. New York: Columbia University Press, 29–68.

Sciolino, E. 2002. Ivory Coast's raging conflict draws France in. *The New York Times*, 26 December [Online]. Available at: Factiva [accessed: 26 February 2012].

Scruton, R. 2002. *The West and the Rest: Globalization and the Terrorist Threat*. Wilmington, DE: ISI Books.

Sengupta, S. 2004a. 25 killed in antigovernment protest in Ivory Coast. *The New York Times*, 26 March [Online]. Available at: Factiva [accessed: 26 February 2012].

Sengupta, S. 2004b. Ivory Coast cease-fire ends with airstrikes against 2 rebel towns. *The New York Times*, 5 November [Online]. Available at: Factiva [accessed: 26 February 2012].

Serot, E. 2002. French military mulls backing peacekeeping force in Ivory Coast. *Agence France-Presse* (*AFP*), 1 October [Online]. Available: Factiva [accessed: 26 February 2012].

Shaw, S.J. and Shaw, E.K. 1977. *History of the Ottoman Empire and Modern Turkey*, vol. 2. Cambridge: Cambridge University Press.

Shea, G. 2002. Ivory Coast govt denies ethnic killings, protestors storm French base. *Agence France-Presse* (*AFP*), 22 October [Online]. Available: Factiva [accessed: 26 February 2012].

Simpson, G. 2004. *Great Powers and Outlaw States: Unequal Sovereigns in the International Legal Order*. Cambridge: Cambridge University Press.

Slomp, G. 2000. *Thomas Hobbes and the Political Philosophy of Glory*. Basingstoke: MacMillan.

Small, M. 2005. *At the Water's Edge: American Politics and the Vietnam War*. Chicago: Ivan R. Dee, Publisher.

Smith, C.S. 2003. French risking prestige as talks open in Ivory Coast civil war. *The New York Times*, 16 January [Online]. Available: Factiva [accessed: 26 February 2012].

Snyder, J. 1991. Introduction, in *Dominoes and Bandwagons: Strategic Beliefs and Great Power Competition in the Eurasian Rimland*, edited by R. Jervis and J. Snyder. New York and Oxford: Oxford University Press, 3–19.

Sonntag, A. 2008. The burdensome heritage of prestige politics, in *France on the World Stage: Nation State Strategies in the Global Era*, edited by M. Maclean and J. Szarka. Basingstoke and New York: Palgrave MacMillan, 77–90.

Soutou, G-H. 2002. France, nations and empires from the nineteenth century to the present day: between Jacobin tradition, European balance of power and European integration, in *Governance, Globalization and the European Union. Which Europe for Tomorrow?*, edited by H. Cavanna. Dublin and Portland, OR: Four Courts Press, 69–85.

*The Standard*. 1882a. 30 May, 5.

*The Standard*. 1882b. 15 June, 5.

Steele, B.J. 2008. *Ontological Security in International Relations*. London and New York: Routledge.

Steele, B.J. 2010. Irony, emotions and critical distance. *Millennium: Journal of International Studies*, 39(1), 89–107.

Steele, D. 1983. Britain and Egypt 1882–1914: the containment of Islamic nationalism, in *Imperialism and Nationalism in the Middle East*, edited by K.M. Wilson. London: Mansell Publishing Ltd, 1–25.

Steinberg, B.S. 1996. *Shame and Humiliation: Presidential Decision Making on Vietnam*. Pittsburgh: University of Pittsburgh Press.

Stewart, F.H. 1994. *Honor*. Chicago and London: The University of Chicago Press.

Stokes, E. 1975. Uneconomic imperialism. *The Historical Journal*, 18(2), 409–16.

Straus, S. 2011. 'It's sheer horror here': the patterns of violence during the first four months of Côte D'Ivoire's post-electoral crisis. *African Affairs*, 110(440), 481–89.

Taliaferro, J.W. 2004a. *Balancing Risks: Great Power Intervention in the Periphery*. Ithaca and London: Cornell University Press.
Taliaferro, J.W. 2004b. Power politics and the balance of risk: hypotheses on great power intervention in the periphery. *Political Psychology*, 25(2), 177–211.
Taylor, A.J.P. 1954. *The Struggle for Mastery in Europe 1848–1918*. Oxford: Clarendon Press.
Taylor, S.C. 1993. Lyndon Johnson and the Vietnamese, in *Shadow on the White House: Presidents and the Vietnam War, 1945–1975*, edited by D.L. Anderson. Lawrence, KS: University Press of Kansas, 113–29.
Temple, R. 1882. Principles of British policy in Egypt. *The Contemporary Review*, 42, 495–508.
Thody, P. 1998. *The Fifth French Republic: Presidents, Politics and Personalities*. London and New York: Routledge.
Thompson, A.S. 2000. *Imperial Britain: The Empire in British Politics, c.1880–1932*. London: Pearson.
Thomson, Jr., J.C. 1988. How could Vietnam happen? An autopsy, in *Domestic Sources of American Foreign Policy*, edited by C.W. Kegley and E.R. Wittkopf. New York: St. Martin's Press, 205–14.
Thornton, A.P. 1966. *The Imperial Idea and its Enemies*. New York: St. Martin's Press.
Tignor, R.L. 1966. *Modernization and British Colonial Rule in Egypt, 1882–1914*. Princeton, NJ: Princeton University Press.
*The Times*. 1881a. 2 June, 4.
*The Times*. 1881b. 23 July, 5.
*The Times*. 1881c. 17 August, 10.
*The Times*, 1881d. 22 August, 4.
*The Times*. 1881e. 6 October, 4.
*The Times*. 1881f. 4 November, 8.
*The Times*. 1882g. 26 May, 5.
*The Times*. 1882h. 13 June, 7.
*The Times*. 1882i. 26 June, 9.
*The Times*. 1882j. 11 July, 5.
*The Times*. 1882k. 28 July, 5.
*The Times*. 2011. Force de Frappe French intervention against Ivory Coast's illegitimate ruler was just and necessary, 13 April [Online]. Available at: Factiva [accessed: 26 February 2012].
Tinker, H. 1967. Broken backed states: chaotic, but a high survival rate. *New Guinea and Australia, the Pacific and South-East Asia*, 2(3), 42–45.
Treacher, A. 2000. A case of reinvention: France and military intervention in the 1990s. *International Peacekeeping*, 7(2), 23–40.
Treacher, A. 2002. Europe as power multiplier for French security policy: strategic consistency, tactical adaptation. *European Security*, 10(1), 22–44.
United Nations (UN) Security Council. 2003. *Resolution 1464 (2003)*, S/RES/1464.

United Nations (UN) Security Council. 2011. *Resolution 1975 (2011)*, S/RES/1975.

U.S. comments on report of Control Commission for Vietnam. 1962. *Department of State Bulletin*, 47(1203), 109–10.

Utley, R.E. 2002. 'Not to do less but to do better …': French military policy in Africa. *International Affairs*, 78(1), 129–46.

Utley, R.E. 2006. A means to wider ends? France, Germany and peacekeeping, in *Major Powers and Peacekeeping: Perspectives, Priorities and the Challenges of Military Intervention*, edited by R.E. Utley. Aldershot, UK and Burlington, VT: Ashgate, 63–80.

Vallings, C. and Moreno-Torres, M. 2005. *Drivers of Fragility: What Makes States Fragile?* Poverty Reduction in Difficult Environments (PRDI) Working Paper No. 7, UK Department for International Development.

Van Evera, S. 1997. *Guide to Methods for Students of Political Science*. Ithaca and London: Cornell University Press.

Védrine, H., with Moisi, D. 2001. *France in an Age of Globalization*, translated by P.H. Gordon. Washington, DC: Brookings Institution Press.

Wallis, W. 2011. Battle for Ivory Coast reaches heart of Abidjan. *Financial Times*, 31 March [Online]. Available at: Factiva [accessed: 26 February 2012].

Waltz, K.N. 1979. *Theory of International Politics*. New York: McGraw-Hill.

Weber, M. 1947. *The Theory of Social and Economic Organization*, translated by A.M. Henderson and T. Parsons. New York: Oxford University Press.

Welsh, A. 2008. *What is Honor? A Question of Moral Imperatives*. New Haven, CT and London: Yale University Press.

Wendt, A. 1999. *Social Theory of International Politics*. Cambridge: Cambridge University Press.

Wesley, M. 2005. Toward a realist ethics of intervention. *Ethics & International Affairs*, 19(2), 55–72.

Wesley, M. 2008. The state of the art on the art of state building. *Global Governance*, 14, 369–85.

Westlake, J. 1882. England's duty in Egypt. *The Contemporary Review*, 42, 823–39.

Wheeler, N.J. 1992. Pluralist or solidarist conceptions of international society: Bull and Vincent on humanitarian intervention. *Millennium Journal of International Studies*, 21(3), 463–87.

The White House. 2002. *National Security Strategy of the United States of America*. Washington, DC.

Williams, W.A. 1972. *The Tragedy of American Diplomacy*. 2nd Revised edition. New York: Dell Publishing Co., Inc.

Wohlforth, W.C. 1999. The stability of a unipolar world. *International Security*, 24(1), 5–41.

Wohlforth, W.C. 2009. Unipolarity, status competition, and great power war. *World Politics* 61(1): 28–57.

Wolf, R. 2011. Respect and disrespect in international politics: the significance of status recognition. *International Theory*, 3(1), 105–42.

Wolfers, A. 1962. *Discord and Collaboration: Essays on International Politics*. Baltimore, MD: The Johns Hopkins University Press.

Wolff, S. 2011. The regional dimensions of state failure. *Review of International Studies*, 37(3), 951–72.

Wood, P.C. 2005. France, in *The Politics of Peacekeeping in the Post-Cold War Era*, edited by D.S. Sorenson and P.C. Wood. London and New York: Frank Cass, 68–94.

Wylie, L. 2009. Valuing reputation and prestige: Canadian foreign policy and the International Criminal Court. *American Review of Canadian Studies*, 39(2), 112–30.

Yapp, M.E. 1987. *The Making of the Modern Near East 1792–1923*. London: Longman.

Yeager, T.J. 1998. *Institutions, Transition Economies, and Economic Development: The Political Economy of Global Interdependence*. Boulder and Oxford: Westview Press.

Yergin, D. 1990. *Shattered Peace: The Origins of the Cold War*. Revised edition. London: Penguin.

Young, K.T. 1967. United States policy and Vietnamese political viability, 1954–1967. *Asian Survey*, 7(8), 507–14.

Youngs, R. 2006. The EU and conflict in West Africa. *European Foreign Affairs Review*, 11, 333–52.

Zavis, A. 2002a. France adds military to Ivory Coast. *Associated Press*, 1 October [Online]. Available at: Factiva [accessed: 26 February 2012].

Zavis, A. 2002b. Second Ivory Coast city evacuated. *Associated Press*, 29 September [Online]. Available at: Factiva [accessed: 26 February 2012].

Zmora, H. 2007. A world without a saving grace: glory and immortality in Machiavelli. *History of Political Thought*, 28(3), 449–68.

# Index

For Product Safety Concerns and Information please contact our EU
representative GPSR@taylorandfrancis.com
Taylor & Francis Verlag GmbH, Kaufingerstraße 24, 80331 München, Germany

www.ingramcontent.com/pod-product-compliance
Ingram Content Group UK Ltd.
Pitfield, Milton Keynes, MK11 3LW, UK
UKHW011012180926
475701UK00004B/692

* 9 7 8 1 1 3 8 2 6 9 2 7 9 *